THE CHEMICAL FEAST

The Ralph Nader Study Group Report on Food Protection and the Food and Drug Administration

The Chemical Feast

BY **James S. Turner** PROJECT DIRECTOR

GROSSMAN PUBLISHERS   NEW YORK   1970

In 1968 a Ralph Nader Summer Study Group did a preliminary report on food protection by the FDA. The report was written by James S. Turner. Research was done by James S. Turner, Robert Rideout, Margery Riffler, Ned Lyle, and Michael Friedman. Based on this first report, a second team studied the FDA's food regulation in the summer of 1969. The result is this book, *The Chemical Feast,* by James S. Turner. Research was done by Peter Gold, Anita Johnson, Jean Levin, Al Levine, Lilian Mohin, Eric Moore, Lowell Schoengarth, Virginia Soret, Michole Starrels, James S. Turner, Frederick Walker, Kenneth Zuckerman. Associate researchers were Gary Greenwald, Fred Hyde, Gloria Kreis, John Monkmon, Elissa Parker. The project secretary was Barbara Moore. At the time the research was done, all these people were students or recent graduates. They came from law schools at The Ohio State University, New York University, Boston University, University of Southern California, and the University of Pittsburgh, from medical schools at the University of Michigan, The Ohio State University, Yale University, and Jefferson Medical College, from graduate schools at Princeton University and Cambridge University (England), and from undergraduate school at Vassar College.

Acknowledgment

This book would have been much more difficult to write without the co-operation of many officials, both past and present, of the Food and Drug Administration.

Foreword

Food is the most intimate consumer product. Back many decades, public concern over contaminates and adulterates led to early regulation by the states. The failure of such regulation to insure safe, pure, and nutritious food in the world's largest breadbasket has been in step with each new ingenious technique for manipulating the content of food products as dictated by corporate greed and irresponsibility.

Making food appear what it is not is an integral part of the $125 billion food industry. The deception ranges from the surface packaging to the integrity of the food products' quality to the very shaping of food tastes. The industry's catering is calculated to sharpen and meet superficially consumer tastes at the cost of other critical consumer needs. These tastes include palatability, tenderness, visual presentability, and convenience. They are met by a versatile misuse of modern chemistry, packaging, and merchandising techniques. But meeting these tastes does not lead, unfortunately, to fulfilling the requisites of purity, wholesomeness, safety, and nutrition. In fact, very often the degradation of these standards proceeds from the cosmetic treatment of food or is its direct cost by-product. For example, the nutritional deception about "enriched white flour" covers up the permanent stripping in the processing stages of most nutrients. Coloring additives, preservatives, seasonings, and tenderizers camouflage the rapid increase of fat content in frankfurters (33 per cent [1969] of weight on the average), their decrease in meat protein, and the substandard quality of the meat. The hazards of hundreds of untested or inadequately tested food additives are about to be given some of the governmental attention that they have so long deserved.

Further, the heavy promotional emphasis on "unfoods" such as near-zero-nutrition "snacks," chemically doused bakery goods, and soft drinks have a serious distorting effect on young people's food habits and concepts of nutrition. Millions of youngsters are growing up watching the television ads and believing their messages that Pepsi-Cola and Coca-Cola provide health and vigor. Small wonder then that the United States Department of Agriculture shows a decline in nutritional adequacy of American family diets. Food tastes and habits are largely the product of cultural determination, and in the United States this means largely the policy of the food industry and its determined effort to shape those tastes that maximize its immediate projects and sales. What Frenchman, for instance, would think of going down to the marketplace to buy a Wonder bread? His concept of bread differs from that which has prevailed in this country since the mid-twenties, when spongy-baked bread began its road to commercial devitalization.

For too long there has been an overwhelmingly dominant channel of distorted information from the food industry to the consumer. There has been almost no authoritative and countervailing force for information as to what is happening to the quality of food and why the Food and Drug Administration has so shirked its duties. This may not be surprising when it is remembered that the country just "discovered" mass malnutrition in its midst in 1967–1968 while the economy was booming. That countervailing force for standards and detailed information was to have been in large part the Food and Drug Administration and the United States Department of Agriculture. As Mr. Turner and his assistants show in this report, the Food and Drug Administration, for a variety of reasons within its reasonable control and for the lack of a public constituency, failed to close out the options for corporate cost reduction and camouflage which the industry developed via additives, adulterants, and numerous deceptive practices. Company economy very often was the consumer's cost and hazard. As a result, competition became a way of beating one's competitor by racing for the lowest permissible common denominator. In allowing the proliferation of these abuses and in declining to develop sound, competitively uplifting food standards, the Food and Drug Administration also did a serious disservice to any scrupulous food processors who might have viewed competition as a drive for quality and nutrition rather than the opposite situation which has prevailed.

In sum, the Food and Drug Administration has acted

as an official sponsor of processing and marketing practices that have transformed the defrauding of consumers
into a competitive advantage—a kind of reverse competition (deceptive packaging alone costs consumers billions yearly).

Predictably, such a pattern has helped the concentration of this giant industry into fewer and fewer corporate
hands. The competition, such as it is, has focused heavily
on massive promotional expenditures (between 16 and
18 per cent of gross revenues) on brand-name identifica-
tion, wasteful nonprice competition, and other marketing expenses that do not provide added value for the
consumer but simply increase food prices. In addition,
the food companies have one of the tiniest research
budgets (for nutrition and food quality) of any United
States industry.

The quantity of food pouring from our farms and
ranches must never be confused with its quality by the
time it reaches the consumers' dinner table or whether
it adequately reaches many poor consumers at all. For
years the Food Group, as the food lobby is known in
Washington, has nearly determined the limits of public
dialogue and public policy about food quality. It is time
for consumers to have information that will provide
them with an effective understanding of the secrecy-
clouded situation. This report proposes to contribute
toward that objective as well as to spur the additional
disclosure of facts and materials.

—Ralph Nader

Contents

Consumption is the sole end and purpose of all production; and the interest of the producer ought to be attended to, only so far as it may be necessary for promoting that of the consumer. The maxim is so perfectly self-evident, that it would be absurd to attempt to prove it. But in the mercantile system, the interest of the consumer is almost constantly sacrificed to that of the producer: and it seems to consider production, and not consumption, as the ultimate end and object of all industry and commerce. . . .

It cannot be very difficult to determine who have been the contrivers of this whole mercantile system; not the consumers, we may believe, whose interest has been entirely neglected: but the producers, whose interest has been so carefully attended to; and among this latter class our merchants and manufacturers have been by far the principal architects.

—Adam Smith
The Wealth of Nations
Book IV, Chapter VIII
1784

THE CHEMICAL FEAST

Introduction

"ASK WHY"
—*Sign in the office of Kenneth W. Kirk,
former Associate Commissioner, FDA*

It is the purpose of this book to examine in some detail how the quality of the American diet has been allowed to deteriorate. For too long Americans have rested secure in the belief that their health surpasses that of all other peoples of the world, that they live longer, suffer less, and eat better than people in any other nation. They are mistaken.

Dr. Jean Mayer, nutrition adviser to President Nixon, has pointed out that twenty-year-old men in thirty-six foreign countries will live longer on the average than will American men. The lifetime of twenty-year-old women in twenty-one nations will surpass that of American women. The 1967 (most recent) vital statistics of the United States show that, from 1900 to the present, only about four years have been added on to the life of an American reaching the age of forty. They also show that there has been almost no increase in the life expectancy of Americans since the 1959–1961 reporting period. Americans do not live longer—either than other people or than they did ten years ago. Black American men actually die younger than they did in 1959.

Some experts on social statistics suggest that "quite possibly infant mortality rates give the best overall measure of national health we have." [1] By that measure Americans have comparatively lower standards than they used to and lower than those of many other people in the world. In 1950 the U.S. had the fifth lowest infant mortality rate in the world; eighteen years later that position had changed to thirteenth. The U.S. Public Health Service reported that in 1966 Sweden, Japan, the United Kingdom, and East Germany, among others, had infant mortality rates lower than the United States'. Men in each of these countries were also expected to live longer than American men.

The American diet has deteriorated in the past decade. On November 25, 1969, the editor of the *Journal of Nutrition Education* held a Washington press conference to announce the results of the most extensive review of nutrition studies ever undertaken in this country. The authors began the study in 1966 (before the problem of hunger in America was discovered), assuming that it would be a routine academic effort establishing that all Americans were adequately nourished. They were shocked to discover "that nutrient inadequacies . . . reach into all income groups and all regions" of the country. "Nearly *all* children under one year of age had an iron intake less than the Recommended Dietary Allowance." The study "found infants of higher income families to be less well nourished than those in lower income families." It concluded, "Dietary habits of the American public have become worse, especially since 1960." [2] In the past decade American life expectancy has not dramatically increased, while those of other nations have. In the same time period Americans have not reduced as dramatically as other nations the number of babies who die each year. And American hunger and inadequate vitamin and mineral nutrition have become the subject of heated debate exposing unimagined national failures.

These facts raise questions about the way Americans organize themselves to provide for basic needs. One of those needs, food, is the subject of this book. Americans should ask why they appear to eat poorly. They should ask if there are authorities assigned to warn of and protect against danger from improper food, and, if so, why they seem to be failing. They should ask why members of the food industry, America's largest retail industry, have been allowed to let the safety, wholesomeness, and value of their products deteriorate.

The Food and Drug Administration of the United States Department of Health, Education, and Welfare should be able to answer these questions. It is primarily to this agency that Americans have given the responsibility of food protection. The Food and Drug Administration (FDA) administers the Food, Drug, and Cosmetic Act of 1938, which means that it is responsible for insuring the quality of all food, drugs, and cosmetics sold in the United States. Twenty-three million dollars of its roughly $73 million annual budget goes to programs designed to protect the food supply.

The Act of 1938 has been amended several times in an effort by Congress to tighten food protection. In 1954 the FDA was given authority to set pesticide tolerances in foods; in 1958 the Food Additives Amendment required the FDA to establish that all chemical additives were proven safe before use in food; and in 1960 the provisions of the 1958 amendment were extended to cover color additives in foods. The addition of drugs to food-producing animals was made the subject of legislation in 1968.

To enforce these laws, the FDA has seventeen district offices across the United States and employs approximately 5,000 people. Some are inspectors who routinely examine food plants, monitor food shipments, and check for misleading label claims on foods sold in retail stores; some are inspectors concerned with drugs and other areas of the FDA's responsibility. Other employees are scientists who conduct laboratory experiments, study the work of scientists outside the agency, and serve as important technical advisers to the public health agencies of other nations. Other jobs of the FDA include the setting of food standards, the development of good manufacturing practices for the food industry, and the evolution of scientific methods for monitoring the quality of the food supply.

In spite of its vast responsibility, the FDA has found its meager although sometimes well-intended efforts continually neutralized by the powerful forces of special interests that include the large, well-funded efforts of Washington law firms, massive trade associations made up of the nation's fifty thousand food manufacturing firms, and a small group of industry-dependent "food scientists" who more often than not routinely produce scientific studies that support the most recent industry marketing decision. In the face of the $125 billion food industry, which is over six times as large as General Motors, America's largest industrial corporation, the FDA is unable to exert any meaningful influence on behalf of the food-consuming public. Impotence has characterized the FDA and its predecessor agencies since passage of the Pure Food Act of 1906. Due to the total collapse of the food protection efforts of the Food and Drug Administration, which has allowed vicious, unchecked battles for profit to wrack the food industry, food restoration has become an important national goal for all Americans to work toward. Understanding the magnitude, meaning, and cause of the FDA collapse may begin movement toward that goal.

1. Cyclamates

"Cyclamates have been more widely and thoroughly studied than any of the food additives in present use . . . more widely studied than any other food substance—natural or synthetic— with the possible exception of the amino acids."

—Joseph C. Lowey, executive, Abbott Laboratories, press conference, Chicago, Illinois, October 8, 1969

"Ladies and gentlemen; I am today ordering that the artificial sweetener, cyclamate, be removed from the list of substances generally recognized as safe for use in foods."

With these words, spoken on October 18, 1969, Secretary of Health, Education, and Welfare Robert H. Finch announced the end of cyclamates as a component of the American food supply. The announcement, affecting more than $1 billion worth of food sweetened with cyclamates, was one of the most dramatic in American regulatory history. The decision was made in response to tremendous public pressure. Nevertheless, the man who made it refused to let the issue of cyclamates bring his agency publicly to grips with any of the broader legal and scientific issues raised by the discovery that an item which for years had been classified among substances generally recognized as safe by the Food and Drug Administration had subsequently been discovered to cause bladder cancer in test rats.

The first official association of the FDA with a cyclamate product came in January, 1950, when Abbott Laboratories filed a new drug application for Sucaryl

Sodium (a cyclamate product). Abbott's new drug tablets were "intended for use in foods and beverages by diabetics and by others who must restrict their intake of sugar," [1] according to the Abbott drug application. It was the original intention of Abbott to use the product as a drug. For strictly food use, a new drug application would not have been necessary. Dr. A. J. Lehman of the FDA reviewed the Abbott Laboratories test data supplied with the application and dismissed it as useless. The application, he said, was "an illustration of how an experiment should not be conducted." The numbers of test animals were too small, control groups were discontinued too early in the experiments, not enough autopsies were performed, and the report itself was vague.[2] On the basis of its own data, Abbott's request to market cyclamates would have been rejected, but the FDA took the unusual position of approving the request on the basis of two-year feeding studies that it had conducted in its own laboratories. Dr. Lehman's report concluded: "If we had not studied this compound I would be quite reluctant to permit its use even for drug use, not to mention as an artificial sweetener for foods. It should be pointed out to Abbott that the evidence to support their case is not contained in this NDA; and that it is on the basis of our own work that recommendations are being made to permit this application to become effective." [3]

It is important to note that, when the pressure on cyclamates came to a head in October, 1969, almost twenty years later, a review of the FDA data relied on by Dr. Lehman revealed "a highly suspicious frequency of lung tumors . . . (which) assumed significant back-up importance." [4] In addition, of the less than one hundred rats tested by the FDA, six had rare ovarian, kidney, skin, or uterine tumors that would ordinarily occur about once in ten thousand cases—making this more than six hundred times the normal occurrence. The appearance of malignant tumors had been clearly noted in the 1950 FDA laboratory sheets on which the conclusions of safety were based. Combining these suggestions of cancer with the shoddiness of Abbott's test should have clearly indicated that more tests of cyclamates were needed before allowing them to be marketed. But the FDA demanded no further tests. This was the first of many danger signals about cyclamates that the FDA ignored.

The next warning about cyclamates came to the FDA officially from the Food Nutrition Board of the National Academy of Sciences-National Research Council (NAS-NRC) in 1954. The FDA took no action to restrict the use of cyclamates at that time. The warning was repeated in 1955, 1962, and in modified form in 1968. In a special communication to the Food and Drug Administration in November, 1954, the Food Nutrition Board said, "The priority of public welfare over all other considerations precludes, therefore, the uncontrolled distribution of foodstuffs containing cyclamate." [5] The board made this recommendation because it was "impressed with the fact that cyclamate has physiologic activity in addition to its sweetening effect, that there is no prolonged experience with its use, and that little is known of the results of its continued ingestion in large amounts in a variety of situations in individuals of all ages and states of health." [6] In 1955 the Food Protection Committee of the board said cyclamates "should be subject to continuing observations for possible deleterious effects under prolonged and varying conditions of use and should be reappraised whenever indicated by advances in knowledge." [7] In November, 1955, following the release of this report, the Food Nutrition Board, in a special recommendation to the FDA, repeated its conclusion that public welfare considerations precluded the uncontrolled distribution of foodstuffs containing cyclamates. Again the FDA made no move to restrict the use of the chemical.

In 1962, seven years later, the Food Nutrition Board revised its policy statement on cyclamates. In a review of the growing use of cyclamates, it pointed out that when the rest of the diet was not controlled, foods containing cyclamates "have no direct influence on body weight," [8] even though this was one of the advertised purposes for use of the substance. In this revised report the board repeated verbatim its warning that "the priority of public welfare over all other considerations precludes, therefore, the uncontrolled distribution of foodstuffs containing cyclamate." [9] In November, 1968, an *ad hoc* committee on cyclamates appointed by the NAS-NRC shortened but retained the essence of the earlier warnings by stating, "Totally unrestricted use of the cyclamates is not warranted at this time." [10] In an effort to cope with the by then over $1 billion worth of food products containing cyclamates developed since the first NAS warning, the *ad hoc* committee recommended maximum daily intakes of cyclamates based on the fact that they caused diarrhea— a fact mentioned in the original new drug application filed eighteen years earlier. The FDA never effectively circulated these limits to the general public; in fact, it used the Food Nutrition Board's revised report, which softened earlier warnings, to justify inaction.

The Food Additives Amendment of 1958 required all chemicals added to food to be subjected to rigorous testing establishing safety before being added to the food supply, unless they were "generally recognized as safe." In order to administer this law, the FDA had to distinguish those chemicals that were generally recognized as safe from those that were not, so in December, 1958, the agency prepared a tentative list of 189 substances that it believed could be exempted from the testing requirement. This proposed list was sent to nine hundred scientists throughout the country "to determine whether these substances were in fact generally recognized as safe." [11] Of the nine hundred scientists, 350 replied, and of that number only 194 "concurred with the list or made no comment." Based on these replies, a revised list, which deleted six of the original substances and attempted to define more precisely the term "generally recognized as safe," became official in November, 1959. Theoretically, this list, known since then as the GRAS list, is made up of the most common and most apparently safe food items— salt, pepper, sugar, vinegar are cited by the FDA Commissioner as examples. They are excluded from the class of substances that must be proven safe before they are added to the food supply. Conversely, exclusion from the GRAS list does not mean that a substance is automatically or indefinitely excluded from the food supply. Exclusion from the list merely means that the company proposing the item for use in foods must conduct scientific tests to establish its safety before it is placed in foods.

Only one scientist responding to the FDA commented directly on cyclamates. That scientist suggested that there was not enough information available to include them safely on the list. But the FDA's final statement read: "Nonnutritive sweeteners—safety has adequately been established for the substances in this category." [12] This blanket comment, covering saccharin and cyclamates, was made on August 10, 1959, three years and nine months after the Food Protection Committee of the National Academy of Sciences recommended against "the uncontrolled distribution of foodstuffs containing cyclamate." (No new evidence to discredit that warning had arisen. The NAS repeated it verbatim two and a half years later.) More startling, the FDA was ignoring its own previous policy on cyclamates. Until they were included on the proposed GRAS list in 1958, cyclamates were restricted to use in special dietary foods, and had to be labeled "should be used only by persons who *must* restrict their intake of ordinary sweets." [13] Abbott Laboratories desired to avoid the premarketing test responsibility in the case of cyclamates, and whether intentionally or inadvertently the FDA indulged this desire by placing cyclamates on the GRAS list. Once on the list, cyclamates could be used in any foods, in any amount, and in many cases without the label warning. In addition, manufacturers began answering consumer inquiries about safety by citing the fact that cyclamates were generally recognized as safe by the FDA. The inclusion of cyclamates (then known as cyclohexyl sulfamate) on the GRAS list marked the beginning of their uncontrolled use in the food supply.

GRAS list status for cyclamates eventually resulted in the consumption of this product by nearly 75 per cent of the families in America, often without any way of knowing they were taking in the chemical. Bacon and ham cured with cyclamates under Agriculture Department regulations required no label declaration. Children's vitamins coated with cyclamates, an inexpensive way to improve their taste, circulated without notice to the consuming public. The FDA adopted food standards for artificially sweetened canned fruit, jams, and jellies that allowed the use of cyclamates or saccharin without any need to mention these ingredients on the label. All of this activity was the direct result of placing cyclamates on the Generally Recognized As Safe list.

Once an item is on the GRAS list, as cyclamates were, it remains there, unreviewed, until questions are raised about its safety. Since 1958 there has been no systematic review of any of the items on the list. There is no individual or group within the FDA charged with the responsibility of monitoring either the kind of use or the amount of use that any substance may have—this in spite of the fact that the FDA officially recognizes that a change in use either of amount or kind of any substance on the GRAS list could be grounds for removing it from the list. The only way that challenges to the safety of GRAS substances come to the attention of the FDA is through what the agency's staff read in newspapers and magazines, both professional and nonprofessional, and, even when these signs appear, it does not mean the FDA will take action. It is a haphazard system at best. Just as the FDA failed to review its own data on cyclamates before placing them on the GRAS list, it also failed to review the scientific criticism of cyclamates that mounted in almost direct proportion to the expansion of the cyclamates market.

The FDA failed to review the listing of cyclamates after they underwent massive changes of use. It also failed to review all available data after the passage of the 1958 Food Additives Amendment to the Food, Drug, and Cosmetic Act, in which the so-called Delaney Clause (named after James Delaney, Democrat of New York, who sponsored it) deems unsafe any additive "found to induce cancer when ingested by man or animal." [14] * After passage of this clause, establishing a particular Congressional concern, the FDA should have reviewed its data on all substances for any indication that they might cause cancer. Such a review,

---

* It was on the basis of the Delaney Clause that cyclamate was eventually removed from the GRAS list and from the market in 1969. Cyclamates caused cancer in the bladders of rats in a test commissioned by Abbott Laboratories in 1967 and completed in October, 1969.

conducted thoroughly and scientifically, would have raised enough serious doubts about cyclamates to make the FDA perform even more thorough studies on them and could have sped their removal from the market.

But the FDA did not just fail to respond to legislation; it actually overlooked or ignored scientific evidence indicating the dangers of cyclamates. Since 95 per cent of all cyclamates ingested are passed out of the system within twenty-four hours of consumption, food and chemical industry scientists have argued that they must be safe. But "the fact that cyclamate has physiologic activity in addition to its sweetening effect"[15] raised early doubts about the safety of the substance. Then, in 1966, two Japanese scientists reported that cyclamates passing through the body of a man could create a different chemical called cyclohexylamine (CHA).[16] Later tests showed that this occurred in about a third of the population. CHA is clearly a dangerous chemical. As early as 1958, long before the relationship between CHA and cyclamates was known, the FDA adopted a regulation that allowed a maximum of ten parts of CHA per one million parts of boiler feed water to be used in certain food-processing procedures. The use of CHA was so limited that water containing the chemical was not allowed to come into contact with milk or milk products.[17] In comparison, according to Dr. Jack Schubert, Professor of Radiation Chemistry at the University of Pittsburgh, in persons whose systems convert cyclamates into CHA, CHA is introduced directly into the system in amounts ranging from twenty to five hundred parts per one million, or even more. For example, one package of artificially sweetened Kool-Aid contained 28.5 per cent cyclamates, which convert to 3,200 parts per million of CHA in a significant portion of the population. In fact, one package of presweetened Kool-Aid, often consumed directly from the package in powder form, contained cyclamates in excess of the daily intake levels recommended for children by the FDA itself. In some cases, the excess was as much as five hundred milligrams, or nearly 30 per cent. Other dry beverage bases contained more than two and one-half times the cyclamates recommended by the FDA for the consumption of one child in one day.[18] It is important to note that the FDA intake recommendations were made *before* there was any official recognition of the ability of cyclamates to cause cancer in rats. It would seem that once the more serious effects of cyclamates were recognized, more stringent warnings would be issued. In fact, the reverse is true. The warning required on products currently containing cyclamates is less stringent than that proposed by the FDA in April, 1969.

Once the relationship between ingested cyclamates and CHA was isolated, the evidence justifying doubts about cyclamates' safety expressed by the National Academy of Sciences in 1954 began to become compelling, but still the FDA allowed cyclamates to remain on the GRAS list. On March 7, 1968, Dr. Jacqueline Verrett, an FDA biochemist, reported to a high-level FDA science seminar that she had discovered a firm relationship between cyclamates injected into chicken eggs and deformities of embryos taken from the eggs. The seminar was convened by Dr. William H. Summerson, then director of the FDA Bureau of Science, because, in his words, "The current [February, 1968] interest in the safety of artificial sweeteners and their use in foods and drugs necessitates a research effort that encompasses many disciplines which are in the Bureau of Science." [19] In her 1968 year-end research summary to her supervisors, Dr. Verrett reported, "It has been found that calcium cyclamate, cyclohexylamine, and dicyclohexylamine are specific teratogens, having the ability to produce phocomelia and similar defects in the [chicken] embryos." [20] On April 2, 1969, a superior of Dr. Verrett's, concerned about the FDA's failure to consider Dr. Verrett's results seriously, carried two deformed chicken embryos showing phocomelia (the thalidomide effect) to the Commissioner's office. He failed to move the Commissioner, Herbert Ley, to action. Again in her 1969 mid-year report, Dr. Verrett informed her superiors of the continuing build-up of evidence against cyclamates, pointing out that "the teratogenic effects of these compounds were reported in the previous progress report." [21] By "teratogenic" Dr. Verrett meant monstrous deformities in the chicks— deformities such as wings growing out of the wrong part of the body, a leg rotated in the socket, and extreme curvature of the spine. In spite of Dr. Verrett's research, cyclamates remained on the FDA Generally Regarded As Safe list, and Abbott Laboratories, the major manufacturer of cyclamates, continued to assure its buyers that "the American housewife need have no hesitancy about using artificial sweeteners in the preparation of foods and beverages." [22] Dr. Verrett's findings were and still are officially disregarded. Even seeing the deformed chick embryos did not impress Commissioner Ley. He claimed not to understand their significance.[23]

But more than Dr. Verrett's findings were ignored by the FDA. On November 15, 1968, the reliable *Medical World News* reported that FDA cell biology research chief Dr. Marvin Legator had discovered that cyclohexylamine could "break a significant proportion of chromosomes in both *in vitro* and *in vivo* animal studies." The magazine went on to report that the doses given to the rats were believed to be comparable to the amounts that humans who changed cyclamate to cyclohexylamine were then getting from regular food consumption. The story went on to quote a high-ranking FDA official as saying, "It's a big one. This is potentially one of the biggest things we've had around here for a long time." Despite their importance, Dr. Legator's facts were not acted upon by the FDA. The reason is suggested in part by the fate of Dr. Legator's effort to inform FDA Commissioner Ley of the importance he attached to a related discovery. On January 24, 1969, Dr. Legator prepared a memo entitled "The Profound Importance of the Isolation of N-Hydroxylated Cyclohexylamine in Human Prisoners Receiving Cyclamates." In the memo the FDA scientist said, "Not all N-hydroxylated amines are carcinogenic and mutagenic, but a sufficient number are to cause serious concern." He closed the memo stating, "The use of cyclamates should be immediately curtailed, pending the outcome of additional studies." [24] The memo was passed to Dr. Legator's superior, Dr. Edwin L. Hove, who disagreed with the recommendation. Dr. Hove claims that he and his superiors decided that the memo should be rewritten. Without informing Dr. Legator, Dr. Banes (to whom Dr. Legator's memo was addressed), or Commissioner Ley, a new memorandum was prepared and forwarded over Dr. Legator's name with the same heading and date, using the original language, but omitting the strong recommendation against cyclamate use. This deceptive action obscured the "profound importance" of the discovery Dr. Legator wished to communicate to the office of FDA Commissioner Ley.

The dramatic findings of Drs. Legator and Verrett were not the only evidence implicating cyclamates which the FDA ignored. At least ten other danger signals, all of which FDA researchers had brought to the Commissioner's attention by December 12, 1968, brought no action. It seems likely that regular use of cyclamates might disrupt the effects of anticoagulants in humans, perhaps through inhibiting vitamin K effectiveness, an effect that could cause bleeding problems. Tests show unexplained effects on the liver. Cyclamates affect the intestinal tract, causing softening of the stool. Cyclamate use causes a change in the way the body absorbs certain drugs, by, for example, affecting the way substances bind themselves to plasma, probably altering the effectiveness of the drug. Cyclamate absorption into the body is increased by the consumption of caffeine, fats, and citric acid, and cyclamates are distributed through breast milk and across the placenta. Each of these effects is cause for detailed scrutiny. It appears that a significant portion of food-grade cyclamates contains the dangerous and untested chemical cyclohexylamine (CHA) so that even that portion of the population that does not convert cyclamates to CHA is likely to be exposed to CHA if they consume foods containing cyclamates. Controlled tests on mammals indicate that CHA affects the reproductive system, causing, for example, some loss of fetuses (fetus resorption) in pigs. There has been only a very limited number of really effective long-term feeding studies with adequate numbers of animals, so it is difficult to assess how likely it is that cyclamates or CHA will cause cancer. A final argument against the continued use of cyclamates in place of sugar as a sweetener is the fact that they have limited effectiveness for weight control even under controlled dietary conditions. Tests on both humans and rats that compared the effects of sugar and cyclamates on body weight showed no significant advantage to cyclamate use. All of these facts were presented to FDA Commissioner Herbert Ley in a detailed memorandum from Dr. John J. Schrogie and Dr. Herman F. Kraybill, of the FDA's bureaus of medicine and science respectively, on December 12, 1968. On December 13, 1968, Dr. Ley issued a press release that, although it said, "Totally unrestricted use of the cyclamates (commonly used as artificial sweeteners) is not warranted at this time," generally implied that there was little in the then widespread general use of cyclamates to be concerned about. On the day of this announcement one FDA laboratory assistant said, "It makes you wonder about the agency. It all seems like politics, not science."

Dr. Ley's conclusions about the safety of cyclamate use were based on the 1968 report of the National Academy of Sciences committee studying cyclamates. Drs. Schrogie and Kraybill, the Commissioner's own experts, reviewed that report when it came out and said:

This report of the Food Protection Committee represents a largely uncritical review of the available material. Conclusions of studies are included without proper regard for the quality of methodology originally used. Studies lacking adequate statistical design are given equal weight with sounder studies; many clinical and epidemiological studies yielding questionable conclusions are given uncritical acceptance. Because such conclusions are included, possibly erroneous results gain added stature and interpretive errors are perpetuated.

It is not our intention to direct attention solely to reports of potentially toxic effects. The quality of studies is often mediocre on both sides of the issue. Although questions of safety have been raised, they have not as yet been resolved satisfactorily in either direction.

This Report, in general, suggests a level of knowledge on many aspects of this topic which simply does not exist. It should have pointed more critically to the current deficiencies in information as a basis for further action.[25]

In December, 1968, acting on this uncritical report based on incomplete knowledge and in spite of serious significant doubts, Commissioner Ley moved to retain cyclamates on the FDA Generally Recognized As Safe list. In taking that action, the Commissioner had to ignore major questions about cyclamate safety raised by Drs. Schrogie, Kraybill, Legator, and Verrett of his own staff and supported by a significant amount of scientific study both inside and outside the FDA.

When HEW Secretary Robert H. Finch finally removed cyclamates from the GRAS list and the market, he too did not mention the doubts contained in fifteen years of scientific writing about the chemical. He misled and confused the American public. He did not warn that scientific knowledge about chemical hazards is severely limited. He did not try to explain that the law requires a food additive to be established as safe before it is used and that the manufacturer of cyclamates had failed to meet this responsibility. Instead he chose to dismiss all but one narrow study suggesting a connection between rat cancer and cyclamates. Rather than clearly asserting his authority, the Secretary backed into an apologetic enforcement of one particular codicil of the law, saying, "I have acted under the provisions of law because . . . I am required to do so." [26] The Secretary's press conference and his subsequent actions suggest that he misunderstands the 1958 Food Additives Amendment and the hazards it was meant to control. He seemed to consider it unimportant that an additive be proven safe before it was cleared for use in food, and he appeared willing to permit modification of the law to allow distribution in food of elements that had not been proven safe. He spoke of the growing scientific concern about the increasing number of chemicals that individuals come in contact with as if it were insignificant. He treated as unnecessary the protection of every scientist's right to communicate his findings to his fellow scientists and the general public.

There is bound to be heated debate when the safety of a chemical as widely used as cyclamates is brought into question. The food industry has a tremendous economic investment in the continued use of the substance. To protect this investment, it can argue that no ill effects have yet been observed in human beings. But the question is: when a food additive presents a possible risk, shall it be allowed in the food supply until proven unsafe, or shall it be excluded from the food supply until proven safe? In other words, shall the safety of a food additive be tested in human beings or in rats? In the case of cyclamates, the position of the FDA has amounted to a belief that the testing should be done on people. If the food industry can use a questionable additive until it is conclusively proven to be unsafe, people will be injured. The pre-testing provisions of the food additive law are designed to avoid this kind of injury, but the FDA has failed to protect the public against such injury, and now Secretary Finch has chosen to minimize the serious danger presented by the FDA's policy.

The purpose of the Food Additives Amendment of 1958 is clearly spelled out in the committee report on the bill. "The purpose of the legislation is to protect the health of consumers by requiring manufacturers of food additives and food processors to pre-test any potentially unsafe substances which are to be added to food." [27] The grave doubts that have been raised about cyclamates clearly bring them within the reach of this purpose as a "potentially unsafe substance." The law itself is explicit about how such a substance *must* (a requirement of law) be treated by the Secretary of Health, Education, and Welfare. It shall only be placed in the food supply in accordance with a regu- lation and "no such regulation shall issue if a fair evaluation of the data before the Secretary fails to establish that the proposed use of the food additive . . . will be safe." [28] The Secretary has dismissed the ma- jority of the data suggesting danger in cyclamates. [29] But even the evidence that he acknowledges, a test commissioned by Abbott Laboratories showing a sig- nificant number of bladder cancer tumors in rats fed cyclamates, cannot be said to establish the safety of cyclamates—quite the contrary. Therefore, if the law is to be applied, cyclamates must not be allowed as an additive to any food.

But this basic authority was not what Secretary Finch invoked in removing cyclamates from the market. He relied instead on what he called "the so-called Delaney Amendment, enacted eleven years ago, which states that any food additive must be removed from the market if it has been shown to cause cancer when fed to humans or animals." [30] By this and subsequent statements, the Secretary and his advisers imply that but for the "so-called Delaney Amendment," cyclamates could legally remain on the market. Thus Secretary Finch has chosen to minimize the basic concept of the food additive law that only items *proven safe* can be allowed in the food supply. There was no need to rely on the Delaney Clause in moving against cyclamates: doing so put his action on the slenderest available legal base. As a result, the decision has been easily eroded by special interests and does not serve as the strong precedent against future industry challenges and interpretations that it should.

The Secretary had only to decide that enough scientific evidence had been raised to refute FDA's contention that cyclamates were generally recognized as safe. Following such a determination, the burden of proving safety, according to the law, rests with the manufacturers of cyclamate: they would have had to prepare a food additive petition alleging safety, which would then have been evaluated by FDA scientists. But sixty-four years of supposed regulation of the food supply by the Food and Drug Administration have shown that when the law allows administrative discretion, industry, not the consumer, benefits. Instead of invoking his discretionary power against cyclamates, Secretary Finch waited until the law forced him to act. Even then he criticized the Delaney Clause under which he was acting: "But who's to say that using Fresca or some other diet drink . . . isn't better for you than the problems of overweight or diabetes?" [31] No more eloquent argument for the retention and expansion of the Delaney Clause can be made than the assertion that without it the unrestricted use of cyclamates in foodstuffs, a use opposed by the National Academy of Sciences for fifteen years, would be continuing uninhibited today. What is needed to provide effective consumer protection is stronger laws—patterned after the Delaney Amendment—which do not allow administrative discretion.

On November 14, one month after the cyclamate ban

was announced, HEW decided that the ban on cyclamates in packaged foods (as opposed to beverages) would go into effect on September 1, 1970, rather than February 1, as originally announced. The delay allowed owners of foods already canned to cut their losses, which would have been close to $100 million. A week later, on November 20, Secretary Finch announced that "cyclamates will be restricted essentially to use in foods, [i.e., not beverages] and as a sugar substitute produced in tablet or liquid form." [32] There would, he promised, be a requirement that "food products and concentrates containing cyclamates be drug-labeled to show the cyclamate content in an average serving" and allowing them to be "sold on a non-prescription basis." [33] This announcement signaled a retreat not only from the original October 18, 1969, ban but from even the less dramatic position of caution adopted by the FDA in April, 1969. At that time the FDA proposed that labels be required to declare the amount of cyclamates in the product, to warn of possible hazards, and to recommend a maximum daily intake level. In order to be at all effective, any cyclamate labeling must indicate the levels at which ingestion of cyclamates might become dangerous. The idea of such a warning is, of course, offensive to the food industry because it might cut into profits. The requirement for a warning never went into effect. Secretary Finch's announcement softening the FDA's position *after* dramatic evidence of hazard became known is at best cynically irresponsible. Giant advertising campaigns were conducted within the food industry, proclaiming "the government has changed its mind on cyclamates." NBC News pointed out that for all intents and purposes "they [foods containing cyclamates] will be available to anyone not frightened away by the warning label." Dr. Frederick Stare, syndicated columnist and head of the department of nutrition at Harvard, said in one column that foods containing cyclamates would be readily available for those people who were diabetic or who desired to lose weight. On the day it was announced the retreat was underlined by Surgeon General Dr. Jesse Steinfeld's revelation that FDA tests using one-sixth the amount of cyclamates as that in the orig-

inal tests for one-sixth the period of time had also resulted in a significant incidence of bladder cancer—this
time in a different strain of rats.[34]

Secretary Finch has publicly identified the usefulness
of cyclamates for diabetics and in control of weight as
important benefits to be weighed against the dangers
of cyclamates. In fact, the FDA told the National
Academy of Sciences and the general public that "none
of the few controlled studies reported to date have established a useful role for nonnutritive sweeteners as
weight-reducing aids except under the most carefully
controlled conditions." [35] In one controlled study carried
out by the Harvard School of Public Health and the
Peter Bent Brigham Hospital, involving 247 obese individuals and 100 diabetic persons, no significant difference was apparent when the weight loss of users and
nonusers of low-calorie diet foods was compared.[36] In
well-controlled animal experiments male rats fed cyclamates in amounts equivalent to that normally consumed
by man actually gained weight.[37] More significant in
light of HEW's decision to allow the use of foods containing cyclamates if labeled for diabetics is the fact
that diabetics appear to have six to ten times the normal
number of grossly deformed offspring, one of the kinds
of harm related to cyclamates by laboratory studies.[38]
In minimizing its legal authority and ignoring significant
scientific evidence, HEW leaders have shown the same
insensitivity as the FDA toward growing scientific concern about the potential destructiveness of the chemical
environment.

When they banned cyclamates Secretary Finch, Commissioner Ley, and other HEW officials took this opportunity to minimize instead of highlight the potential
danger of the chemical. Dr. Jesse Steinfeld, speaking for
Secretary Finch at the October 18, 1969, press conference said, "We have no indication that human bladder
cancer from whatever cause is increasing to any significant degree. Our data to this effect are obtained from
studies underway for at least two decades in the state
of Connecticut. It is the only good source known to us
for such data, and it was brought up to date two days
ago by what we have obtained in the way of data up to
now." [39]

Ten days after the press conference an HEW official, Dr. Joseph A. Lieberman, stated in an internal HEW memorandum calling for further study of the possible hazards related to cyclamates, "Dr. Steinfeld refers to data from the Connecticut cancer registry that indicates no significant increase in human bladder cancer has occurred over the past 20 years. Retrospective registry data on a single type of cancer in one state might not at this point in time provide a sufficiently sensitive index on the carcinogenic effect of a chemical agent if a latent period of 10–20 years is operable, such as is the case for other amine bladder turmorigens in man. Cyclamates have come into wide-scale dietary use only in the past ten years. Therefore, sufficient time probably has not elapsed for any significant increase in humans to be manifested." [40] On October 30 Dr. Steinfeld learned from scientists at the National Institute of Cancer that in fact the Connecticut registry data showed that between 1945 and 1965 the incidence of bladder cancer in that state doubled. Of course, this rise in bladder cancer cannot be traced to cyclamates for the reasons cited by Dr. Lieberman, but it certainly contradicts the figures cited twelve days earlier by Dr. Steinfeld.

HEW, again following the lead of the FDA, dismissed as insignificant data showing chromosome breakage and embryo deformity in laboratory tests with animals given doses of cyclamates. When the decision to take cyclamates off the market was announced, Dr. Steinfeld explained, "The decisions being announced here today are based on bladder tumors obtained from feeding massive doses of cyclamate throughout the life span of rats. It has nothing to do with previous studies of the effect of cyclamates on chick embryos or on studies of rat chromosomes in tissue culture or rat chromosome studies *in vivo* experiments to that time." [41] The studies referred to were those of FDA scientists Legator and Verrett, which together received wide publicity leading to an October convening of the National Academy of Sciences Committee on Non-nutritive Sweeteners. In the FDA presentation to that committee, Dr. Verrett reported that when very small doses (.5 parts per million) of calcium cyclamate were injected into fertile eggs, 13 per cent of the chick embryos from those eggs were grossly (i.e., visibly) deformed. The same test using cyclohexylamine at the extremely low level of .05 parts per million produced 25 per cent deformities.[42] At some higher but not excessive levels, Dr. Verrett's experiments produced teratogenic deformities at a rate approaching 100 per cent. In fact, both cyclamates and cyclohexylamine produced more chick embryo deformities than thalidomide did when it was applied in the same tests. When taken by pregnant women, thalidomide caused gross (teratogenic) deformities—including lack of arms, legs, or fingers, and inoperative limb joints—in over ten thousand European babies.

The NAS Committee on Non-nutritive Sweeteners received as an official submission from Dr. Legator data suggesting that cyclamates might cause genetic damage. Dr. G. B. West, identified by *Medical World News* as a "prominent British government investigator" from the British Industrial Biological Research Association, was impressed by Legator's findings. Dr. West explained that "any effect on chromosomes is a major item, and the low-dose discoveries of the FDA study are right in the danger zone. These findings should be borne in mind by everybody researching cyclamate." [43] (The dose level was ten milligrams per kilogram of body weight, which was one-fifth of that recommended as a safe daily intake level by FDA in its December 13, 1968, warnings on cyclamate consumption.) Interestingly enough, the NAS committee failed to take notice of the Legator data even though the committee's chairman had been unofficially provided a copy shortly after the information was presented to a seminar of 150 cytogeneticists and biologists run by Oak Ridge National Laboratory at Gatlinburg, Tennessee, in the middle of October, 1968. Dr. Julius Coon, chairman of the committee, explained that his group's policy was "to evaluate only material that is in the published literature or has come to it through official channels." [44] Apparently, the FDA did not think enough of Legator's data or its implications for the health of the American people to allow it to be evaluated by the NAS committee until 1969, one year after it had first been made public. That was the last official action that the FDA took on Legator's or Verrett's data in spite of the fact that Dr. Lieberman singled them out in his memorandum. Specifically, he said the Verrett-Legator data strongly suggested that cyclamates might cause mutations, teratogenic deformities, or cancer, and that in this regard cyclamates were an example of a potential chemical hazard causing increasing concern among scientists. Dr. Lieberman suggested that the FDA undertake studies to determine if cyclamates already consumed had had any observable negative effects in humans. Another HEW scientist, Dr. Umberto Saffioti, recommended that persons who had consumed great quantities of cyclamates should seek periodic clinical examinations to detect possible developing bladder cancers. But Saffioti elicited no more response from the FDA than Lieberman had.

A great deal of evidence suggests that cyclamates are hazardous. By ignoring most of it and minimizing the rest, Secretary Finch and Commissioner Ley allowed an atmosphere of dangerous confusion to prevail. The room for a justified difference of opinion on cyclamates could have been considerably narrowed if the entire story had been accurately told by the Commissioner and the Secretary. In fact, "in England, private-label foods containing the artificial sweetener cyclamate have been (voluntarily) banned from the shelves of at least 27 department stores and 270 supermarkets" since late 1968, *Medical World News* reported.[45] American grocers have been uncertain how to deal with the remaining products containing cyclamates.

More distressing than the confusion of grocers, however, is the confusion of doctors and scientists. On November 18, 1969, an advisory committee reported to Secretary Finch that the medical benefits of cyclamates (to diabetics and to patients to whom weight control is essential) outweighed the hazards of the chemical. Although this report significantly eroded the decision to ban cyclamates, neither the recommendations nor the method used to arrive at them can be justified. None of the researchers critical of cyclamates were on the committee or consulted by it. There was no evidence presented showing that cyclamates could be useful in either diabetes or weight management. Some evidence to the contrary exists and apparently was not considered.

Surgeon General Steinfeld has continued to participate in misleading the public and the scientific community. In the February 20, 1970, issue of *Science,* Dr. Steinfeld, along with former FDA Commissioner Dr. Ley, representatives of Abbott Laboratories, and an independent research laboratory that does testing for Abbott, repeated without variance a version of the cyclamate ban that was scientifically misleading and legally inaccurate. Although Dr. Steinfeld knew of and had publicly explained the results of FDA tests showing bladder cancer in rats at relatively low dosage and in a second strain of rats, he did not mention this study in the *Science* article. Instead, he signed a report of the high-dosage studies originally done, leaving the impression that there was little evidence to implicate cyclamates as dangerous. Legally he repeated the inaccurate contention that the FDA was forced to remove cyclamates from the market only because of the Delaney Clause. Even if there were no prohibition against substances that cause cancer in animals, cyclamates would have to be removed from the GRAS list and from the market under the remaining requirements of the law. Distortion of the law and of reported test results on cyclamates by government and industry spokesmen writing and speaking in concert is a most dangerous practice. By directing cyclamates to the diabetic population, the Surgeon General and the advisory committee might subject diabetics to certain serious hazards. Assistant Surgeon General Arthur S. Wolff, in a memo drafted "for the record" three days before the dramatic and unexpected cyclamates ban, pointed out that the "diabetic state itself appears to be etiologically associated with a higher prevalence of congenital defects as well as still births and neonatal mortality." In short, the diabetic appears to be particularly sensitive to the very kinds of hazard suggested by research to be related to cyclamates.[46]

Scientists at Albany Medical College, who have been conducting tests on cyclamates, insisted that their contracts for human feeding tests of cyclamates not be stopped. It was their intention to feed large doses of cyclamates, even more than the liberal safety levels recommended by the FDA, to prisoners at the New York State Penitentiary, in spite of the scientific evidence of hazard and in spite of vigorous opposition from FDA scientists. Commissioner Ley thought he was bound by the testing contract to allow the research on humans to continue and to expand. Dr. Leo Friedman, head of the FDA pharmacology branch, commenting on these tests, illustrated how bad decisions multiply. He said it was not necessarily immoral to feed cyclamates to prisoners at the Dannemora State Penitentiary in New York because "after all, we're now committing physicians to making this decision every time they advise patients to use cyclamates." [47] Since physicians are being allowed to give cyclamates to patients, it is all right to give the chemical in large doses to prisoners. This argument was not persuasive and the tests on prisoners were halted as "immoral" and "unjustified experimentation."

Each of the scientific problems raised by the FDA research on cyclamates is part of a broader problem first brought to the attention of the agency in a 1963 speech by Nobel Prize-winning scientist, Dr. Hermann Muller. He said, "Today we human beings are exposed to a great number of substances not encountered by our ancestors, to which we therefore have not been specifically adapted by natural selection. Among those substances are food additives, drugs, narcotics, antibiotics, cosmetics, contraceptives, air pollutants, and water pollutants." [48] Dr. Muller was afraid these could cause chromosome breaks, leading to mutations, birth deformities, and cancer. Secretary Finch and Commissioner Ley ignored this possibility when they dismissed the work of their own scientists. Finch actually criticized FDA scientists for speaking out of turn. The following lines were exchanged at a press conference on October 18:

QUESTION: Mr. Secretary, could you tell us if you are satisfied with the Food and Drug Administration's handling of this cyclamate issue?
SECRETARY FINCH: By and large, yes. I was unhappy and expressed my unhappiness about the subject doctor [sic] in the Food and Drug Administration who chose in the case of

the eggs to go directly to the media without having consulted with their superior and with the office. That is not a procedure I approve and certainly they did not act in a very ethical way.

DR. STEINFELD: These experiments must be communicated, but the problem is that people to whom they should be communicated are other scientists working in the field who do have the ability to interpret them and relate them to other ongoing research.

I think it unfortunate to publish them in general media along with interpretations which at this moment certainly are far from justified.[49]

The unjustified interpretation referred to was given by FDA scientist Dr. Jacqueline Verrett on a Washington, D.C., television station on October 1, 1969:

ANNOUNCER: FDA scientists are reluctant to offer their opinions on sensitive matters, but Dr. Verrett was asked what her experiments should mean to women who are pregnant.

DR. VERRETT: It would seem that at least here, an effect on reproduction has been demonstrated. It's only in the chicken embryo. However, I think the prudent thing is to avoid anything which is unnecessary and which is not given under medical supervision perhaps, until further information has been gained.[50]

This televised interview began the chain of events that culminated in the banning of cyclamates. To dismiss its conclusion as unjustified and call Dr. Verrett unethical for raising her doubts in public is to demonstrate an insensitivity to the need for the responsible presentation of scientific information to the general public, who are, after all, the potential or actual victims of any industry negligence or venality. Dr. Verrett's conclusion was no more dramatic than those of other doctors and scientists. Dr. Claire Dick, an Abbott Laboratories cytogeneticist, appeared as a representative of that company on KDKA-TV in Pittsburgh, September 4, 1969, nearly one month before the Verrett presentation in Washington. Interviewer Maria Torre asked Dr. Dick, "Do you use cyclamates, doctor?"

DR. DICK: Yes, I do.

TORRE: If you were pregnant, would you use them?

DR. DICK: Well, pregnancy is another matter because the National Foundation suggest, and I would agree with this, that no pregnant woman should consume any kind of chemicals unless she's advised to by her doctor.[51]

Dr. Verrett's warning was not only justified, it was generally concurred with by the scientific and medical community. Dr. Verrett did not, as Secretary Finch alleged, "go directly to the media." In fact, Paul Friedman of NBC News in Washington approached her on September 29, 1969. Dr. Verrett did not proceed, as the Secretary alleges, "without having consulted with her superiors." Actually, she immediately informed the press office of FDA, which in turn informed Deputy Commissioner Winton Rankin, who was acting as Commissioner while Dr. Ley was out of town. Mr. Rankin approved the interview. His only comment about it subsequently was that he did not know that the chick deformities caused by cyclamates would be related to similar deformities caused by thalidomide. The comment illustrates his misunderstanding of the problem, not his failure to be consulted on the proposed interview. If Dr. Verrett's conclusion was a generally accepted health warning and her procedure proper, it was irresponsible to say she acted unethically. In fact, any other action on her part, which could have resulted in withholding a serious health warning from the public, would have been a transgression of her profession's ethical standards.

Though Dr. Legator was not directly referred to during the October 18 press conference, Secretary Finch and Dr. Steinfeld indirectly criticized his wide publicity in the popular press. The Washington *Post* (November 17, 1968), *Newsweek* (September 29, 1969), and a number of other publications have presented popular versions of Dr. Legator's discovery that cyclamates break the chromosomes of rats—an effect that could cause cancer. Dr. Steinfeld's belief that scientific studies done by government researchers "should be communicated [only to] other scientists working in the field" would seem to apply to Dr. Legator as well as Dr. Verrett. But Dr. Legator's experience within the FDA should be an instructive warning to both HEW and the general public.

He presented the findings of his study in a technical paper to a technical scientific gathering—the Seventh

Conference on Mammalian Cytology and Somatic Cell Genetics—in October, 1968. His findings were passed over (because he had not *officially* and directly submitted them) by the National Academy of Sciences Committee on Non-nutritive Sweeteners a month later. In January Legator's recommendation to Commissioner Ley that cyclamates be removed from the market at once was excised from his memo without Legator's—or the Commissioner's—knowledge. Dr. Legator then prepared his findings for publication, and they appeared in *Science* magazine on September 21, 1969. In spite of the fact that Dr. Legator's information had not been considered by the NAS-NRC committee on cyclamates in November, 1968, and in spite of its acknowledged importance, it was not until eleven months later, after the public had been alerted to the potential dangers of the chemical, that the FDA prevailed on the NAS-NRC to consider it officially. In the meantime, Dr. Verrett's findings, first officially reported to her FDA superiors in March, 1968, were also being officially ignored by the agency. When the unexpected call from NBC-TV came to Dr. Verrett's office in September, 1969, ethics, against the background of official lack of interest, left little room for the scientist but to seek permission, which she did, to tell her story publicly.

The dangers of cyclamates and the way they were obscured by the FDA and Secretary Finch should serve as a warning to the public. It should now be common knowledge that it is possible for the Food and Drug Administration to call a potentially hazardous substance safe. The cyclamates case establishes the fact that the FDA has been less than diligent in applying the food protection laws. It should now be clear that uncritical reliance on the pronouncements of professional scientists cannot be substituted for enlightened public inquiry into serious health-related food problems—particularly when the FDA distorts or withholds altogether scientific reports. That Secretary Finch has chosen to relax the ban on cyclamates, saying that "cyclamates will be restricted essentially to use in foods" (i.e., not in beverages), should cause grave doubts about both HEW's ability to apply scientific evidence and the procedures the agency uses to set policy. Unfortunately, the treatment of cyclamates is not an exception; it is a representative case study of how the FDA fails to provide the kind of protection for the food supply which the American consumer expects and often thinks he is getting.

The dramatic removal of cyclamates from the marketplace was necessary because the FDA failed to do its job. It did not heed the frequent early warnings against the general use of cyclamates made by the scientific community. It did not periodically and systematically review the safety of substances on its GRAS list. It dismissed or distorted the warnings of its own scientists. Secretary Finch compounded these failures by ignoring the accumulated doubts about cyclamates and minimizing the importance of removing the chemical from the market rapidly. He did not connect this removal with the legal requirement that all chemicals must be proved safe before being added to food. He never mentioned evidence that birth defects and genetic damage that were related to cyclamates in tests on laboratory animals are a more serious danger than cancer. And he denied the importance of free scientific inquiry, expression, and interchange between scientists and the public. In spite of this negative stance on the part of the man most responsible for regulating what the food industry puts into the American food supply, Louis Harris reported that 50 per cent of the American people supported the ban. Given clear-cut information and responsible leadership by individuals in government and industry, public support for the action would doubtless have been far stronger. By attempting to avoid, then delaying and finally distorting the ban on cyclamates, the FDA and Secretary Finch undermined confidence in the American food supply and left the impression that neither government nor industry is primarily concerned with protecting the public interest.

The impression is quite accurate. The cyclamates decision must be viewed as the beginning, not the end, of public concern about chemicals in the food supply.

2.

Enforcement

*"The Food and Drug Administration is
charged by Congress with an onerous
responsibility—that of protecting this
Nation's health. Instead of shouldering
this heavy responsibility,
we find the agency engaged
in bizarre and juvenile games
of cops and robbers."*

—Senator Edward Long

The FDA has often responded to major health problems such as the propriety of using cyclamates in the food supply with lethargy, but, when faced with the relatively minor transgressions of individuals it particularly dislikes, the agency has managed to exhibit a frightening vigor. Take the case of Dr. Wilhelm Reich, the well known avant-garde psychoanalyst.

Dr. Reich became known in this country during the 1940's for his unique set of theories on the nature of sexuality. Reich was already famous as the author of the generally recognized psychiatric classic, *Character Analysis,* which set the framework for his theories on sex, and as the man who had first described the function of the orgasm. By 1947 his ideas had become faddishly fashionable, and a number of so-called Reichian groups (which greatly distorted and vulgarized the psychiatrist's theories) were establishing communities, particularly in California. In May, 1947, *The New Republic* reported on the developing Reichian movement, criticizing Reich for his apparent claim that he had found a way to cure cancer and for developing and selling devices (orgone accumulators, orgone blankets, and orgone boxes) that he claimed could improve personal health. It was at this point and in response to *The New Republic* article that the FDA first became officially interested in Reich.

For the next thirteen years the FDA conducted a

vicious campaign to discredit him and his ideas, distorting facts in its possession to achieve that goal. The agency fundamentally misstated the results of a State Department background check on Reich, conducted at the FDA's request. The State Department reported in June, 1952, that the author of a rumor that Dr. Reich had not received a medical degree had officially retracted it, that Dr. Reich had in fact received a medical degree in Vienna, and that he had worked with Sigmund Freud, becoming senior analyst at Freud's Berlin Institute.[1] Sixteen months after this State Department memorandum was filed, John Harvey of the FDA summarized the FDA argument against Reich for government attorneys preparing to prosecute the psychiatrist, saying that "Although he [Reich] lays claim to having graduated some thirty years ago from the University of Vienna Medical School with an M.D. degree, we have not been able to confirm this and the opinion has been expressed in scientific circles in Norway that the character of his medical education is to be questioned." The Harvey memorandum even referred directly to the State Department investigation which it so grossly distorted. Harvey also slurred Dr. Reich's character by referring to Ilse Ollendorff as the woman he lived with.[2] Ilse Ollendorff was in fact the doctor's wife.

In this frame of mind, the FDA finally went to court. There is little doubt that the use and sale of the orgone devices (which by best estimates brought in approximately $100,000 of income over the fifteen years of their use) raised serious legal questions under the Food, Drug, and Cosmetic Act, but the FDA was after much more than the devices. Under the act, Reich's books could be legally construed as descriptive labels or direction for the use of the devices. Because of this, the FDA obtained a court injunction that barred the orgone devices from interstate commerce, prohibited the sale of ten different works written by Reich (including the classic, *Character Analysis*), and decreed the "destruction of all documents, bulletins, pamphlets, journals and booklets" of Reich's research foundation.[3] In accordance with the third part of this injunction, an FDA inspector called on Reich in July, 1956, and proceeded to enforce the order by *burning Wilhelm Reich's books.* "During the

burning of the books Dr. Reich found himself just about
to throw some of the literature on the fire," noted the
FDA inspector in his office memo recording the event.
"He stopped short and remarked, 'I promised myself
that I would have nothing to do with the burning of this
literature.' Dr. Reich was very friendly, and the conversation was pleasant during my visit. He also stated that
his books had been burnt in Germany, and he did not
think it would ever happen again, but here they were
being burned once again." [4]

For refusing to obey certain parts of the injunction,
Reich was sent to the Federal penitentiary at Lewisburg,
Pennsylvania, where he died seventeen months later. As
late as 1960 agents of the FDA were still seeking out
and burning various Reich publications owned by his
heirs. Altogether, the FDA spent thirteen years on the
case.

Was this a proper use of Federal regulatory authority?
The American Civil Liberties Union described the
court injunction upon which the FDA acted as "a
serious challenge to the freedom of scientific inquiry
and to the freedom of the press, principles of free
thought on which our democratic government is
based." [5] The FDA's campaign against the sale of Reich's
books as well as the burning of his papers and pamphlets was a grievous misuse of its power, regardless of
the merits of Reich's writings. The FDA is charged with
protecting the nation's health through regulating its food
and drug supply, not with suppressing opinions it finds
offensive. It is an irony that in the case of Wilhelm Reich
much of the work that the FDA wished to suppress was
highly thought of by members of the psychoanalytic profession, and that the FDA knew this to be the case before
the prosecution of Reich was launched. The State Department document filed four years before the action had
said, "It is of interest that all but one of the psychiatrists [in Norway] consulted for information about Dr.
Reich spoke of his psychiatric work with the greatest
respect while without exception denying the validity of
his biological work." [6]

It is a further irony that the Food and Drug Law,
through the FDA's enforcement policy, tends to catch
not those guilty of fraud, but those who sincerely believe

in their theories and works. Unlike cynical shakedown artists, the true believer is reluctant to admit his error in return for a suspended sentence. If Dr. Reich had been willing to admit that his orgone devices were useless and to cease selling them, he would have escaped all further harassment, including the burning of his papers and the suppression of his books. Thus the FDA policy has resulted in the reversal of one of the ancient tenets of law, that evil intentions are an important part of the crime of fraud.

In 1965 Senator Edward Long of Missouri conducted hearings which, according to him, "uncovered instance after instance of FDA raids on small vitamin and food supplement manufacturers. These small, defenseless businesses were guilty of producing products which FDA officials claimed were unnecessary for the average human diet. Here again, we have the same Federal agency setting itself up as the judge of what should and should not be eaten by the general public." [7] The Long hearings on invasion of privacy by government agencies revealed that the FDA had one of the largest and most sophisticated inventories of snooping devices in the Federal government. Asked about these devices by a special subcommittee of the House Committee on Interstate and Foreign Commerce in 1966, Dr. James Goddard, then Commissioner of Food and Drugs, said, "We do have equipment that is used . . . to record oral promotional claims made by health food lecturers at public meetings and by door-to-door salesmen who offer such things as vitamins as cures for disease." [8] Dr. Goddard did not explain in detail how these devices were used, but the description can be supplied from a brief filed in the United States Supreme Court:

FDA agents testified that certain premises of the Fort Wayne Hotel had been leased to the defendants and that before the lectures were open to the public the agents entered upon the premises, dropped a microphone down an air vent which was in the ceiling of the premises directly in front and above the lecture stand, ran wires out of the windows and across the roof of the second floor, and connected the wires to a tape recorder which had been set up in other rooms of the hotel. The record further shows that the agents had gained access to the defendants' leased premises before they were open to the public by flashing official credentials to the Assistant Manager of the hotel and that they had entered the premises on another occasion prior to the time they were open to the public. The agents confirmed that the eavesdropping equipment was Government-owned.

A similar access was made with respect to defendants' business premises in Masonic Temple. There, an FDA agent entered defendants' leased premises before they were open to the public, obtained a tape recorder from the manager of the building and placed it in the manager's office which was in a room separate and apart from defendants' business premises.

The Trial Judge (ruled) . . . that the recordings (though Constitutional) were obtained as a direct consequence of an unlawful trespass and physical intrusion into defendants' business premises.[9]

Senator Edward Long had strong words for such methods:

We have had startling and shocking disclosures during these last three days of hearings. The hearings have revealed police-state tactics ranging from possibly perjured testimony to gain a conviction, to abusive law-enforcement practices including intimidation and gross disregard for the constitutional rights guaranteed to all American citizens by the first, fourth, and fifth, and sixth amendments. In short, an agency of the Federal Government has been accused of attempting to gain convictions at any costs.

Prior to the commencement of these hearings, this same agency saw fit to be unco-operative, misleading and evasive with this committee.

The unfortunate ramifications of such conduct on the part of a Federal agency are overwhelming. The Food and Drug Administration is charged by Congress with an onerous responsibility—that of protecting this Nation's health. Instead of shouldering this heavy responsibility, we find the agency engaged in bizarre and juvenile games of cops and robbers. Instead of a guardian of the national health, we find an agency which is police-oriented, chiefly concerned with prosecutions and convictions, totally indifferent to the individuals' rights, and bent on using snooping gear to pry and invade the citizens' right of privacy.[10]

The FDA's concept of law enforcement is not the creation of evil and destructive inspectors; it comes from higher up in the organization. In fact, the enforcement personnel of the FDA have shown a consistent sensitivity and dedication. But agency policy has channeled their work into relatively unimportant areas and away from areas in which strong enforcement activity is clearly needed. For example, it has been only because of sheer administrative ingenuity by relatively non-influential officials that the Fair Packaging and Labeling Act of 1967, affecting all packaged goods sold in the United States, has received any enforcement at all by the FDA—and then only two men work for its enforcement, while an entire plan of attack for its enforcement is allowed to languish because of inattention or a decision to de-emphasize it from top agency leadership. In place of emphasis on packaging and labeling, FDA enforcement officials, who could be used to speed up consumer protection in the packaging field, agonize over the problems raised by trying to prosecute the supposedly fraudulent religion of Scientology on the grounds that its practitioners use a misbranded "quack" device in their religious activities. In fact, the agonizing proved to be justified when after eight years of FDA work on the Scientology case the United States Court of Appeals for the District of Columbia reversed a district court conviction of Scientology with even the dissenting judge suggesting that the FDA had swept too broadly in its seizure of Scientology literature.[11] Undaunted, the FDA is now preparing to try again.

FDA inspectors are often troubled by the ethical implications of what they are required to do. In a series of interviews conducted by Nader Summer Study Group students in August, 1969, a number of inspectors spoke of their worries over FDA actions. One inspector closely associated with the case against Dr. Reich said he had kept himself informed on its aftermath. Noticing the recent upsurge of responsible debate over the doctor's ideas, he commented, "I hope we did the right thing." (Nathan C. Hale, a New York author and sculptor, is preparing a detailed analysis of Dr. Reich's involvement with the FDA, which may clear up many of the doubts about the case that have troubled doctors, scholars, and students as well as FDA inspectors for the past fifteen years.) Another inspector was asked why, when Dr. Reich's books were burned, more books than the court had ordered were destroyed. "Oh, that happens quite often," he said. "The burning is done by U.S. Marshals, and they burn everything in sight." Yet another inspector commented that when he had personally blocked further action on fifteen cases in which FDA inspectors had tricked people into violating the law, his superiors ordered him to pass the cases on to someone else. Fortunately, William Goodrich, the Department of Health, Education, and Welfare Assistant General Counsel, who oversees FDA legal activity, blocked prosecution of the cases because they would have probably been thrown out of court.

In a fourth conversation an inspector commented on Royal Lee, a dentist and health-food purveyor, long a target of FDA enforcement activities that finally led to Lee's conviction for violation of the Food and Drug Law as well as an injunction against selling mislabeled vitamin preparations, a cease-and-desist order from the Federal Trade Commission, and withdrawal by the Post Office Department of the right to solicit money through the mails. One of Lee's customers, the inspector said, had been Richard M. Nixon, but then he admitted that in eight years of checking the return addresses on Royal Lee's mail he had never seen Mr. Nixon's name. This meant that the FDA was routinely examining the return addresses on Lee's incoming mail, a practice attacked by Senator Long as an offensive breach of the right to privacy. When asked about this procedure the inspector was quick to say that it is done only on fourth-class mail and then only with the permission of the district director, as if this answered the Senator's charge.

The FDA leadership does not consult its enforcement staff on matters of policy. When the much-touted but seriously lacking Kinslow Report, on the consumer protection failures of the FDA, was prepared, only one enforcement official was consulted and he on a very minor point. The Kinslow committee, made up completely of agency personnel, contained no officials whose prime or sole responsibility was for enforcement activities of the agency. The heavy influence of Deputy Commissioner Winton Rankin and Associate Commissioner Kenneth Kirk was responsible for the failure to consider the opinions of people currently working in the agency's enforcement programs. Generally recognized as the most

powerful career men in the FDA, these two former inspectors set enforcement policy based on their combined
total of more than seventy years of working for the FDA.
Unfortunately, their general policies were distinctly different from those of their enforcement staff; in spite of,
or perhaps because of, their tenure, they were the ones
who appeared to be out of touch.

The FDA has founded its enforcement policy upon
the belief that all but a tiny number of the food and
drug manufacturers of the country can be trusted to
place the public interest ahead of their own profits. Alfred
Barnhard, former Director of the FDA Bureau of Regulatory Compliance, speaking in 1968 of the "willingness
to try to comply on the part of the vast majority of the
regulated industry," said: "I have been advised by both
financiers and sociologists that, if it were in fact true
that as many as 15 per cent of the people in this country
really could not be trusted, it would be totally impossible
to carry on the business of the society." [12]

It is curious that Mr. Barnhard should have made a
point of that 15 per cent figure in his speech, because in
fact the FDA estimates that many more than 15 per cent
of the food companies it regulates do not comply with its
guidelines. Here are some of the agency's own statements on this point: "In the food area over 80 per cent of
the establishments subject to the provisions of the Food,
Drug, and Cosmetic Act are in substantial compliance
with its provisions." [13] (I.e., close to 20 per cent of the
establishments are not in compliance.) "FDA's major
food objective is to achieve compliance with good manufacturing practices in at least 90 per cent of the industry or industry segments where the potential of microbiological contamination producing disease states in the
consumer is the highest. Present compliance levels in
this area are estimated to be approximately 65 per cent."
(I.e., approximately 35 per cent of the food industry
does not comply with good manufacturing practices designed to eliminate microbiological diseases.) [14] An enforcement policy that proceeds on the assumption, as
FDA's does, that there is little need for vigorous action
to assure compliance by major manufacturers is doomed
to failure.

Once it is assumed that major producers are anxious

to comply with the law the next step is the development of co-operative agreements. One food trade publication was full of praise for former FDA Commissioner Herbert L. Ley's desire to have "more extensive two-way communication with food manufacturers." Its article stated:

Some of the Commissioner's enthusiasm comes from a recent achievement. FDA officials sat down at the conference table with executives of member companies of Grocery Manufacturers of America. The purpose was to solve common problems and iron out differences. Resolution of one worrisome question is cited. Agreement was reached on a definition of "withdrawal." When a food product is still under the control of the manufacturer, taking it off the market does not constitute an FDA "withdrawal." In the absence of legal action, such a move is merely a voluntary removal. This is to the benefit of the industry in a public relations way.[15]

But why should the Commissioner protect the "public relations" image of the food industry? By doing so he may be keeping accurate consumer information from his constituency—the public. If the FDA discovers a putrid, dangerous, or adulterated food condition requiring recall of the product, why should that news be kept from consumers? These recalls used to be published as part of the official record of FDA action. But now it will be impossible for the public to find out that they have been made because they will no longer be published publicly as part of the FDA recall list.

A report to the Secretary of Health, Education, and Welfare, the Department Task Force on Environmental Health and Related Problems, headed by Ron M. Litton, supports doubts about the inherent willingness of industry to comply with the law:

In 1965 a total of 711 firms suspected of producing harmful or contaminated consumer products refused to let Food and Drug Administration conduct inspections. Some 515 refused to furnish quality or quantity formulas to the Administration; 26 denied the Administration the opportunity to observe a manufacturing procedure. And 153 refused Food and Drug Administration personnel permission to review control records. Also, 111 would not permit the Food and Drug Administration to review complaint files, and 216 refused permission to review shipping records.
The consumer was the victim.[16]

The reason why the FDA persists in the strange practice of proclaiming and relying upon the trustworthiness of the food industry is suggested in its resolution of the heated controversy about how to label the fat content of foods. The FDA decided to avoid any positive action because, in the words of William W. Goodrich, HEW Assistant General Counsel for FDA, "Pressing this matter to hearing would involve us in a controversy between the dairy industry and the corn and vegetable oil interests." [17] The FDA moves cautiously against major components of the food industry because it is much smaller and weaker than they are.

The FDA's problems of enforcement have been consistently misrepresented as a choice between stricter police activities leading to more seizures, arrests, and convictions, or a more informal educational approach leading to voluntary compliance with the law. Wallace F. Janssen, the official staff historian of the Food and Drug Administration, bluntly stated the problems as " 'Education' vs. 'Enforcement'—a basic issue" in the title of one section of his history of the FDA during Lyndon Johnson's Presidency. Janssen points out that the Second Citizens Committee to evaluate the FDA, convened in 1962, recommended that "FDA should put major emphasis on promoting industry self-regulation through greater use of education and co-operation, as contrasted with reliance on court proceedings to insure compliance. . . . A basic question—what kind of agency should the FDA become—was still to be answered. Should it be more educational and scientific—less of a policeman? Industry had long been in favor of this. The 'cop and robber' image of FDA's relation to business was highly distasteful, as was publicity about law violations. But enlightened industry also recognized the need for enforcement—if only to back up education." [18]

No idea has damaged the effectiveness of the FDA more than the thought that law enforcement can be separated from compliance with the law. It has divided industry, the FDA, and observers into vigorously warring camps partisan to one side or the other—education or enforcement—diverting energy and resources away from fundamental issues. The suspicion and division have led to a marked deterioration of both FDA's science education *and* law enforcement. The dichotomy was described in 1955 by the First Citizens Committee convened to evaluate the effectiveness of the FDA. In December, 1969, it was still playing a vital role in discussions of the latest agency reorganization. The *Food, Drug and Cosmetic Reports,* a private weekly publication for executives in the drug, cosmetic, and related industries, described the new FDA commissioner by saying, "COMMISSIONER EDWARDS IS MANAGEMENT-ORIENTED, TO STRESS EFFICIENCY, NOT COPISM: FDA's new commissioner, Dr. Charles Edwards, is a management-oriented former surgeon who will try to turn FDA into a more efficient agency that handles its business more rapidly. His regime is expected to de-emphasize the 'cop' aspect and stress a businesslike organizational approach to handling regulatory and product clearance problems." [19]

If the FDA is going to conduct an effective enforcement program, its officials, beginning with the Commissioner, must eliminate the notion that police activities cannot be done with speed and efficiency. It must earn a reputation as a businesslike, rapidly moving "cop." To create this image it must become more sensitive to the rights of the public, including those it regulates, and it must re-examine ways in which it expends its meager resources. A continued debate over education versus enforcement will be disastrous.

The FDA combines an implicit belief in the honesty of big food interests and a caution about engaging in big fights with a vigorous and unrelenting pursuit of relatively minor hazards which use up large portions of its resources. Thus, it has conducted two great anti-"quack" campaigns, one against fraudulent cancer cures and the other against fraudulent vitamin sales. Dr. Reich was caught in the first crusade and the health food stores defended by Senator Long in the second. The crusades were misconceived because the Food and Drug Law was not designed to deal with the problems raised by sharp and strongly held differences of opinion about how to live and what to eat. It was designed to send to jail that group of human misfits who callously and crudely mislead unsuspecting consumers into reliance on their products in spite of adulteration or lack of value, by cleverly organized and massively circulated sales campaigns. Rather than plan big campaigns against major firms that routinely break the law, the FDA pursues small violators.

Its tenacity in chasing people it considers to be "quacks" is the result of delusion and laziness. The delusion arises from the glamour of stake-outs, two-way radio cars, and clever undercover work, all of which are a part of the quack-abatement activities of the FDA. Laziness is one of the causes because it is much easier to catch a small-time operator, whether venally or innocently destructive, than to tackle the giant corporate frauds. It was FDA policy for years to prove its success by getting convictions, and a little conviction counts as much as a big one on an anonymous scoreboard. The application of major amounts of the agency's limited resources to a relatively unimportant problem is typical of the FDA. The massive effort to stamp out the alleged frauds of the vitamin and health food industries has occupied the time and energy of lawyers, inspectors, scientists, and administrative personnel for years. Yet this is a relatively minor fraud if it is a fraud at all. Former Commissioner James Goddard, who personally adopted this crusade, claims that "$500,000,000 annually is wasted on unnecessary or falsely represented vitamin products and so-called health foods." [20] In contrast, the President's Committee on Consumer Interests said in its 1966 report that "In one study, college-educated shoppers who were directed to select the least expensive package in 20 product categories, failed 43 per cent of the time at an extra cost of 9.0 per cent." [21] If stricter enforcement practices by the FDA caused consumers to save even 1 per cent, rather than 9 per cent of their retail food bill (i.e., 1 per cent of the food industry's estimated $125 billion annual sales), the savings to the American public would be more than twice the total value of the alleged vitamin and health fraud. Yet, the FDA has only two men working to enforce the Fair Packaging and Labeling Law. Even the $500 million figure is suspiciously high because many experts say vitamins are not worthless. Dr. Stanley N. Gershoff, Associate Professor of Nutrition, Harvard School of Public Health, who has worked long and hard to alert the public to the problems of hunger in America, has said that FDA's position on hunger and vitamin supplements is based on "absolutely absurd comments about nutrition." He was speaking at a press conference at the National Press Club in Washington on November 25, 1969, to announce that a survey of nutrition studies conducted between 1950 and 1968 showed a deterioration in American diets, particularly since 1960, that a significant proportion of the population examined were taking in less than half of the recommended daily allowance of vitamins, and that many had biochemical indices in the "deficient" range. In short, the people studied, primarily middle-class, could effectively utilize vitamin supplements. However, it is not difficult to find fraudulent or misleading packages. Still the FDA pursues the vitamin industry in an apparent effort to stamp it out while only two FDA enforcement employees wage a lonely battle against misleading food packages.

Except for their basic assumptions, the great quack campaigns of the FDA are well thought out and co-ordinated. The Post Office Department is relied on to help in the effort to watch the mail of a suspected violator and to challenge the mailing privileges of the accused. The FDA has a working protocol with the Federal Trade Commission that allows the FDA the choice of urging that agency to seek a cease-and-desist order against offending activities when its own authority for seizures is deemed inadequate to stop alleged offenses. The Bureau of Investigations of the American Medical Association is called upon to investigate suspected medical quacks and maintains files on those organizations and persons it believes are encroaching on the legitimate practice of medicine. All parts of this apparatus have been brought together from time to time in national conferences on medical quackery, jointly sponsored by the FDA and the AMA. James Ridgeway, then of *The New Republic*, described the atmosphere of the second annual conference, held in 1963. "You left this two-day convention with the feeling you had been at a training camp for finks who on their return home could make a collect telephone call anytime to the Food and Drug Administration to rat on any doctor not a member of the American Medical Association." [22]

Fraud of this kind that the FDA tackles is a serious

problem causing economic and health problems for many people. However, the emphasis given to fighting it and the methods used by the FDA are far out of proportion to the threat it presents. The single-minded vigor of the FDA antifraud campaign has hurt the agency in three ways. First, it has led the agency into excesses of law enforcement, including the use of snooping, harassment, and prying techniques that it could not effectively defend against charges from Congress and the general public. These excesses have led to the demand by two citizen advisory committees, members of Congress, and many other FDA observers that the enforcement image of the agency be de-emphasized and that a more educational approach to compliance be adopted. Unfortunately, these attacks on enforcement urging that legal activity be replaced with persuasion were wide of the mark. The real problem at the FDA was the failure to develop sophisticated methods to go after meaningful violators. Instead of building a thorough knowledge of the food industry's technology and economics so that it could deal on a basis of equal knowledge with industry personnel, the FDA spent its time developing spying techniques. As a result, between 1950 and 1965 the food industry went through its period of fastest growth almost completely unmonitored. In that time a brand-new series of problems—including the hazards involved with the chemical environment through the use of food additives, the threat of food contamination becoming nationwide through a modern mass-distribution system, the monitoring of dangerous pesticide residues in widely distributed foods, the introduction of brand-new synthetic foods made up entirely of chemicals—developed without serious and effective attention from the FDA.

The second undermining effect of the quack campaigns was their diversion of already existing agency resources away from serious economic and health problems in the larger and more traditional areas of the food industry. The vitamin and health food business, which may not be a fraud at all, was called the "most widespread and expensive type of quackery in the United States" by former FDA Commissioner George Larrick at the 1961 conference on medical quackery. But this "fraud" is minor compared to the routine practices of other segments of the food industry. If the Fair Packaging and Labeling Act were properly enforced, the savings to the American consumer would be between $1 billion and $10 billion. This act alone, properly enforced, might save between two and twenty times more money for Americans than elimination of the most important "fraud" problem now pursued by FDA. Some orange juice processors claim that mislabeling, false advertising, and adulteration in the orange juice industry cost American consumers between $100 million and $300 million each year. Juice is routinely watered. Juice made from concentrate is labeled fresh. And advertising makes claims of freshness and purity that are untrue. The FDA claims it is unable to regulate these abuses because it lacks the ability to analyze the contents of orange juice purchased in stores and does not have the manpower to inspect every plant. The orange juice *drink* business needs more attention from the FDA also. Orange juice drink is sold—at present legally—as a competitor to orange juice, and its advertising claims it is even better than the juice. In fact, it is required to contain only 50 per cent orange juice. The FDA has failed to meet the problem of orange juice drink distortion because, according to Mr. Alvin Gottlieb of the HEW General Counsel's office, the lawyer handling the orange juice drink standard had left the agency in the middle of the problem and there was no one to take his place. In the meantime two HEW attorneys have been spending full time since early 1968 trying to eliminate the vitamin fraud. Salmonella food poisoning costs the American public "at least $300 million annually and probably more," due to days lost from work and medical costs, according to the National Academy of Sciences' 1969 evaluation of the salmonella problem. If the FDA had devoted as much time, energy, money, and people to salmonella as it did to stamping out vitamin frauds, the major portion of that $300 million would have been saved. The entire diet food industry (advertised as an aid to weight control), selling lightly sweetened foods and beverages and costing the American public between $1 and $1.5 billion a year, was based on factual distortions and overt violations of FDA standards by the food industry. The FDA has taken only tentative steps to stamp out this fraud. At the same time, ironically, the problem identified as the vitamin fraud by FDA officials remains roughly the same from year to year in spite of the vigor of the FDA's campaign against it. One reason is that too many reputable scientists and doctors do not agree with the FDA's basic assumption that all vitamins are unnecessary for healthy people.

The third and probably most seriously undermining effect of the quack campaigns has been to obscure serious limitations in the FDA's legal authority and to provide effective arguments against eliminating them. The Litton Report to Secretary Gardner in 1967 described the limitations clearly:

Unlike most government regulatory agencies, the Food and Drug Administration does not have subpoena authority, either to summon witnesses or to require firms to divulge pertinent records. It has requested this investigative authority to allow it to do a better job of protecting the American public. To this date, the request has been denied. With respect to foods, the Department must have considerably more authority to assure adequate protection of the public health. The Department must be able to evaluate the synergistic effect of food additives so that the consumer is protected from threats that cannot be detected by the separate analysis of individual food additives. This means evaluating the sum total of the toxicological effects of a mixture.

Furthermore, the Department must have, as it does not now, adequate authority to inspect and evaluate the processing of foods to make certain that their safety is not impaired through the effect of a process which may or may not involve the use of additives.[23]

A story told by the FDA's legal representative, William W. Goodrich, illustrates just how limited the FDA's authority is. He claims that in one case brought to improve the sanitation standards of a food-producing plant, he showed that there were a large number of flies getting into the food and that there were no screens on the plant windows. He sought a court order to install screens. He claims to have lost the case to the defense, which argued that the screens had been permanently removed from the windows for sanitary reasons—i.e., to let the flies out. The FDA should have the authority to require screens in all food plants.

The Food Safety Panel of the December, 1969, White

House Conference on Nutrition and Health stated that "additional legal authority and resources are urgently needed to expand and improve inspection of food plants." In fact, there is little disagreement that effective food protection by the FDA is severely limited by its lack of enforcement and inspection authority. However, as long as the FDA insists on squandering what powers it has in back-room meetings with industry representatives it cannot expect to have its powers expanded. The FDA cannot effectively protect the food supply of the American consumer without a badly needed expansion of authority. Conversely, it cannot expect to receive expanded powers as long as it acts so irresponsibly that it gives opponents of regulation strong arguments against expanded authority. Whenever supporters of more vigorous regulation of the food industry, both on the inside and outside of government, seek broader FDA authority from Congress, they are faced with convincing arguments from strong food lobbies that the FDA is not responsibly handling the authority it already has. The very people who most benefit from FDA weakness use that weakness as an argument against strengthening the agency. They point to inspectors who leave the FDA to go into industry jobs, harassment of small and relatively defenseless businesses, and foolish wastes of energy such as the vitamin hearings, and convince Congress that the FDA cannot handle more authority.

The program to strengthen the FDA's authority must be implemented in two steps. First, a concerted effort must be made to change the agency's enforcement posture. A beginning could be made by reappraising the agency's present stance against the Church of Scientology, which the FDA still intends to prosecute, and replacing the vitamin hearings with a more reasonable effort to eliminate false vitamin advertising. A reappraisal should lead to more clearly defined and legally acceptable positions on Scientology. At the minimum, the charges and public pronouncements should be narrowed to include reference only to those activities that allegedly violate the Food and Drug Law. But the agency might even consider dropping the entire case, as some of its inspectors suggest. As desirable as stopping Scientology might seem to some, it is not a goal intended by the Food, Drug, and Cosmetic Act. Action to restore the FDA's sanity in the Scientology case could go a long way in beginning the process of restoring the enforcement reputation of the FDA. Eliminating the vitamin hearings would free badly needed resources. At the same time the agency should begin to build a positive image by vigorous enforcement of the Fair Packaging and Labeling Act. While restructuring its enforcement methods and shifting its aim to new targets, the FDA should not give in to pressure to de-emphasize enforcement. In this regard, the agency should overlook the recommendations of the Second Citizens Committee, which called for more emphasis on voluntary compliance. Those recommendations obscure disagreement within the committee. As one member subsequently wrote to the Secretary of HEW, "I am specifically disturbed by the portion of the recommendation that says FDA ought to move from a philosophy of police power enforcement, to health education and thence, to a grand finale of 'mandated self-inspection and self-regulation.' It conveys the impression that FDA should work toward the progressive abandonment of its responsibilities." [24]

The second step in strengthening the FDA's authority must be to begin an information campaign to alert consumers and the Congress to the severity of the limitations placed upon the agency. For example, the names of all plants refusing FDA inspection should be published along with the periodic list of food recalls. Each industry action to remove food from the market after prompting by FDA inspectors should be published publicly as a food recall regardless of the marketing stage at which it occurs. Each case in which the inspection of records would have aided in the elimination of a health or economic danger should be widely publicized to illustrate the importance of obtaining such authority. The number and details of effective enforcement actions thwarted by the FDA's lack of subpoena power should also be made publicly available. Inspection reports on food plants showing the true level of food protection should be made part of the public record. Each of these activities would create an awareness which in turn would spur Congress to take a closer look at the poor state of food protection in 1970 America.

At the same time efforts such as the conferences on medical quackery and meetings designed to notify consumers of the dangers of vitamins should be replaced or paralleled by conferences and meetings on the dangers of food-borne disease. The meaning of the cyclamates ban and the use of food additives generally should be explored in these meetings of consumers, business officials, and representatives of the FDA. This kind of education campaign would be essential in any effort to refine and strengthen the FDA's authority to act against real food-borne hazards. Without it, the FDA will continue striking out in isolated directions without adequate facts or even in spite of the facts. With new enforcement techniques and targets and strengthened authority the FDA might, in the future, successfully avoid the temptation to burn the books of a Dr. Reich while letting the cynically crooked escape.

3. Hidden Ingredients

"Coke got theirs, why can't we get ours?"

—Comment made to an FDA hearing
examiner by an industry lawyer
during 1965 peanut butter hearings

On January 21, 1966, four days after he took office, FDA Commissioner James Goddard issued a food standards regulation for nonalcoholic beverages. One sentence in it ended a controversy that had been simmering since passage of the 1938 Food, Drug, and Cosmetic Act: "Soda water designated by a name including any proprietary name . . . which includes the word 'cola' or a designation as a 'pepper' beverage that, for years, has become well known as being made with kola nut extract and/or other natural caffeine-containing extracts, and thus as a caffeine-containing drink, shall contain caffeine in a quantity not to exceed 0.02 per cent by weight." [1]

The effect of this sentence was to allow cola drink manufacturers and the makers of Dr. Pepper to add caffeine to their products without saying so on the label. All other soft drink manufacturers were required to label added caffeine. After twenty-eight years of stalling against proposals to require caffeine labeling the cola manufacturers—particularly Coca-Cola—were able, with White House and Congressional intervention and over the nearly unanimous objection of FDA staff personnel, to convince the FDA Commissioner to grant an exemption from the labeling requirements of the law.

The authority and guidelines for the establishment of food standards such as that defining Coca-Cola are contained in Section 401 of the Food, Drug, and Cosmetic Act, which reads: "Whenever in the judgment of the Secretary such action will promote *honesty and fair dealing* in the interest of consumers, he shall promulgate regulations fixing and establishing for any food, under its common or usual name so far as practicable, a reasonable definition and standard of identity. . . ." (Emphasis added.)

In a 1935 message to Congress, President Franklin D. Roosevelt outlined the purpose behind the food standard section of the Food Act: "Every enterprise in the United States should be able to adhere to the simple principle of honesty without fear of penalty on that account. Honesty ought to be the best policy, not only for one individual or one enterprise, but for every individual and every enterprise in the nation. In one field of endeavor there is an obvious means to the end which has been too long neglected: the setting up and careful enforcement of standards of identity for food we eat and the drugs we use, together with the strict exclusion from our markets of harmful or adulterated products." [2]

Theoretically, food standards are supposed to insure that the consumer is informed about what he is buying. The standards define cheese, milk, bread, eggs, nuts, ice cream, and all other major food products; each is supposed to consist of mandatory and optional ingredients as spelled out in the food standard, which becomes a part of the United States Code of Federal Regulations. Any ingredient that is mandatory need not be listed on the food package. However, the law intended that all optional ingredients be identified on the label so that a consumer could learn what the product he was buying consisted of by reading the label and checking the Code of Federal Regulations. But the disorderly promulgation of food standards by the FDA has destroyed the consumer's ability to know what he is buying. First, the FDA has created a third category of ingredients—"permissible ingredients"—which can be added to a product if the manufacturer desires but which need not be named on the label. As a result, it is impossible for anyone—the FDA, doctors, or consumers —to know if certain chemicals are present without analyzing the product in a laboratory. The food standards list 223 of these permissible ingredients. Second, there is no consistency in the food standards. Some items must be labeled in some foods but not in others. Emulsifying agents, for example, must be labeled in pasteurized process cheese food, but the same agents need not be labeled in a different product called pasteurized process cheese. There are dozens of examples of this kind of confusion. Third, vague general categories that have no meaning to FDA inspectors or to consumers are prescribed by many standards. "Batter and breading ingredients" must be listed on the package of breaded shrimp, and ingredients identified only as "other foods suitable for blending with cream cheese" are mandatory with certain cream cheese products. In dressings for food, a permissible ingredient not requiring labeling is "any suitable harmless food seasoning or flavoring." The nut products standard allows "seasoning and stabilizing ingredients." All of these categories are vague and uninformative.

By almost any guidelines, food standards have been a failure. The way in which the labeling exemption was granted for the cola and "pepper" beverage industries demonstrates how this breakdown has occurred.

The failure to label caffeine on cola drinks and Dr. Pepper does not necessarily present a health hazard. It does demonstrate an insensitivity toward honesty and fair dealing with consumers. Some consumers wish to avoid consuming caffeine for various reasons. Mormons reject caffeine on religious grounds. Others consider it a health risk. At least one doctor, Dr. Samuel Bellet, Chief of Cardiology of Philadelphia General Hospital, has suggested that "caffeine may be more important than smoking in setting the stage for heart attacks." [3] Certain individuals, sensitive to caffeine, report markedly noticeable heart palpitations following a single cup of coffee or a single bottle of cola beverage and may wish to avoid it. Caffeine is a mild stimulant which appears to create a slight physical dependency in regular users; withdrawal headaches have been associated with cessation of heavy coffee drinking. This combination of health factors has caused some researchers to suggest that caffeine, a food additive generally recognized as safe, ought to be looked at more carefully by those concerned with public health and welfare. For all these reasons many individuals may wish to avoid ingesting caffeine. But they may now consume it in cola and Dr. Pepper drinks without even knowing it.

The vigor and effectiveness of the cola industry effort

to block caffeine labeling on its products demonstrate one way in which the food standard concept has failed. The cola drink manufacturers sought to have caffeine declared a mandatory ingredient of all cola drinks in order to avoid fair, complete, and honest labeling of their product. They succeeded because of the FDA's interpretation of one sentence in Section 401 of the Food, Drug, and Cosmetic Act which reads: "In prescribing any definition and standard of identity for any food or class of food in which optional ingredients are permitted, the Secretary shall, for the purpose of promoting honesty and fair dealing in the interest of consumers, designate the optional ingredients which shall be named on the label."

In characteristic fashion, the FDA interpreted this sentence in the industry's favor, to mean that the agency was prohibited from requiring manufacturers to list mandatory ingredients on their labels. Under this reading of the law, all a business interest needed to do to avoid labeling an embarrassing constituent of its product was to get the FDA to declare it a mandatory ingredient. With the adoption of the nonalcoholic beverage standard, a cola drink was not legally a cola drink unless it contained caffeine.

Also, as a result of this interpretation, the manufacturers of artificially sweetened jams, jellies, and fruits obtained standard definitions that required them to add either saccharin or cyclamates to the product without identifying which sweetener was used and allowed them to label the product "artificially sweetened." These standards were in force at the time the FDA proposed a warning setting out a limited recommended daily intake of cyclamates for health reasons. But it would have been difficult for the public to comply with the warning when the presence of cyclamates was not identified in some of the products in which it appeared. In setting standards for mayonnaise, French dressing, and salad dressings, monosodium glutamate was listed, not as an optional ingredient, but rather as a permissible ingredient— thereby eliminating the requirement that it be declared on the labels of these products. This was done at a time when disturbing questions had been raised about certain suggested adverse effects of the additive. One FDA official even recommended privately to superiors that "like individuals who have adverse symptoms from eating other food items, the individuals who are susceptible to MSG should learn to stay away from food such as soups, with large amounts of MSG." [4] But it is difficult to avoid monosodium glutamate when its presence in three major food categories—salad dressing, French dressing, and mayonnaise—is not labeled on their packages. In fact, the FDA has so confused the wording of its food standards that it has become necessary for persons interested in understanding them to retain a lawyer to discover their meaning. Directing itself specifically to the elimination of this industry-inspired FDA abuse of the law, the Panel on Food Safety of the December, 1969, White House Conference on Food, Nutrition and Health stated, "The existence of definitions and standards of identity for any food should not exempt that food from all requirements for listing ingredients on the label, including such food additives as would be required on the label in the absence of a standard." If the value of food standards as a device for honesty and fair dealing with consumers is to be restored, FDA complicity in food-standard manipulation must be eliminated.

Even if the legal loopholes (many of them created by the FDA itself and correctable without Congressional actions) are closed, the consumer interest faces formidable opposition within the FDA. Again the way "Coke got theirs" illustrates the problem. With passage of the Food, Drug, and Cosmetic Act of June 25, 1938, the FDA obtained the power to set food standards. Caffeine in Coca-Cola had been a controversial subject since the passage of the 1906 Pure Food Law, and a food standard for the drink was expected to be one of the early pieces of business under the new law. But, in fact, twenty-eight years passed before action was taken. Asked about the delay, one FDA official blamed it on the intervention of the Second World War. When it was pointed out that this explanation could account for only seven or eight of the twenty-eight years, he had no further comment. During this entire time, nonalcoholic beverages did not label *any* of their ingredients. The FDA took no action whatsoever until June 16, 1961, when FDA Commissioner George Larrick published an announcement in the *Federal Register* saying that, in accordance with the law, all ingredients on nonalcoholic beverages would have to be labeled beginning one year later, on June 15, 1962. The pressure was on the cola manufacturers and they responded vigorously.

They sought and obtained a fifteen-month extension on the effective date for termination of the exemption. On September 14, 1963, one day before the end of the extension, the American Bottlers of Carbonated Beverages, spokesman for the cola and Dr. Pepper industries, officially proposed a standard for nonalcoholic beverages that did not require the labeling of caffeine. The proposal effectively suspended all labeling requirements in spite of the lapse of the exemption, until the disposition of the proposed standard was determined.

The bottlers (with a twenty-five-man board made up of twelve from Coca-Cola, three from Dr. Pepper and ten from assorted bottlers) supported their position against labeling caffeine with two major arguments. They claimed that it was well known that all colas contained caffeine, saying that cola equals caffeine. They argued that consumers were perfectly satisfied with the practice of not labeling caffeine. FDA personnel then began to gather the facts to aid the Commissioner in deciding whether to embrace or reject the bottlers' proposal.

Between September 14, 1963, and October 1, 1964, seventy-three comments on the bottlers' proposal were received at the FDA. "All who mentioned caffeine (four state officials and thirty-four consumers) requested that it at least be named on the label of all beverages in which it is used," said one summary memo.[5] The rest of the comments opposed the food standard on various grounds, including several that did not mention caffeine specifically, but requested that all ingredients be labeled. Based on these comments, the FDA Bureau of Scientific Standards and Evaluation proposed a new regulation, which was never adopted, that stated that "the optional ingredients caffeine, quinine, artificial color, artificial flavor and preservatives are to be declared on the label when used." [6]

Both arguments of the bottlers—first that all colas contained caffeine, and second that consumers knew this—received serious setbacks on June 7, 1965, when the FDA district offices reported the results of a survey of the caffeine content of samples from 160 colas. That survey, which continues to be the most significant document in the entire controversy, revealed that ninety-six of the samples examined contained either a barely measurable amount of caffeine or no caffeine at all.[7] On the basis of the consumer comments and the results of the survey which demonstrated the weaknesses of the bottlers' two major arguments, the bureau and division leaders of the FDA joined in an effort to convince Commissioner Larrick to issue an order requiring the labeling of caffeine on cola drinks and Dr. Pepper. Their opinion had been succinctly stated in a memorandum to the Commissioner: "It is therefore obvious that the evidence does not support the basic premise that caffeine is a well known and accepted component of cola beverages. On the contrary, it would seem that the evidence supports the formal comments which we received urging that we reject the proposal to authorize the use of caffeine without label declaration." [8]

Several of these officials are still convinced that Larrick had definitely made up his mind to require caffeine labeling. A draft order to that effect initialed by several FDA officials and prepared for publication, but still lying unused in FDA files, supports their conviction. It was never made public. Shortly after the preparation of this draft order, Commissioner Larrick retired.

Every indication from the files of the FDA and extensive interviews with participants in the decision suggests that the agency had decided to require the labeling of caffeine on cola drinks and Dr. Pepper as well as on all other nonalcoholic beverages. However, when James Goddard entered office on January 17, 1966, Deputy Commissioner Winton B. Rankin presented him with a memorandum that completely distorted the history of the controversy. He recognized caffeine labeling as the main issue but proposed "an order that does not require such a label declaration on cola beverages, but does require it on other types of beverages." He stated that "while some consumers will not approve of the action, there appears to be a marked lack of interest on the part of consumers." Most FDA officials recall the consumer interest in setting this standard as very high and the standard as very controversial. Few other food standards had received as much consumer comment. Rankin closed the memo with telling political overtones, saying, "We recall your attention to the order because Mr. Jim Jones of the White House has expressed interest. Senator Russell of Georgia has asked that the decision be conveyed to him as soon as possible, and we believe the Secretary's office will want to know of developments." [9] Rankin, in an interview with a Nader team member, claims that Goddard directed him to prepare the memo prior to his taking office. Goddard, according to Ron Kessler, then of *The Wall Street Journal,* believes that he made a mistake in promulgating the new standard allowing the non-labeling of caffeine.

Why the FDA has consistently ignored consumers has been unwittingly explained by H. Thomas Austern, a powerful Washington lawyer who specialized in arguing that cigarettes are not unhealthy and that food standards should be eased through the FDA. Describing what food standards mean to him—suggesting that they are ultimately economic and political—he said:

An economic judgment remains one, no matter how much technical clothing it wears. How to determine the fat or moisture content of cheese, or the specific gravity of tomato puree, are technical questions. Where to put the permissible level of moisture or what label name to prescribe for a product, or whether a cheaper ingredient may be substituted for a more expensive one, are questions largely answered by economic judgments. With all deference, one need not be a chemist or bacteriologist, and might even be a lawyer, in order to exercise judgment as to what will "promote honesty and fair dealing in the interest of consumers." It is because they are not objective technical questions, but rather issues as imponderable as any in the field of government, that their resolution is often difficult.[10]

It can also be suggested that one might even be a consumer and still have an informed judgment as to what will promote honesty and fair dealing in the interest of the consumer. For example, a consumer might ask: If a food company puts MSG or cyclamates or caffeine in its products, does asking that company to name that additive on its label raise "issues as imponderable as any in the field of government" whose "resolution is often difficult"? If so, then corporate lawyers have made more of a mess of the legal system than is already apparent.

Or a consumer might ask: If heart specialists agree that diets high in fat are dangerous to the heart, or if hot dogs are made in part out of chickens, is it really promoting "honesty and fair dealing in the interest of consumers" to allow companies not to list fat or chicken content on the products or even worse, in some cases, to require nonlisting? An inquiring consumer might ask: If standard-setting in the food field is merely an exercise of political and economic power, then why not boycott or picket those products that are offensive— particularly those that fail to label their ingredients? When one considers the crudeness of the food industry's power-flexing in the field of food standards, consumer boycotts and pickets seem quite reasonable.

During the debates on the labeling of added caffeine, a representative of Coca-Cola suggested that if Coke was forced to list all added caffeine it would change its process so that it would naturally end up with the same amounts of caffeine that it now adds. In these meetings between Coke officials and the FDA there were no consumers present and no consumer interest represented. The dozens of consumer letters—a large response over what was publicly an obscure issue—asking for caffeine labeling carried no weight in that league.

Corporate manipulation and the weakness of the FDA, spurred on by the constant threat of implacable industrial power, smothered the consumer demands. According to the FDA, the consumer requests were not worded properly. By this cynical citation of a legal technicality consumers were robbed of a public hearing. The inclusion of Dr. Pepper by name in the final standard illustrates how feeble rights are when someone else is bargaining them away. When the inclusion of Dr. Pepper by name in the exemption was first mentioned, "the Commissioner explained why this could not be done because it would be class legislation and thus not in accord with the Constitution. Mr. Bradshaw Mintener [of the bottlers and formerly of HEW] agreed with this view." [11] This Constitutional position fell to a more compelling argument. The FDA proposed that the way to avoid the Constitutional problem was to call Dr. Pepper a cola. But it seems that Dr. Pepper is bottled on a franchise basis in plants that also bottle Coca-Cola and Pepsi-Cola. Part of the cola companies' franchise agreement is that their bottler will not bottle other colas. Therefore, since calling Dr. Pepper a cola would lose it a number of bottlers, the FDA suggestion was put aside. Thus was minted a new rule: When a franchise agreement collides directly with the Constitution of the United States, it is the Constitution that must give way.

The Gatorade story even further shows how useless the FDA's food standards are. After Stokely-Van Camp (the makers of Gatorade) obtained the rights to the drink from the Florida professor who had developed and patented it with money provided by a grant from the National Institutes of Health (a questionable practice in itself) the famous pork-and-bean company sought to market it. One would think, as did the Vice President of Coca-Cola, that Gatorade would have had to meet the requirements of the nonalcoholic beverage standard, but Stokely officials found another loophole in the standards; they merely called their product something other than a nonalcoholic beverage—they named it a "thirst-quencher." A new product category was thus created for which theoretically a new food standard can be developed someday. If in addition to all its other weaknesses the FDA food standard system gives industry the option of avoiding the entire program, there seems litle value in it for consumers.

The FDA has not been content just to undermine whatever value the food standards might originally have held for consumers. The agency has tried to use them in what appears at times to be a campaign of dietary tyranny. The FDA's food standards give legal sanction to the article of faith that "American consumers enjoy a food supply that is unsurpassed in quantity, in variety, and in nutritional value. Americans, generally, have to go out of their way to avoid being well fed." [12] To give this opinion the force of law, in December, 1966, the FDA proposed a special dietary food standard requiring the label of most vitamin preparations to contain the statement: "Vitamins and minerals are supplied in abundant amounts by commonly available foods.

Except for persons with special medical needs, there is no scientific basis for recommending routine use of dietary supplements." [13]

Dr. Stanley N. Gershoff, who called the FDA's vitamin regulations "absurd," has also said that "nutrient inadequacies are not confined to the poor or the old, but reach into all income groups and all regions." [14] Dr. W. H. Sebrell, Chairman of the National Academy of Sciences–National Research Council Committee on Recommended Dietary Allowances, attacked the label proposal saying it was a contention of "no relevance . . . which taken out of context creates a false impression." [15] Assistant Secretary of Agriculture George L. Mehren called the proposed label statement "inaccurate and misleading," said it would give "a false sense of security" to a consumer regardless of his eating habits, and urged that it not be used. He also pointed out that an Agriculture Department survey indicated that "48% of households do not fully meet approved intake of one or more nutrients." [16]

A current FDA food standard prohibits labeling a product as low in certain kinds of fats: "It is therefore the opinion of the Food and Drug Administration that any claim, direct or implied, in the labeling of fats and oils or other fatty substances offered to the general public that they will prevent, mitigate, or cure diseases of the heart or arteries is false or misleading, and constitutes misbranding within the meaning of the Federal Food, Drug, and Cosmetic Act." [17] The fat-labeling requirement, adopted in 1959, has been continuously and consistently attacked by cardiologists around the country. Dr. Irvine Page, a Cleveland heart specialist who was honored as Heart Doctor of the Year by President Nixon early in 1969, criticized the regulation, saying, "There is no reason why the public shouldn't know about the fats in food that they buy." [18]

An article in the January 10, 1969, issue of *Time* magazine suggests that misconceived government action in one direction can lead to revolutionary reaction in the opposite direction, causing fundamental changes that might be both necessary and unfortunate. "Medical researchers studying heart disease are coming reluctantly to a revolutionary conclusion. The Federal

Government, they suggest, may have to intervene and decree a radical change in the prevailing American diet. This would involve taking most of the fat out of those marbled steaks and from those billions of gallons of milk, as well as altering the chemical constitution of cooking oils and fats." [19]

The governmental power necessary to carry out such a program would be vast and unprecedented. Ironically, whatever need there is to take government action to remove fat from the American diet results in part from the government's own action (through the Food and Drug Administration's ban on fat labeling), making it impossible for fat-free food to compete on the open market. The FDA's action has discouraged businessmen from developing low-fat candy, pastry, cheese, and other potentially healthful foods since they wouldn't be allowed to advertise the advantages. The FDA has been spurred to take this unfortunate action primarily by the efforts of the giant meat and dairy industries. Thus, in addition to failing to protect the rights and pocketbooks of the consumer, the FDA is guilty of using food standards to try to control the American diet and may have contributed to serious diet-related health problems.

These failures do not exhaust the weaknesses of the FDA food standard program. When the FDA is convinced that a serious and deceptive practice exists which could, in part at least, be resolved by the issuance of a food standard, the agency still does not act effectively. First, there are interminable delays while the affected power interests jockey for the best possible position to protect their profits. Then, even if by some chance a standard is issued, the agency has almost no effective tool for its enforcement. Finally, since it is impossible to control deception either because of the difficulties of promulgating a standard in the first place, or of enforcing one that might be promulgated, the consumer is harmed by the fact that legitimate businessmen who do not desire to deceive consumers find it difficult to compete with adulterated products which are cheaper to manufacture. Each of these three additional weaknesses of the food standard program is dramatically illustrated by the great orange juice drink standard debate which has raged between orange juice producers and regulators for the past seven years.

In May of 1968 a set of eight standards for diluted fruit juice detailing the differences between a juice drink (at least 50 per cent juice), an ade (at least 25 per cent juice) and a drink (at least 10 per cent juice) was proposed by FDA. In April, 1970, twenty-three months later, the standards still had not been adopted because the Florida and California fruit juice industries could not agree on what was in their best interest and the FDA has thus far refrained from acting because the industries have not agreed. Again, there is little chance that the interest of the consumer will predominate as the law says it should. The fruit juice debate illustrates what a weak tool the FDA food standard program is for the protection of the public interest. The proposed standard issued in May, 1968, was the result of a five-year debate among the FDA, state regulatory officials, and the California and Florida fruit juice industries. The FDA food standards committee agreed to the draft in principle in the summer of 1963. One year later, a briefing memo was forwarded to the Commissioner, saying, "We believe that state regulatory officials are more interested in, and more concerned over, standards for diluted fruit juice beverages than they are over standards for any other category of foods." [20] This information did not move the FDA to action. The debate that in January, 1969, was approaching its seventh year revolved around three major issues. The Florida interests sought the right to add color to its diluted orange juice since it is naturally paler than California juice. When the California interests indicated they were concerned about losing the competitive advantage the deeper color of their juice gave them (and so opposed the adding of artificial color), the Florida interests suggested that all labels be required to state the percentage of real juice contained in the product so that the deep color would not give California an advantage. The third issue developed when the industry indicated its desire to add additional components besides orange juice, color, and water to its diluted juice products. The proposal caused one FDA official to write:

The 10% o.j. [orange juice] 90% water drink is hardly even fit to drink. What makes these products palatable? It is the addition of substantial and noticeable quantities of pulp, orange oil, acid sugar and color. These "incidentals" are what make the product. It certainly isn't the o.j. content. Therefore, there is little reason to call 10% or 20% o.j. products anything but flavored water. It is also true that by manipulating the orange oil, color, and pulp content, a person can produce all four products, i.e., nectar, juice drink, ade, and drink as entities identical in appearance, taste, and overall "attractiveness." . . .

If people want diluted o.j., the most sensible way is to buy orange juice and add water to it. Actually, most people do not want this. To add water in the cannery, and dress it up with orange essence, added pulp, color, acid, etc., has only one function. It fools the public.[21]

A series of memoranda never before made public show that in 1967 the FDA conducted a consumer survey that indicated clearly that the consumer interest lay with percentage labeling of the valuable juice constituent. "Eighty per cent of the respondents want names on the labels to include the per cent of juice declaration." [22] The survey also revealed that "the majority of respondents estimated the level of orange juice in orange juice drink at the eighty per cent level." [23] With the consumer interest and the need for action clear, the FDA should have moved rapidly to enforce the law. Actually, it is still awaiting the outcome of conversations between the California and Florida orange juice interests to decide what action to take.

The consumer survey illustrated an interesting side issue. The FDA has been so ineffective that it is often unfairly blamed for deceptive actions that are the fault of industry. "Because the majority of people thought that orange drink contained 80 per cent or more orange juice when they were asked to comment on the acceptability of 30 per cent or 50 per cent orange juice, they implied that the federal government was trying to reduce the amount of juice they estimated was in the product." [24] Such unfortunate assumptions, nurtured by FDA timidity and inaction, widen the damaging credibility gap between consumers and government regulators.

The difficulty of enforcing a food standard after it is

finally adopted is illustrated by the orange juice conspiracy trial. Whatever confusion exists about diluted fruit drink standards, it is clear that pure orange juice is supposed to be 100 per cent orange juice. In spite of this, the practice of dilution is widespread in the orange juice industry. In 1958 the FDA became involved in a complicated legal battle with the Caltec Citrus Company after having staked out the company's warehouse and observed sugar, vitamin C, and other substances not allowed in pure orange juice being carried in a back door. It was estimated that the watering and adulterating practices of the company cost consumers $1 million in lost value—$1 million of pure company profits. The outcome of the case (defended by attorney Percy Foreman, acting for the company) was a total fine of $6,000 and a suspended sentence for the violators. A man who could return $1 million on a $6,000 investment would be considered brilliant in any business circle. It is widely rumored in "orange juice circles" that at least one major producer has built itself to prominence by routinely watering its juices as much as 10 per cent.

Consumer confusion brought about in part at least by FDA delay and inaction in establishing food standards and the inability of the FDA to enforce effectively those standards that do exist lead to the third great consumer loss that can be traced to the faulty food standard program. If two orange juice companies begin operations on an equal financial footing, but one of them gets away with expanding its sales by adding 10 per cent water to juice products, it will have a distinct competitive advantage. It will be able to apply the increased revenue to market development, advertising, and distribution, rapidly outselling its competitor. The good money paid for orange juice which is in fact water is part of the inflationary spiral that is undermining the value of the consumer dollar. The diminishing quality of a number of American food items can be traced directly to the ineffectiveness of the FDA food standards program. In fact, the consumer might be more wary, and therefore better off, if there were no programs of food standards designed to protect him.

As it now stands, consumers mistakenly assume that they are being protected when, in fact, it is unscrupulous businesses that are being protected in their fraud.

The entire food standard program should be completely overhauled. The FDA must organize its resources and orient its food standard policy toward the original food standards goal of promoting "honesty and fair dealing in the interest of consumers." For the past ten years, 70 per cent of all proposed food standards have been initiated by elements of the food industry. As a result, the FDA has grown passive, becoming dependent on the ability of various antagonistic industry elements to resolve their controversies. In this atmosphere the consumer's interest has usually been lost. The Lipton Company's Beef Stroganoff, one of a series of easy-to-serve foods made primarily from soy beans, illustrates how a food standard can be manipulated to fool the consumer. The Department of Agriculture (which sets standards for meat products) requires that Beef Stroganoff consist of 45 per cent meat, the rest being noodles, garnish, and sour cream. Lipton's, with government acquiescence, adds much less than 45 per cent beef to its Stroganoff product. It packages the Stroganoff ingredients in three subpackages: one contains noodles, one garnish, the third beef, sour cream, and soy protein meal. Forty-five per cent of the third package is beef. When prepared, Lipton's Stroganoff contains approximately 20 per cent beef rather than the 45 per cent required by the food standard. Approximately 25 per cent of the end product is soy bean meal, which sells for ten cents a pound. Under the food standard provision of the Food, Drug, and Cosmetic Act, the FDA has the authority to require that such a product be labeled "imitation" Beef Stroganoff. But the FDA has not taken action.

Each of the food standard distortions—ingredients which can be used if desired and not labeled, inconsistently requiring an additive to be labeled on some items and not others, and vague uninformative categories—has been the product of interference and maneuvering by the food industry and has caused consumer deception. The obvious immediate remedy, well within the law, would be for the FDA to require that all ingredients be clearly stated as mandatory in the food standard or labeled on the product. The obvious long-range remedy would be to require chemicals to be named on product labels. To achieve these goals the FDA must regain the initiative from industry. The food standard program must be given Commissioner-level co-ordination with the scientific, medical, and enforcement elements of the agency. A general policy of comprehensive and informative labeling must replace the piecemeal, product-by-product battles such as the mozzarella cheese fight, the eight-month peanut butter standard hearing, or the losing battle to get caffeine on the label of colas. The FDA should require across-the-board percentage labeling of the most valuable constituent (the percentage of orange juice in orange drink, peanuts in peanut butter, and strawberries in strawberry jam and other such products). Health as well as economic considerations should inspire food standard efforts; for example, there should be an immediate re-evaluation of fat and vitamin product labeling. A general rule should be adopted that when consumer communications to the FDA indicate a general consumer preference, that preference should be publicized and given careful consideration. Fifty thousand post cards, no matter how opposed to agency policy, should not be dismissed as the work of "quacks." When 80 per cent of consumers contacted desire percentage of the valuable constituent of orange juice drink to be labeled, that fact should be weighed more heavily than the selfish interests of orange drink producers. By itself the reorientation of the food standard program will not be sufficient to undo all the damage done by the misdirected food standards program of the past two decades. But without that reorientation none of the damage will be undone.

A number of other changes must be made in addition to redirecting the food standards program toward consumer protection and providing leadership from the Commissioner's office for the food standards battle. The food standards activities of the FDA should be moved out of the Agriculture Department building, which is ten blocks away from the FDA's downtown Washington office, to the FDA headquarters. As one former FDA Assistant Commissioner, Theodore Cron, said, "I don't know what's going on in food standards. And I can't find out. It's closed tight as a drum. Somebody should look at those guys." FDA food standards people have been unable to escape the industry-protection bias of their fellow workers in the Agriculture Department. While protecting industry is part of the avowed purpose of the Department of Agriculture, it has no place at the FDA. Moving the food standards branch of the FDA out of the Agriculture building and into the FDA building would allow more co-ordination between the agency's food standards program and its fair packaging and labeling program.

Once the FDA has redirected a significant number of its resources toward consumer-protection goals, it then can seek more funding from the Congress to expand those activities. Until it does move to make the food standards program effective, any requests for additional money in the food field should be viewed suspiciously by Congress. The food standard program at the FDA has long been an enigma to both internal and external observers. Until the food standards activities of the FDA are opened to public scrutiny, made into a tool to protect honesty and fair dealing in the interest of consumers, and used to eliminate instead of promoting widespread and expensive consumer ignorance and industrial fraud, FDA cannot be viewed as an effective consumer protection agency. But there is no sign of any such reform beginning.

4. Food-Borne Disease

"With respect to food, the Department of Health, Education, and Welfare must have considerably more authority to assure adequate protection of the public health."

—"Strategy for a Livable Environment." Report to HEW Secretary by the Task Force on Environmental Health and Related Problems, June, 1967

The Food and Drug Administration will not acknowledge the relationship between deteriorating American health and the limited availability of safe and wholesome food. In fact, American food consumption patterns play an important role in the nation's disgracefully high infant mortality rate, low rise in life expectancy, and seemingly insoluble problems of stroke, heart disease, and cancer. But the FDA repeatedly asserts that the American food supply is the best in the world. "Today's scientific knowledge, working through good laws to protect consumers, assures the safety and the wholesomeness of every component of our food supply," ran one example of official dictum from the agency.[1] This blind faith contrasts strongly with the picture seen by public health experts. In 1966 the National Commission on Community Health Services sponsored by the American Public Health Association and the National Health Council and chaired by Marion B. Folsom, former Secretary of Health, Education, and Welfare, released an exhaustive report on the state of American health services. Speaking of food protection, this commission said: "The current level of support being given to food protection at all levels of government is grossly inadequate. It does not even permit the responsible agencies to apply available knowledge to prevent . . . illnesses, much less to cope with the multitude of new and emerging problems. In fact, there is an enormous and rapidly increasing disparity between the number of problems arising and the amount of effort directed to their resolution. Changes in the production and processing of foods, increasing exposure of foods to chemicals, and changes in food preparation and nationwide distribution methods and techniques, together with inadequate public health controls, have created the potential for massive nationwide outbreaks of food-borne illnesses." [2]

Statistics support the picture of deteriorated American health. In 1964, the President's Commission on Heart Disease, Cancer, and Stroke reported that in the previous year those three diseases accounted for 71 per cent of all American deaths.[3] The economic cost of those deaths and the diseases that caused them was computed by the commission to be $31.6 billion.[4] The National Commission on Community Health Services reported in 1966 that "heart disease and stroke are indubitably related to an individual's way of life, and their toll could be reduced by broader observance of well-established guidelines of exercise, *diet*, and weight control." [5] (Emphasis added.)

The tremendous toll of the major killers is indicated by the relative stability of American life expectancy figures. Although the effects of tuberculosis, pneumonia, influenza, and other infectious diseases, which were the major cause of death in the United States a few decades ago, have been minimized, life expectancy has not made significant gains. Vital statistics of the United States for 1967, the most recent figures available, show that a forty-year-old man could expect to live only 4.1 years longer than a forty-year-old man had in 1900. A twenty-year-old American male today will have a shorter life than twenty-year-old men in thirty-six other countries. American women at the age of twenty have a life expectancy shorter than that of their counterparts in twenty-one countries. In 1950 only four countries had lower infant mortality rates than the United States. Today about fifteen countries have lower infant death rates.[6] Currently, one in every forty-three babies born in the United States dies before his first birthday—eighty thousand a year. According to the *Christian Science Monitor*, "the infant mortality rate, largely due to malnutrition, in some parts of this country was [found to be] one in ten—as high as much of Asia's." [7] Malnutrition in the expectant mother causes infant death because it leads to prematurity. Also it now appears that malnutrition during the mother's childhood can inhibit her ability to carry a child for the full nine months. Prematurity and the respiratory and other diseases that accompany it are the major cause of infant mortality. In spite of this dramatic evidence of the effects of malnutrition, poor dietary habits and diet related health problems, the FDA still officially asserts that "the American consumer —whatever his age and whatever his financial condition—has an excellent chance of taking in the recommended daily requirements of vitamins and minerals through the foods he eats, *without* resorting to any . . . supplements." [8]

The official FDA failure to emphasize the relationship between health and diet falls into four general areas of inaction: the hazards of the chemical environment (that is, the increasing number of chemicals an individual is exposed to) are minimized; the existence of undernutrition is officially denied; the food poisoning hazards related to new methods of food production and distribution are given low priority; and research on the causes of heart disease and stroke is ignored.

Hazards of the chemical environment are minimized:
The FDA has so minimized the dangers from food additives that it has effectively destroyed the letter and spirit of the Food Additives Amendment of 1958. The working philosophy of the FDA was stated in the agency's 1967 Fact Sheet on Nutrition, which said: "Dangerous food preservatives were a major concern of the Food and Drug Administration when it began operations on January 1, 1907. Today's scientific knowledge, working through good laws to protect consumers, assures the safety and the wholesomeness of every component of our food supply." [9] Operating on this article of faith, the agency failed to take action against cyclamates in spite of significant evidence of their possible dangers. In 1951 studies on saccharin were reported to show an unusually high incidence of unusual combinations of cancers. This reported discovery has not yet

been followed up by the FDA. Nor has the warning that monosodium glutamate in baby foods might be dangerous. The agency has just begun a thorough review of sixty-four food additives that it now, after being subjected to mounting public pressure, thinks should receive closer attention. Vitamin D was sharply curtailed as an additive to milk six years after the FDA had rejected scientific evidence that it was unsafe and allowed its use. Saforale, the main flavoring ingredient of root beer, was found to be a cancer-causing agent after having been cleared as safe by the FDA. An antioxidant compound called NDGA, added to fatty foods to prevent deterioration, had to be removed from the FDA's GRAS list nine years after having been declared safe. On January 27, 1970, the FDA required industry to remove brominated vegetable oils, used as a stabilizer in citrus-base soft drinks, orange juice, ice cream, and bakery products, because when they were fed to rats in high doses they caused heart lesions and impaired heart function, but industry was given six months to accomplish the removal. In the meantime it is impossible for those who wish to avoid these oils to do so since they appear in many foods without labeling.

In the face of these failures to protect or even warn the public adequately, the FDA's current attitude about food chemicals is depressing. "For the most part," says the FDA memorandum ordering review of the GRAS list, "the judgments made ten years ago in compiling the GRAS list, on the basis of evidence then available, have stood the test of time very well." [10] The FDA memorandum says that "additional techniques for assessing safety have been developed" since the original list was prepared, causing some need for re-evaluation. It is misleading to call the discovery of bladder cancer in rats that were fed cyclamates the result of an "additional technique." The FDA discovered the cancer when it examined the rat bladders, a procedure not considered routine until recently. In many other cases the problems the FDA finally recognized had been clearly suggested by independent researchers but originally rejected by the agency.

Concerning cancer, the FDA reluctantly accepted and reluctantly enforces the legal requirement that any substance that causes cancer in animals should not be added to the food supply. Official spokesmen of the agency have embraced the widely criticized belief that carcinogenic response increases with increasing dose levels of the carcinogen—i.e., that there is a dose level below which it is safe to consume cancer-causing chemicals. Scientists, both inside and outside the FDA, have termed this notion "pure bunk." As a consumer protection agency, the FDA should err toward consumer safety— particularly when directed to do so by law—and exclude all suspected cancer-causing chemicals from the food supply, but the agency has not actively pursued many indications that certain food additives may cause cancer.

The FDA is currently repeating the mistake it made in 1958. The mounting evidence that birth defects, cancer, hereditary change, and heart disease may be related to food additives has been sometimes reluctantly embraced, sometimes ignored or distorted by FDA decision-makers. The tragedy of the current FDA policy is that although it has finally recognized that the GRAS list must undergo close scrutiny in an effort to untangle the errors of the past, it is failing to look to the future. The agency is still skeptical about tackling the serious and profoundly disturbing questions raised by chemicals that cause genetic damage to rats and birth deformities to chick embryos. Today the FDA is treating the genetic and birth defect threat of chemicals the way it treated the cancer threat ten years ago—skeptically. Just as it begins to dig out of the mess created by its 1958 skepticism about the dangers of cancer from chemicals it plants the seeds for disaster in 1980. A few reassuring press releases in that year will not be able to undo the kind of genetic damage that may result if the FDA continues to be as ineffective in regulating food chemicals as it has been in the past decade. If the ingestion of certain chemicals can cause changes in the genetic structure of human beings, as new tests are now implying, this generation of Americans may be sitting on a mutagenic time bomb. Scientists in this field say that compared to this possibility, cancer—which appears only in the victim, not endlessly into the generations that succeed him—is a minor concern.

The existence of undernutrition is officially denied:

The FDA has spent close to $200,000 since early 1968, compiled twenty-six thousand pages of testimony, and used thousands of FDA man-hours to prove that there are no problems of mal- or undernutrition in America that require the use of vitamin supplements. This position has been increasingly embarrassing for the agency to maintain as areas of poor nutrition have been turned up across the country by the United States Department of Agriculture, the United States Senate Select Committee on Nutrition and Human Needs, and even in a thorough review of nutrition studies conducted largely in middle-class neighborhoods. The FDA found itself opposing vitamin supplementation just at a time when vitamin deficiencies were becoming a major national concern. Scientists and researchers in the field of nutrition have been appalled by the FDA's activities in the vitamin field almost since they began. In the area of vitamin regulation, as in the areas of fat labeling and food sanitation, the FDA has used the power it has been given to protect the food supply in a way that works against public health.

Food poisoning is given low priority:

The Food Safety Panel of the December, 1969, White House Conference on Food Nutrition and Health identified the problem of microbiological contamination—food poisoning—as a major American health concern and recommended wider surveillance of food-borne disease plus development of new testing methods to detect food poisons. The panel urged wider reporting of the problem and said: "Not only do we need public awareness of the extent of food-borne illness, but also a mechanism is essential to get the practicing physician and individual citizens to participate in the reporting system. In fact, by conservative estimates between 2,000,000 and 10,000,000 cases of food poisoning occur in the United States annually. The National Academy of Sciences estimates that salmonella, only one of the food poisons, alone costs Americans $300 million annually." [11] Kenneth R. Lennington, the FDA salmonella project officer, pointed out that in 1967 "on a nationwide basis, the total number of reported salmonella food-borne outbreaks are running staphylococcus [staph] a close second." [12]

Salmonella and staph are not the only disease-carrying organisms found in food. Poliomyelitis and infectious hepatitis have been caused by viruses contained in fluid milk, raw shellfish, cooked and cold-cut meats, salads, frozen strawberries, and reconstituted orange juice.[13] Meat, fish, and poultry have been associated with Clostridium perfirgens food poisoning causing profuse diarrhea, frequently accompanied by abdominal pain, within eight to twelve hours after eating the contaminated food.[14] Gastroenteritis (any inflammation of the stomach or intestines) resulting from Shigella infection, which had for years been assumed to be a disease associated with filth "endemic in some mental institutions, and in some lower socio-economic communities," has been reported in at least one elementary-school lunch line, affecting 201 children, and in one army mess affecting 240 personnel.[15] These are only some of the disease-carrying organisms that appear in food.

In his speech outlining in detail a number of specific food poisonings, Kenneth Lennington also explained why the problem was likely to get worse and not better: "Our mode of living and technology probably renders us more susceptible to food-borne infection today. The convenience foods, ready-to-eat items, and frozen prepared dinners requiring only minimum heating prior to serving open avenues for mass infection. Our production and distribution system is such that today the output of a plant may be distributed nationwide, or even worldwide. This means that an infected employee or a breakdown or deterioration of some phase of plant sanitation can infect thousands of consumers instead of a limited surrounding community. Our population concentration, human and food animal, with the resultant waste disposal and pollution problems, is likewise conducive to spread of infection. . . . Effective control of the food-borne infections, whether they be bacterial or viral in nature, entails a much higher and more rigid level of sanitation than generally has been practiced, or required, by industry, or by health and regulatory officials." [16]

The Food and Drug Administration has tended to minimize publicly the food-borne disease problem and industry's role in creating it, and has set program priorities that seriously hamper any effort to clean up the offending industries. In May, 1968, the FDA issued a fact sheet entitled "To Keep Food Clean." It purportedly explained the problems of providing clean, wholesome food for the entire nation. Actually, it presented the official agency position, which implies that the problem is well in hand. It took no notice of the grossly inadequate support being given to food protection programs by state and local as well as Federal government agencies. No mention was made of the fact that hepatitis outbreaks associated with food consumption had increased measurably in the previous year or of the two to ten million salmonella cases that occur each year. Worse, the fact sheet implied that industry was effectively enforcing sanitation in its establishments. It said, "Food processors as a whole are aware of their responsibilities to maintain adequate sanitation control in their factories . . . through the years this [the FDA inspection program] has led to many voluntary corrections, such as plant improvements and the destruction of unfit ingredients. There is growing consciousness of the high sanitary standards demanded of food processors and handlers . . . there are approximately 64,000 interstate food establishments subject to FDA inspection. Last year [1967] there were inspections of these food factories and warehouses."

This cheery communiqué did not exactly describe the full situation. The fact sheet might have cited, instead, the kinds of abuses uncovered. For instance, the Stokely-Van Camp plant in Lawrence, Kansas, was inspected by the FDA on August 2, 1966. The inspectors found that after packing, cans of food were cooled in bacteria-laden water. The plant manager maintained that if any can had a hole in it and the bacteria from the water got into the food, it would cause the can to swell and explode before it was eaten. But this was not a foolproof defense since the bacteria might not cause the can to explode. The FDA urged that the practice be stopped. The memo also might have mentioned the dozens of offensive items that consumers have found in soft drinks. That list includes decomposing mice, maggots, used condoms, and cigarette butts.[17] There are hundreds of FDA inspection files showing such violations but no files, of course, to show violations in plants that have not been inspected.

FDA inspection data from fiscal year 1968 (July 1, 1968, to June 30, 1969) showed that in establishments producing products with a potential for microbiological contamination, with the FDA good manufacturing guidelines designed to minimize microbiological contamination, compliance was only 61 per cent.[18] This low compliance rate should suggest a serious problem, particularly in view of the fact that the FDA routinely inspects only about 40 per cent of the food-producing plants in the country each year,[19] and that in some districts these plants are inspected only once every six years.[20] The compliance level in plants that know they will not be inspected is probably lower than 61 per cent.

The FDA guidelines being violated seem like commonsense rules:

1. Promote personal cleanliness among employees.
2. Provide adequate hand-washing facilities throughout the plant.
3. Train employees to prepare, handle, and store foods in a sanitary manner.
4. Use effective cleaning and sanitizing procedures.
5. Inspect incoming raw materials and reject any showing decomposition.
6. Destroy bacteria during processing by approved methods, and handle finished packaged products in a manner that avoids contamination.
7. Maintain proper storage temperatures.
8. Indicate refrigeration labeling directions on packaged perishable items requiring cold temperatures.
9. Rotate raw and finished stock and destroy spoiled foods.[21]

In setting regulatory priorities, the FDA divides its efforts into three areas: health, sanitation, and economics. (Note that health is separated from sanitation.) Food regulation responsibilities are divided into ten priorities by the 1970 operating plan; so-called non-hazardous problems of food sanitation are the eighth priority. These consist of (1) the use of filthy or decomposed raw materials, and (2) unsanitary conditions in the manufacture, processing and/or storage of foods whereby the finished product may become contaminated with such filth as insect fragments, rodent hairs, worms, flies, bird excreta, etc.[22] This definition of sanitation embraces what most public health officials would call an important health problem that is a major contributor to microbiological contamination, yet it ranks eighth on the list of priorities, below, for example, economic fraud (under which the FDA prosecutes health food stores), and only two priorities above tea-testing. Various comments from FDA district offices on the 1970 operations plan point out the dangers of such a low priority for sanitation and show once again the split between those FDA officials who set policy and those who must carry it out.

Kansas City
We have sufficient information to demonstrate that industry is reacting to the low priority placed on sanitation. As an example, we recently inspected 21 warehouses with State of Nebraska Inspectors for State training purposes. These warehouses represented those not inspected for two or three years and which, for the most part, would not have been planned. As a result of the inspection, 16 of the firms are now classed out of compliance. More than 20,800 pounds of food items were destroyed under Nebraska State supervision due to rodent, bird and insect contamination.

These 21 firms represent less than 1% of our inventory in this problem area but demonstrate an impressive regressive trend in sanitation basics which we believe is directly attributable to our decreased priority and coverage.

The trade press has given widespread publicity of FDA's nonemphasis of sanitation. . . . We are receiving increasingly frequent complaints regarding filth in foods from state and local agencies as well as consumers. . . .

Additionally, we think that such low priority on our part is inconsistent with the emphasis placed on this problem by our sister agency the Environmental Control Administration [another HEW agency], and with increasingly frequent reports linking rodents to the spread of disease.

Minneapolis
It has always been difficult to separate potential microbiological problems associated with rodents and insects from sanitation, but under our present planning concept we are required to do so. Rats and mice are known to be vehicles for the transmission of serious disease conditions such as plague and there is a distinct potential for health hazards associated with rodent-contaminated foods. More recently, university research has established that insects are also car-

riers of pathogenic organisms. This distinction between sanitation and microbiological contamination appears to be inconsistent with the general goals of the Consumer Protection and Environmental Health Service, whose responsibilities include rodent and insect control in the total environment.

New Orleans
We are not satisfied that rodent contamination of food should be classed in the "non-hazardous" program area. Numerous papers and tests on subjects of public health and preventive medicine state that rats are implicated in the transmission of many diseases—including marine typhus, which is endemic to the Gulf Coast region. Our sister agency ECA has just begun to administer a law aimed at rat control, and we understand that they regard rats as a public health problem.

The rate of industry compliance in FY [fiscal year] 1968 was 72% as compared with 59% for the first half of FY 1969. Rodents were the major cause of noncompliance thus far in FY 1969.[23]

Research on the causes of heart disease and stroke is ignored:

Since 1959, the Food and Drug Administration has vigorously denied the most significant relationship between diet on the one hand and deaths from heart disease and stroke on the other—the danger in saturated fats. It has threatened to prosecute any manufacturers of food products containing unsaturated fats who even suggest the possibility of such a connection in their advertising. This campaign has been called "unscientific, unrealistic, harsh, and archaic" by heart specialist Dr. Jeremiah Stammler, speaking for a large number of cardiologists across the country.[24] Many heart specialists assert that foods high in saturated fats tend to build cholesterol in the body and thus contribute to the possibility of heart disease. Therefore, they say, the diet of many persons should be altered by replacing large quantities of saturated fats with polyunsaturated fats. The National Academy of Sciences-National Research Council,[25] American Diabetes Association,[26] the American Heart Association,[27] the American Medical Association,[28] and the National Diet-Heart Study of the Executive Committee on Diet and Heart Disease [29] have all urged accurate fat labeling and the elimination of the FDA's prohibition of the advertising of products on the basis of the fact that they contain unsaturated fats. Experts consulted by the FDA have unanimously agreed.[30] Canada,[31] Sweden, Finland, and Norway have adopted official policies recognizing the importance of cutting down on saturated fat intake as part of a program to ease the threat of heart disease.[32] But the FDA maintains that fat content labeling "is false or misleading, and constitutes misbranding within the meaning of the Federal Food, Drug, and Cosmetic Act."[33]

The prime consideration underlying any regulatory decision by the FDA is not scientific merit; it is not public interest; it is not even a concerted effort to make the agency look good. What motivates FDA decisions is the desire to insure that whatever is or is not done will not make the FDA look bad. The agency moves agonizingly slowly, hoping not to be noticed or, if noticed, hoping not to offend anyone who cares and can do anything about it—which primarily means well-organized economic interests. Six years after the issue of fat labeling first arose, an FDA official recommended that a decision still be put off. Here was his reasoning: "Any information that may come out of such a delay would either be in favor of the Food and Drug Administration's 1959 policy or [opposed] to it. Either way, I do not believe the Food and Drug Administration could look very bad; the most that could be said would be that the FDA moved cautiously until the evidence supported the claims."[34] The FDA took no action itself to find information that would resolve the controversy. No FDA research on fats was begun; no literature search was undertaken; no effort to prod others into research was made. Any additional useful information was expected to appear spontaneously ("come out") from the delay.

The tremendous organized power of certain segments of the food industry, capable of stirring up just the controversy the FDA likes to avoid, was used to support the argument that the link between saturated fats and heart disease had not been conclusively established. Under these circumstances, the argument went, the labeling of fats according to whether they were saturated or unsaturated would give manufacturers of products containing *un*saturated fats an unfair advantage in the marketplace. The conflict between this position and the public health interest inspired the continuing delay of a decision by the FDA. In 1965, after re-evaluating its long-standing controversial position against labeling of fats, the FDA decided to *continue* the ban. The major internal memorandum supporting this decision, inaccurate in both its facts and its arguments, hinted at the reason. "Perhaps the present answer lies in the opinions of a considerable number of large firms who believe more time is needed to study the problem." [35]

Two years later, the new FDA Commissioner, James L. Goddard, was once again in the midst of a review of the policy. Once again, a delay was ordered. This time the decision followed a December 1, 1967, meeting between FDA officials (including Commissioner Goddard) and representatives of the Ivorydale Technical Center of the Procter and Gamble Company. The Procter and Gamble people were concerned that fat labeling would be ordered, and they proposed a voluntary education program, to be carried out by the Nutrition Foundation and the Grocery Manufacturers Association, as one alternative. After that meeting, the official policy position of the FDA was forwarded from Assistant Commissioner Kirk to Commissioner Goddard. It concluded, "in the light of the meeting in Dr. Goddard's office . . . we will not undertake to resolve the differences at this time, but will await the reaction from the Nutrition Foundation and the Grocery Manufacturers Association people, as discussed in the report of that meeting." [36] Dr. Goddard's successor as Commissioner, Dr. Herbert Ley, when faced with the same decision, also relied more on the position of industry than on science to justify a postponement to review the fat-labeling policy. Although as director of the FDA Bureau of Medicine he had signed a vigorous recommendation that fat labeling be required, he reversed his position when Commissioner and continued the agency policy against fat labeling. In an August, 1969, interview, he explained that certain aspects of the controversy had not been known to him when he signed the original memo. Specifically, he referred to the position stated by the agency legal counsel in a memorandum prepared in 1965. It said, "Pressing this matter to hearing would involve us in a controversy between the dairy industry and the corn and vegetable oil interests." [37] Bowing to the pressure that such a controversy could bring on the agency, Dr. Ley sought to establish a committee of scientists to advise him on the fat-labeling question. It is at this point that the eleven-year-old controversy rests today.

Even though several FDA officials were aware that prohibiting fat labeling exceeded FDA authority, their doubts were overcome by the zeal of their diet-fraud campaign and the proddings of industry. In 1963 one official wrote, "I personally doubt that we will ever be able to remove the word 'polyunsaturated' and similar words (lineolates, etc.) from the labeling of foods where they are now being employed with 'good' reason. How to contain the representations is the main problem. Perhaps the fad will go away voluntarily in a few years." [38]

In 1968 Commissioner Ley was informed by his own Bureau of Regulatory Compliance that the Justice Department had refused to file charges in the fat-labeling cases because it doubted that the government could prove that foods high in polyunsaturated fats would not be of value in the prevention of heart disease.[39] In fact, major producers of polyunsaturated-fat products have been advised by their attorneys to continue the kind of labeling that FDA has tried to ban, and several have. But the FDA ruling has had a damaging effect on the development of new products such as pastries, candies, cheeses, etc., low in saturated fats. Most companies do not wish to include the cost of legal conflict as part of the total risk of new product development. Since the law bars them from labeling new products as high in polyunsaturated fats, they are robbed of their chief potential selling point, and thus discouraged from developing products of considerable value to American public health. In defense of the FDA position, Dr. Ley said, in July, 1969, "The scientific correlation between fatty acids ingestion and arteriosclerosis is an extremely tenuous one . . . although there is a great deal of publicity there is very little scientific fact that clearly links the ingestion of fat in one form or another with heart disease." [40]

This is the same Dr. Ley who, two years earlier, had sent a memo to the then FDA Commissioner Goddard urging that fat labeling be permitted. He said then, "The Bureau of Medicine recognizes that this position represents a major change of policy. Nevertheless, the position is recommended as the only reasonable one at this time." [41]

Chemical additives, vitamins, fat labeling, and filth in food all have important health implications for the American public. All are major responsibilities of the FDA food protection program, yet none has received the kind of scientific and regulatory attention that will advance the quality of American health. In the place of sustained action to advance health by helping to improve the American diet, the FDA substitutes a naïve faith that the way American food is produced, preserved, and distributed is exceptionally fine. It maintains this faith in the face of increasing scientific evidence that chemical additives can be extremely dangerous, that the vitamin content of the American diet is deteriorating, that saturated fat in food may be a contributing factor to more than 70 per cent of all American deaths, and that American food is getting filthier. Faith has a way of withstanding fact. But while the FDA goes through the ritualistic exercise that it passes off as regulation, it is the food consumer who is injured.

5.

The Food Industry

"*[Most] manufacturers recognize that consumer interest and producer interest are inseparable, and that practices adverse to consumer interest are likewise adverse to the interest of industry; . . . most manufacturers make sincere efforts to meet all legal requirements not only because they are the law . . . but because it is the right thing to do.*"

—*"Creed of the FDA," Commissioner Paul Dunbar, October, 1947*

The food industry is the largest retail industry in America, having total sales of approximately $125 billion in 1969. Like all industry, its job is to make money, and because it does the job well, other giant moneymakers are buying into it.

Economically, the industry is moving toward monopoly. The report of the National Commission on Food Marketing, released in 1966, reported a "sharp rise in conglomerate type acquisitions by large food manufacturers in the past two decades." The report continued, "The size and diversity of the large food conglomerate gives it great ability to survive its own mistakes or intense competitive struggles in particular food fields. It can engage in reciprocal trading arrangements not available to conventional firms. Food conglomerates are likely to grow, to reduce the number of independent competitors in the industry as a whole, and to lace the various segments of the industry more neatly into a single system characterized by the kind of non-price competition in which they excel." [1]

The trend toward concentration described in 1966 has continued as predicted. The Greyhound Corporation, known for its buses, is taking over Armour, the nation's second largest meat packer. International Telephone and Telegraph has taken over Continental Bakery. As part of these giant corporations, the subsidiary food firms gain near immunity from competition. The Marketing Commission described in general terms what the decrease in the total number of food firms means to the consumer. "High concentration in the food industry is undesirable because it weakens competition as a self-regulating device by which the activities of business firms are directed toward the welfare of the public at large. When large firms dominate a field, they frequently forbear from competing actively by price; competition by advertising, sales promotion and other selling efforts almost always increases; and the market power inescapably at the disposal of such firms may be used to impose onerous terms upon suppliers or customers." [2] For example, 85 per cent of American breakfast food is produced by four firms (Kellogg, General Foods, General Mills, Quaker Oats) at a profit nearly double the average for all food manufacturing. Between 1954 and 1964, the retail price for breakfast food per pound increased 45 per cent. The retail price for breakfast cereal rose more than any other food. One major reason for the price rise was the 19 per cent of cereal manufacturers' sales spent on advertising and sales promotion. Advertising and sales are the primary concern of the concentrated food firm; food is secondary.[3]

In addition to concentration of the breakfast cereal market, 95 per cent of all prepared soups are sold by Campbell Soup, more than half of American cheese is sold by Bordon and National Dairy (Kraft), and most salad dressing is sold by National Dairy and Corn Products. By 1958, according to the Food Marketing Commission, 80 per cent of all food companies were classified as oligopolies. The major distinctive product promoted and sold by these large concentrated firms is their brand name. Massive amounts of money are spent for this purpose. As a comparison, twenty-two of the largest food manufacturers in the nation spend about 18 per cent of their sales on advertising (compared with less than 3 per cent for the automobile companies). A fascinating example of money spent on brand-name protection is the fact that Campbell Soup maintains and displays an expensive collection of antique soup tureens. The purpose of the collection, according to William Murphy (Campbell's President), is to counteract the bad image given his products when Andy Warhol painted a famous pop art picture of Campbell Soup cans. "You know what kind of a sex life that man has," the company executive was overheard to say. The cost of the tureen collection is passed on to consumers.

The emphasis on advertising costs the consumer additional money. Food products of identical quality cost significantly different prices depending on whether they are national brands or local product labels, according to the Food Marketing Commission. In 1969, G. E. Brandow recalled this fact to the Senate Select Committee on Nutrition and Human Needs. "The Commission found that retail prices of nationally advertised brands of such common foods as frozen peas and orange juice concentrate averaged 20 per cent higher than private label products of comparable quality." [4] This 20 per cent goes right back into advertising promotion, and market development, along with the profit gained by fraudulent practices like orange juice watering, and extra money raised through misleading labeling and packaging. Profiteering practices, like these, lead to the kind of inflation that has the consumer price index on food leading all other categories. Food industry spokesmen like General Foods President C. W. Cook and the Grocery Manufacturers of America try to put a good face on the situation by pointing out that in 1966 the United States spent only 18 per cent of its income on food, compared to 23 per cent in 1939.[5] This figure, like many others cited by special interest groups, is misleading. The commission points out that in real terms the total amount of food consumption per person has remained stable since 1939, while consumer food expenditures per person have increased, on a scale of 100 from 78 in 1939 to 106 in 1965—or over 37 per cent.[6] A significant part of this increase pays for advertising, packaging, promotion, and product tampering which does not add real food value to the diet. Viewing the over-all situation in the food industry, the commission concluded: "Controlling concentration in the various branches of the food industry is essential to maintaining a competitive environment favoring an acceptable distribution of market power and a socially useful employment of resources. A horizontal merger or acquisition by a large firm in an already concentrated field tends to break down conditions necessary for effective competition—perhaps in purchasing as well as in selling—even when specific restraint of trade cannot be demonstrated. An effective policy to limit concentration requires acceptance of the view that such general impairment of competition is a sufficient reason for vigorous anti-merger action." [7]

Most of the recent growth in American food sales has been in processed foods; for the first time in 1969 their sales exceeded that of unprocessed food. Processed food, featuring its food additives, new foods, massive distribution systems, and minimal home preparation, presents major problems to the FDA. Quaker Oats marketed a diet cereal that violated labeling requirements. One FDA official believes that Kraft has been responsible for a major decline in the quality of cheeses made in the U.S., but the agency can do nothing about it in spite of various cheese standards. Precooked breakfast cereals have the food value toasted out of them, according to Dr. Jean Mayer, but the FDA does not try to regulate their nutritional claims. Summarizing the situation, the agency's own study group on consumer protection said, "The American public's principal consumer protection is provided by the Food and Drug Administration, and we are currently not equipped to cope with the challenge." [8] The reason given for the failure is limited legislation, manpower, and money. But as long as the FDA believes that the food industry wishes to provide the safest, highest-quality food possible to the American people, no amount of legislation, manpower, or money will turn the agency into an effective food regulator. Viewed against the food industry's economic power and vigor and avowed money-making goal, the FDA's faith in industrial self-regulation is ludicrous, if not tragic. The food industry has vigorously set about its task of making profits. It is time the FDA set about *its* assigned task of insuring that profits made by the food industry are not the result of fraud, deception, adulteration, or misbranding. Until the FDA recognizes the food business for the profit-making giant that it is, this public agency will continue to be the vassal of an industry that through callousness, ignorance, or greed routinely mauls the public interest.

The story of the purposeful and economically motivated pollution of baby foods by their manufacturers should dispel all beliefs in food industry self-regulation. If baby-food producers are not motivated to police themselves, it is unlikely that any food producers are. Twenty years ago a jar of baby food contained a given amount of fruit, vegetables, or meat. As the costs of these ingredients rose, baby-food companies began to replace part of them with starch and sugar—each of which is less expensive than the ingredient it was replacing. Naturally, foods thinned out with starch or sugar tasted blander or sweeter than the originals, so baby-food makers began adding salt and monosodium glutamate to please mothers who tasted their babies' food. Then it was discovered that the starches added to the food would break down and become watery if a mother fed her baby some of the bottle's contents and let the remainder sit, even in the refrigerator, overnight. The baby's saliva, which got into the food on the spoon the baby was fed with, was "digesting" it. The answer provided by the baby-food companies was to find a starch that saliva could not break down and add it to the bottle's contents. So now baby food contains not only added sugar, salt, and monosodium glutamate, but also added modified starch which baby saliva does not break down in the jar or the mouth and which some researchers fear may not be completely digested even by the rest of the baby's system. None of these additives in the food for purely economic reasons has been proven safe for consumption by babies.

Industry justifies the addition of sugar to baby foods by the assertion that it will make them tastier to infants. But, actually, most baby food is fed to infants early in their life, before they have developed the ability to discriminate by taste. One of the most unfortunate aspects of the addition of sugar to baby foods has been its effect in nullifying efforts of pediatricians to keep mothers from adding sugar to milk. It is not true that a fat baby is necessarily a healthy baby. According to nutritionists, sugar supplies "empty" calories and makes the baby used to consuming it. From the simple beginning in baby food may come the mother's constant fight against excessive candy eating. Researchers are looking more and more into possible health problems related to excessive sugar consumption, including areas yet to be adequately explored, like the effects of hypoglycemia which may be related to the onset of diabetes.

Salt, too, has come under increasing attack as a component of baby food. In October, 1969, Dr. Jean Mayer said that removing salt from baby food would be the statesmanlike thing for the baby-food companies to do before they are forced to remove it. The reason for the concern is a series of studies by Dr. Lewis Dahl, chief of the Brookhaven National Laboratory, which suggest a relationship between hypertension and high salt consumption. Dr. Dahl points out that there is a high incidence of death (66,819 in 1966) from hypertension and that the disease is appearing in patients in their teens or twenties now rather than in patients in their thirties or forties, as it used to. Dr. Dahl states, "A child gets a salt appetite [from eating salted foods as an infant] which then must be satisfied the rest of his life. If there is a family history of hypertension, and he takes a lot of salt in his food, he may get it early in life." [9]

The food industry's rebuttal to this charge relies on the benefit-vs.-risk argument. Dr. Robert A. Steward, director of research for the Gerber Products Company, made the point, "Before the boon to mothers of preserved baby food is jeopardized, several questions must be answered." [10] Boon? Why not real meat and vegetables in a blender for modern American mothers? "Does excess dietary sodium chloride cause human hypertension?" Dr. Steward asked, and answered: "Several mechanisms affect hypertension. Salt may be involved in one of them. . . . If salt does cause hypertension in the adult, will it produce changes in the infant leading to hypertension later in life? There is no evidence one way or another. . . . Is there a strain of salt-sensitive people (and, therefore, infants) resembling rats? No one knows. . . . Until these questions are answered definitely, too few data are available to invoke some hypertension later in life." [11] The questions raised by Dr. Steward have not been answered. The safety of baby food additives has not been established. But the manufacturer expected his product to be considered innocent until proven guilty. Mothers are asked to accept the "boon" of processed baby food on the strength of inconclusive answers. Dr. Jean Mayer suggests that babies should not be exposed to the levels of sodium now in baby food "proportionally higher than those of adults and enormously higher than those resulting from breast feeding." [12] Unless the safety of a food additive can be assured, its use should be avoided. This is not only prudence, it is the law.

The most vocal controversy about baby food has been created by the addition of monosodium glutamate (MSG) to such foods. The manufacturers' side of the situation was laid out in a letter from Dan Gerber to Gerber share-owners on November 14, 1969:

On May 9, 1969, John Olney, an associate professor of Psychiatry at Washington University in St. Louis, reported that MSG injected under the skin of 2 to 10 day old mice caused a specific type of brain damage and speculated that similar damage might result in human infants fed foods containing MSG. He and others later testified before the Senate Select Committee of Nutrition and Human Needs, citing this work and the conclusions drawn. A considerable amount of publicity was generated from this testimony. This publicity has been kept alive by continuous television appearances of one of the principal consumer protection crusaders, Ralph Nader, and was further augmented by the publication of a report on October 17 by Olney to the effect that MSG injected into a single monkey caused similar brain damage.

Although a committee of experts was appointed as an ad hoc committee to the Food Protection Committee to study the scientific data on MSG and make recommendations for its use in foods, public pronouncements by Dr. Olney and by Dr. Jean Mayer, nutrition adviser to the President of the United States, denounced the use of MSG in baby foods. These statements were publicized on TV and in the newspapers and the U.S. public became very concerned. An attempt was made to counteract the adverse publicity by presentation of the accumulated data demonstrating the safety of MSG when used in normal feeding procedures, but this information, although its validity was recognized by the scientific community, received little coverage in the news media and came too late to head off the public's reaction. Qualified scientists who have reviewed the written work of Dr. Olney as well as unpublished data in his laboratory are not convinced that his work is relevant to human feeding. It is the generally accepted consensus that further work must be done with different species of animals in order to validate the conclusions drawn by Dr. Olney.

In these two relatively short paragraphs the Gerber Products Company demonstrates why food companies cannot be relied upon to police themselves. First and most basic is the assumption that a product can remain on the market until definitively proven dangerous. After attempting to present the best possible case for discrediting the importance of Dr. Olney's work, the company is forced to conclude that "further work must be done." But it is the intention of the law to require an industry to establish the safety of a food additive *before* using it. Clearly MSG should not be used in baby food until proven safe and it should have been removed as soon as doubts were raised about its safety. (It was not removed until October 24, 1969, five months after the report of the brain damage by Dr. Olney, three months after Senate hearings on the potential danger, one day after Dr. Jean Mayer denounced the use of MSG in an address at the Women's National Press Club in Washington, D.C. It is not clear that MSG would have been removed from baby food without public pressure, which means that the FDA, which should have taken legal action to force the removal, was not doing its job.)

Next, implying that a thorough study of Dr. Olney's test has been carried out by qualified scientists, the Gerber letter states that they "are not convinced that his work is relevant to human feeding." It is clear from this statement that these scientists are also not convinced that his work is *not* relevant to human feeding. If they were you can bet the letter would have said so, loud and clear. The doubts about the relevance of animal testing to human problems are real doubts that must be lived with. Some dangers that show up in animals are not dangers to men. Conversely, some dangers to men do not show up in animals. But tests on animals are still the most widely accepted way to get the best prediction of safety for human beings. Whenever a company argues for the safety of a food additive it says that the additive did not harm the animals it was tested on. So when an additive does harm to animals the validity of animal testing should not be challenged. The Gerber letter not only raises questions about the most basic kind of practice for testing the safety of additives, it also mistakes the nature of Dr. Olney's test. It claims he got his results only by *injecting* rats with MSG, but this was not the case. On September 22, 1969, after an FDA scientist visited Dr. Olney's laboratory, the FDA wrote Senator McGovern to correct several misrepresentations it had made about those tests, and MSG in general, during testimony on July 22, 1969. One correction it made was, "Other unpublished work by Dr. Olney indicates that similar lesions were observed after *oral* treatment of weanling mice and rats with doses of 0.5 to 1.0 gram of MSG per kilogram of body weight." [13] (Emphasis added.) The "qualified scientists" referred to in the Gerber letter (but not mentioned by name) should have called this very important fact to the attention of Gerber, and Gerber should have reported it to the share-owners. This should be especially true since getting the same damage from oral treatment strengthens the warning that the original test provided and because the injection tests had been severely criticized by industry scientists.

Another distortion of the Gerber letter lay in the subtle omission of Dr. Olney's chief observation on the basis of his tests. The letter states that Dr. Olney "speculated" that MSG could cause damage in infants. In fact, Dr. Olney did make this speculation, but his main point, merely a restatement of the law, was: "So long as there is any doubt as to the safety at all, I think it the better part of prudence not to have it [MSG] in baby food." [14] In his final distortion, Gerber says that "little coverage" was given to the many tests "demonstrating the safety of MSG" though their "validity was recognized by the scientific community." The MSG studies cited by Gerber suggesting MSG is safe when moderately used by adults were not relevant to the baby-food problem because babies are not merely small adults. What the Gerber letter did not point out to its share-owners was that *no tests* other than Dr. Olney's had been conducted on animals less than twenty days old—the period about which the controversy raged. That was a telling omission. Dan Gerber misled his share-owners by not reporting Dr. Olney's test correctly, by ignoring the gap in the industry's own research on infant animals, and by not acknowledging the importance of the doubts raised by the MSG tests. Some Gerber share-owners are disturbed by having been misled and by the practice of undermining the quality of baby food.

Unfortunately, the FDA cannot be counted on as a major ally in the battle for better baby food. In an interview, the Director of the Bureau of Science of the FDA responded to the assertion that "baby foods are made largely to be pleasant for mothers" by saying that it was important for the baby that his mother enjoy baby food. If she did not, the assessment went, the baby might not eat it. That sounds like industry reasoning.

Salt, sugar, MSG, and modified starch in processed baby food have turned the product into a relatively unnutritious food which may possibly be dangerous, according to Dr. Jean Mayer and other nutritionists. Another potential danger in some processed baby foods was identified by Canadian reports in 1968 that showed high levels of nitrate in baby foods containing spinach, beets, and wax beans. The Washington *Post* reported the comments of Dr. Barry Commoner, a biologist at the Washington University in St. Louis. "In an infant's intestine, he said, nitrates often encounter certain bacteria and are converted to nitrites which combine with hemoglobin [the blood's red oxygen-carrying matter] to cause an asphyxiating disease called methemoglobinemia. German pediatricians have associated a number of cases with infant consumption of spinach. (Certain leafy vegetables tend to concentrate nitrates.)" [15]

The health and nutrition problems related to baby foods have been pointed out to the baby-food companies, mostly by the company's own researchers. But the baby-food producers have not been moved to correct the situation except under pressure—as in the case of MSG.

Dr. Thomas A. Anderson, while serving as chief of the Heinz Nutritional Research Laboratory, tried unsuccessfully to convince his company that they should seriously modify the content of their baby food products because of their lack of quality and potential danger. The company felt that it need not follow the recommendations because the data presented supporting them did not show conclusively that the foods as constituted presented any hazard. In addition, Heinz felt that it would be placed at a competitive disadvantage if the cheaper and possibly dangerous ingredients were removed from their foods and not from their competitors'. In order to make a profit on the improved baby food, Heinz would have to raise prices, and that would lose them customers. So the company set aside Dr. Anderson's recommendations. Furthermore, Heinz tried to block him from testifying before the McGovern Committee on Nutrition and Human Needs and from serving as a member of the Food Quality Panel of the White House Conference on Food Nutrition and Health. Discouraged by this treatment, Dr. Anderson has left Heinz. He expressed his dismay at the company's attitude in a letter to Dr. Jean Mayer. "I rather naïvely thought this . . . guidance of the McGovern Committee during the recent hearings would have resulted in a serious reappraisal by the Heinz company of its approach to baby food formulations. It is now obvious to me that I was wrong in this assumption and that the company is back to a 'business as usual' attitude, probably fostered by the hope that the Committee is now interested in other matters. . . . Regardless of how strongly management may deny any internal pressure it is becoming increasingly clear to me that I can no longer function effectively as nutritionist for . . . the company (if, in fact, I ever did)." [16]

Clearly an industry cannot be expected to regulate itself when it minimizes the quality of its product by adding nutritionally unimportant and possibly unsafe components, then distorts or dismisses the warnings of responsible scientific critics against those components, and finally tries to pressure into silence those critics over whom it has some direct control. Here is another not so unusual example of the food industry's reaction to criticism from scientists. At the height of the battle to remove cyclamates from the market in May of 1969, Dr. Jack Schubert, professor of Radiation Chemistry at the University of Pittsburgh, was asked to prepare a statement on his doubts about the use of cyclamates for a magazine called *Odontological Bulletin.* This dental journal, published for six counties of Pennsylvania, wished to present more information to its readers, many of whom were dentists who had been suggesting the use of food containing cyclamates to cut down tooth decay. Dr. Schubert's article was published and then widely reported in Pittsburgh newspapers and television, including the University of Pittsburgh student paper, *The University Times.* Showing an amazing lack of understanding about academic freedom and scientific independence, Charles S. Brown, Executive Vice President of Abbott Laboratories, the major manufacturer of the sweetener, wrote a letter of complaint to the Chancellor of the University of Pittsburgh, saying in part:

I most strongly protest the use by a faculty member of publications of the University of Pittsburgh to make unwarranted misleading statements about a product of Abbott Laboratories. . . . The scientific information we have—and it is extensive—tells us cyclamate, at currently used levels is safe and useful in the human diet. . . . The prime corporate interest of Abbott Laboratories is Health Care World Wide. . . . In Dr. Schubert's statements, our product—and thus our reputation—is unjustifiably attacked. For these reasons, we must protest when a respected academic institution like the University of Pittsburgh is used to make an unwarranted attack on the product of a corporation that is highly respected for its scientific reputation and integrity. We request that you take appropriate action to correct the misleading statements made in the name of your University.[17]

In spite of Abbott's unequivocal assertions of the sweetener's safety, cyclamates were off the market three months later. Answering the Abbott letter, Dr. F. S. Cheever, the university's Vice Chancellor for Health Professions, explained why it was important for the university not to carry out Abbott's wishes:

I am sure you realize that, as a faculty member, Professor Schubert is entitled to express his opinions freely and without prior clearance by the University administration. The concept of academic freedom is of immense significance in assuring open and free discussion of scientific and policy issues.

You mention Professor Schubert's lack of personal research on cyclamates. From our standpoint, there is no reason why a scientist must remain silent on a technical matter simply because he has not himself done research on the particular subject. Professor Schubert's opinions are based on his evaluation of papers and data appearing in the open literature and in technical reports that have been available to him from a variety of sources. The opinions he has expressed are his own, and they are subject to the peer group evaluation that always exists in the world of science.[18]

After visits from representatives of the public relations firm representing Abbott Laboratories and one public attack by Abbott distorting his comments, Dr. Schubert retained a lawyer to protect his interests.

What lies at the heart of the deterioration in food regulation is a series of fundamental misconceptions and conflicts about the operation of a democratic society and economy. First, there is a polarization between the food industry and its consumers, causing a kind of industrial hysteria that limits the food executive's ability to perceive or acknowledge legitimate consumer concerns. For example, when Donald Kendall was chairman of the Food Safety Panel of the December, 1969, White House Conference on Food, Nutrition and Health, he received a detailed telegram from Nelson C. White, the President of the International Minerals and Chemical Corporation, makers of MSG:

Mr. Murphy of Campbell Soup has told me of your interest in seeing that the upcoming White House Conference on Nutrition is kept within bounds of its stated purpose and that it not be used for rubber stamping the unrealistic thoughts and proposals of completely uninformed and biased so-called protectors of the consumer.

This communication is to assure you of the complete support of this corporation by any means or on any facet of the task you and other leaders face in the conference next week. As the nation's leading producer of MSG we know full well the magnitude of the task. We have for eighteen months found ourselves in the position one time after another of being tried by the press on the unjustified and too often utterly distorted statements of not only pseudo-scientists, but those in government circles who sought political favor with the public through association with the so-called consumer protectionism.

We have in every instance had to project ourselves aggressively into the picture to present the true facts, first to be heard by the Senate Select Committee on Nutrition and Human Needs, when monosodium glutamate became a target as an ingredient of baby foods, a national emotional medium for garnering publicity, and second, when the flurry of publicity on cyclamates resulted in MSG being dragged once again into the consumer spotlight on the basis of limited and inconclusive experiments being taken as proven findings against a quarter of a century of true scientific research.

We again commend you for your interest in the industry's side of the coming confrontation. We urge your most spirited participation and commit this corporation's total support.[19]

Mr. White's assertions can only add to the already accelerating number of dissatisfied food company nutritionists and their colleagues outside the industry, support the doubts of increasingly suspicious food company stockholders, and intensify consumer alienation.

This telegram reveals the attitude that has caused consumers of food to become alienated from its producers and contains most of the assertions that increase doubt about food industry commitment to the public interest. That there is consumer doubt and that it is growing cannot be denied. Mr. White's telegram itself is evidence of the doubt. But rather than view the MSG controversy as an opportunity to exchange concerns with critics and use it to restore confidence in food industry intentions, spokesmen (including scientists) for the food producers retreated into their alienating defensiveness. Officials of International Chemical, makers of more than 70 per cent of the MSG used in the United States, demanded free prime television time to rebut the charges and sent their telegram attacking "unrealistic . . . consumer protectionism" and reliance on "inconclusive experiments." Scientists sympathetic to industry directed angry verbal attacks toward researchers who suggested that MSG might not be safe.

More and more food industry critics of divergent points of view are being heard. At the public sessions of the Food Safety Panel, Olga Mader, speaking for the American Labor Alliance of the United Auto Workers, the Teamsters, and the Chemical Workers of America, defended the Delaney Clause. She said, "As bad as the Delaney Clause is, it has given us some protection. We ought to at least keep the protection we now have." [20] At the other end of the political spectrum, Governor Claude Kirk of Florida has been upset by General Foods Corporation advertisements that Tang, an imitation orange drink, is better than orange juice. According to the Governor (and the company, by the way), it is nothing but a series of chemicals, and he is promising a boycott against all General Foods products.[21]

Boycotts are not new to the food industry. In the fall of 1966, housewives organized to boycott stores that were engaging in practices that the Food Marketing Commission showed raised the price of food.

In New York a "Truth Squad" started a procedure whereby Tuesdays were to be known as "Don't Buy Day." The custom spread until eight hundred communities in six states were involved. In towns where unlimited local telephone calls can be made without raising the bill, housewives were enrolled to make ten calls each, asking everyone they could think of not to patronize markets that made use of gimmicks like trading stamps . . . Mrs. [Esther] Peterson, President Johnson's Special Assistant for Consumer Affairs, cordially hated by Campbell Soups and General Foods and described by the Advertising Association of America as "the most pernicious threat to advertising today," soon found herself getting such objects in the mail from consumers as pictures on packages of shrimp far larger than the edibles inside, and thousands of letters every day.[22]

Donald Kendall, President of PepsiCo, and the recipient of Mr. White's telegram, himself provided an example of how industry responds to criticism. He resigned from the White House Conference after Conference Director Jean Mayer in an article in *Life* magazine attacked fat-fried snacks like those made by a PepsiCo subsidiary, Frito-Lay, saying, "Fried worms would be better. At least you'd get some protein." [23]

Another indication of industry defensiveness is the language it uses in response to evidence that threatens a valuable product. Arthur T. Schramm, known as a spokesman for the food industry, provided a perfect example of such language in a letter he wrote about new information on cyclamates and MSG to the chairman of the National Academy of Sciences' Food Protection Committee, Dr. William J. Darby. He wrote:

The entire atmosphere growing out of such TV programming [news reports about scientific experiments conducted on cyclamates and MSG], coupled with politically oriented Congressional hearings and careless statements by apparently qualified publicity-seeking individuals, is one of economic terrorism. Many of the members of the Industrial Liaison Panel, recognizing this sinister development, have expressed strong feelings on the subject and have asked me, as Chairman of the Food Protection Committee, to take steps necessary to secure time for qualified members of the scientific community to put this matter in proper perspective for the public.

While I do not favor the airing of scientific disagreements in public, I feel we have no choice in this particular case, if we are to avoid the type of blackmail that is now occurring under the guise of freedom of speech.[24]

"Sinister," "terrorism," and "blackmail" are not words designed to convey an attitude of tolerance about doubts raised by scientific tests. Without that tolerance the alienation of consumers will grow. Schramm's letter, which began "Dear Bill" and was signed "Art," was written under the letterhead "Industry Committee of the Industrial Liaison Panel, Food Protection Committee, National Academy of Sciences," of which Schramm was chairman. That the National Academy of Sciences, a semipublic institution, should have a food industry committee is remarkable. The NAS has no "Consumer Committee" nor "Consumer Liaison Panel" and Dr. Darby is not "Bill" to the average consumer.

Another cause of deterioration in American food production is the industry's insistence that the consumer must accept risks to gain the benefits of its products. The same Arthur T. Schramm quoted above, in a 1957 article on food colors, said, "Man in his present generation has inherited a wealth of mechanical conveniences

to supplement his quest for the fuller satisfaction of
his higher nature. Whether he realizes it or not, these
conveniences are not without cost, that cost being the
element of risk. Probably the most impressive example
of man's willingness to expose himself to hazard for a
convenience is his continued use of the automobile—
were the automobile considered in the same manner
as the certified colors, the shocking toll of 42,000 killed
in 1956 would most certainly demand its delisting." [25]

Three assumptions run through Schramm's short
paragraph—that the "risks" cannot be avoided, that
man has a "willingness" to accept the risks, and that
he has obtained a "convenience" in return. They are
made in every defensive food industry argument, but
consumers are challenging them more and more. For
example, consumers said that despite its convenience
they were unwilling to accept the risk, however slight,
posed by MSG in baby food. As a result, the baby food
companies ultimately removed the additive. Congress,
which is supposed to speak for the public in this
society, has clearly stated that no additive shall be
placed in the food supply unless it is proven to be safe,
i.e., presents *no* known risk. Not only public opinion
but the intent of the law condemns the use of MSG
in baby food until its safety is established. In the field
of food additives, the country has legally abolished the
concept of balancing risks against benefits. Food additives *must* be safe. The fact that industry officials and
regulatory agents still apply the risk/benefit argument
to food additives merely widens the gap between them
and those who support the law.

Food industry hysteria and belief in the necessity of
risks join a third industry attitude that contributes to
consumer distress. Food industry spokesmen and their
supporters believe that food safety policy should be
set by themselves in conjunction with the small group
of scientists who have done the actual laboratory
testing of items that might not be safe. Even this group
is reduced as the industry tries to exclude men like
Dr. Olney when, based on their own laboratory research,
they make statements critical of a food industry practice. Excluded from the group by definition are men
such as Dr. Jack Schubert of the University of Pitts-

burgh, whose criticism of cyclamates was dismissed because he had not done any basic research on the chemical. And, of course, consumers are excluded from the group. As both the White telegram and the Schramm letter make clear, anyone outside the narrow group is thought to be a "pseudo-scientist," a seeker of political favor, a spokesman of "so-called consumer protectionism," "politically oriented," "careless," or only "apparently qualified." The assumption appears to be that there are no valid criticisms of the food supply to be made. Industry gets into this position in an effort to protect its economic interest. The scientists who defend the position, however, do so on mistaken grounds. Food scientists believe that only they are qualified to determine what is safe for the food supply. In this assertion, they are confused about the meaning of the term "safety." Scientists are trained to isolate certain sets of facts. This training does not make them particularly or singularly qualified to develop the policy that makes use of those facts. In the field of food safety, scientists can describe the effects of certain additives. For example, cyclamate causes bladder cancer in rats; MSG causes brain damage in infant mice. Once these facts are discovered, the issue to be debated is: Do we want such items in the food supply? There is no particular reason why the answer to such a question should be the province of scientists. If the people who consume the products to which these substances are added do not wish to consume them, that wish must be considered, and if made the law, as is now the case, enforced. If the food industry and its supporting scientists desire to put a different rule into effect, they should try to convince consumers and critics that adding to the human food supply substances that cause cancer or brain damage in animals is not necessarily dangerous. If they hope for success in this task they cannot exclude these consumers and critics from the debate or dismiss their opinions. Doing so, as is their present tactic, encourages the presumption that their case is weak. In fact, as the White House Conference on Food, Nutrition and Health Food Safety Panel said, "It is not possible to determine with absolute certainty the safety of the ever-increasing number of chemicals added to or present in our foods." This comment should be accepted as a warning to treat food chemicals with caution and not as a license to dismiss doubts. It also should make abundantly clear that more than scientific judgment must be called upon to determine what the food protection policy of the nation should be. Scientists can give an appraisal of what the risks are likely to be. Citizens must decide whether the risks are worth taking. Through their representative bodies, citizens currently have decided that any potential risk, however small, justifies excluding an additive from food. Industry, the FDA, and food scientists are obliged to follow that law until it is changed.

While the food industry has amassed its power and ignored its critics, the Food and Drug Administration has made no attempt to restrict it. It is often difficult to distinguish the agency's assumptions from those of the industry. The FDA demonstrates its deference toward industry by basing important regulatory decisions on the discussions held at agency meetings with private industry. The listing of caffeine on the labels of cola beverages and on Dr. Pepper was blocked after private meetings between agency officials and representatives of the American Bottlers of Carbonated Beverages—a cola-dominated trade association. Labeling of fat content was blocked after a private meeting between the FDA Commissioner and his staff and the representative of a Procter and Gamble research subsidiary. Food standards are routinely issued or modified to comply with industry interests or desires after meetings with industry representatives. In fact, the FDA has constructed an elaborate and self-deceiving rationale to justify its general reliance on industry guidance.

The assumption that manufacturing and consuming interests coincide, that manufacturers generally do what is right and obey the law, and the additional often-repeated belief that benefits must be weighed against hazards in deciding to market new and potentially dangerous products are the basic convictions held by the FDA as it begins to negotiate law enforcement with the industries it is supposed to regulate. Each of the convictions is either wrong or misleading. Manufacturing and consumer interests do not coincide. Manufacturers want high profits, which mean highest possible prices with lowest possible costs of production. Consumers, on the other hand, want high quality and value, which means the lowest possible prices and the highest possible expenditures on product improvement. Denying the antagonism between consumers and manufacturers has allowed the FDA to single out and advance the interest it is most aware of—that of industry —and to minimize the interest of the more silent consumer. If the FDA hopes to be effective it must single out, protect, and advance the consumer interest, the purpose for which Congress created it. Industry has the resources to protect its own interests more than adequately. The FDA cannot hope to engage in this kind of consumer protection until it begins to doubt its second conviction that business generally does what is legally and morally right. In reality, food companies are motivated by the prime objective of maximum profit. A glimpse of what motivates food company executives was given in a 1966 Special Supplement on Food Additives in *Chemical Engineering News,* a publication not known for its bias against the food industry. "As one food industry man points out, 'If an established product is grinding out millions of dollars a year for a company, you know darn well the company is not going to mess around with it.' Another food company spokesman points out, 'The marketing of many standard food items—the bread-and-butter items that have been around for years—has by now degenerated into a profitless price squeeze. . . . Therefore, food companies simply must make innovations to maintain growth." [26]

"Grinding out millions," "price squeeze," and "sales growth" are the important motivations in the food executive's world. A National Dairy Council letter to members explaining why they should oppose accurate fat labeling regulations illustrates how these economic motives can distort reality and raise doubts about veracity. The letter, which was inadvertently mailed to the FDA along with the form letter of complaint conveniently provided to members by the Council, said, "We feel that this regulation, if adopted, could pose many problems to the dairy industry." Specifically suggested were fear of "decreased sales of milk and dairy products" and concern about "circumstances such as this [fat labeling] the possibility of which require action if we are to maintain the favorable image of dairy products." [27] The Council wished to discourage accurate health information which might cut into profits.

When it became economically necessary for the Dairy Council to attack imitation milks, however, the Council's argument was that they were high in harmful fats. They even cited Ancel Keys, a leader of the fight for fat labeling, in their argument that imitations were dangerous to health because of their fat content.[28] At the same time that the dairy industry has opposed the labeling of fats because they do not present a health problem, it has cut the butterfat content of homogenized milk from 8 per cent to 3.5 per cent and greatly reduced the use of high-fat-milk-yielding Jersey cows. Economics, not health or science, is the prime determinant of dairy industry policy and practice. The dairy industry is not unique in the food business. All are after profits. Once the FDA recognizes that economics motivates the food industry it might begin to bring about higher quality, fewer possibilities of hazards, and more honest labeling by making any other alternative economically unpleasant.

The third conviction of the FDA, that the benefits of proposed new food products must be weighed against their possible hazards, has misled the FDA into allowing many products on the market in spite of their known potential danger. But the law does not ask for a balance; the Food, Drug, and Cosmetic Act unequivocally states that *no* food additive can be introduced into the food supply *unless its proposed use is shown to be safe*.[29] The potential hazards of food chemicals are too great to allow the use in food of any item which has not been shown by laboratory test to be safe. It is also important to note that the possible hazards of a new chemical are most often balanced against benefits to industry, not benefits to the consumer. Most food additives are used to enhance the profits of industry. (The United States could get along perfectly well without the use of the two to three thousand additives now routinely added to food. In fact, it could probably get along, as do many other nations, using fewer than 1 per cent of the current food additives.) The law is clear that there is to be no weighing of benefits and risks—only established safety qualifies chemically treated food for sale. The many mistakes about food chemicals made by the FDA in the past few years show the foolishness of balancing known risks against possible benefits for industry. Deference to industry's economic interests in the field of food safety is not compatible with the law.

If the FDA could learn to distinguish consumer interests from manufacturer interests, if it could understand that money motivates industry, and if it could apply the law as it was intended to be applied, it could *begin* to eradicate the inadequacy of its food protection policy. Before it can make that beginning it will have to learn a great deal more about the food industry than it now appears to know.

So little serious and original scientific activity is undertaken by the FDA that it is virtually dependent on the research work of industry, which, apart from its obvious bias, is meager and ineffective. Seventy per cent of all food standards are initially proposed by the food industry. Nearly all research on food additive safety is conducted by industry, not the FDA. The abysmally low amount of money that the food industry applies to basic research makes this FDA reliance particularly offensive. In 1968 Representative Craig Hosmer asked why the FDA relied on research data other than its own and pointed out, "The food industry is notorious in its unwillingness to put money up for research and development. It is the lowest industry on the ladder in R&D expenditures." [30] The food industry spent $135 million on research and development in 1964, which represented only 0.4 per cent of their net sales.[31] One result of this small application of research is the fact that "Almost half of the food additive petitions as originally submitted to the Food and Drug Administration have been incomplete or have not adequately supported the regulation requested and, therefore, have required subsequent supplementation, amendment, withdrawal, or denial." [32] At the 1968 food radiation hearings, FDA Associate Commissioner Kenneth Kirk surprised the committee and laid bare the real impotence of FDA. He pointed out that FDA does not do its own research on food additives, that it does not even review the research of industry, but rather reviews summaries of that research. He concluded his comment saying, "As time goes on I find our scientists are asking for the raw data more and more than they used to. I think it goes to what [Associate Commissioner] Dr. [Daniel] Banes said, that science marches on and you learn a lot of things. Of course, we in FDA never feel that anything is closed." [33] The FDA does not understand that fulfilling its responsibility is nonnegotiable, essential to the effective running of the economy, and easily lost sight of in the intense argument of well-financed special interest groups. Not recognizing or understanding the nature of this responsibility, the FDA continues to negotiate away its tools for meeting it.

When the FDA sought the authority to inspect food company records in 1962, it was defeated by the industry argument that such authority would endanger the secrecy essential to the running of the industry. The argument was that personnel transfers from the FDA to industry are so regular that inspectors seeing secret records of one company would automatically pass them on to their new and competing employer.

Employee transfer from the FDA to its regulated industries was serious enough in 1964 (83 of 813 retiring or transferring took such jobs) to prompt Representative Melvin Laird of Wisconsin to ask Secretary Celebreeze and FDA Commissioner Larrick if they had considered adopting conflict-of-interest rules preventing FDA employees from taking jobs in the food or drug industries for a certain period after their departure from FDA. Representative Laird said, "I strongly incline toward a requirement of this kind with respect to FDA personnel. . . . These two items [two FDA officials who left their jobs to work for drug companies] reawaken a concern I have had for several years that individuals in Government who exercise regulatory authority over major segments of American industry may so position themselves as to obtain lucrative positions with the regulated enterprises and open themselves and their agencies to perhaps valid accusations of conflicts of interest." [34] Dr. Louis Lasagna of Johns Hopkins University described the situation in his 1962 book, *The Doctors' Dilemmas:* the "subtle and potentially most dangerous aspect of the FDA setup [is] the well traveled, two-way street between industry and Washington. Men from the drug industry have gone on to FDA jobs and—more important—FDA specialists have gone on to lucrative executive jobs in industry. . . . It does not seem desirable to have in decision-making positions, scientists who are consciously or unconsciously always contemplating the possibility that their futures may be determined by their rapport with industry." [35]

The FDA's own policies encourage its closeness to industry. Under the FDA's voluntary compliance program, thirty-four thousand representatives of five thousand regulated firms have attended 325 workshops and forty national conferences between 1965 and 1970. The purpose of this massive effort was "to help give industry a better understanding of the law and FDA regulations, to make available to industry benefits of FDA research and methodology to help solve contamination and other problems, and to encourage maximum self-regulation. . . ." [36] The purpose of this program as explained by its director is to encourage industry to recognize the importance of quality. "Effective industry-assured compliance requires that most food, drug and cosmetic firms understand and appreciate the consumer's concern with quality and make efforts to satisfy it, the keystone of their operation." [37] To use persuasion as the primary tool in the campaign to replace profit with quality as the keystone of food industry operations is futile. It would seem that a program trying to make industry responsive to consumers would include consumer seminars and national conferences designed to determine exactly what does concern consumers, to inform consumers of the law, and to develop ways for them to aid in its enforcement. The meager consumer information program undertaken by the FDA is nothing like the massive agency effort to "educate" industry. As long as the FDA does not redress this balance it will continue to fail further in its mission. The effects of not understanding the importance of this balance were demonstrated in one of the first actions taken by former Commissioner Ley. "FDA officials sat down at the conference table with executives of member companies of the Grocery Manufacturers of America and agreed to redefine the meaning of the word 'withdrawal' which was to the benefit of the industry in a public relations way," reported *Food Engineering* in October, 1968. The decision, its effect, and the way it was arrived at all were of doubtful value in advancing the consumer interest.

The FDA relies on industry science, believes in industry honesty, and does not consult consumers in making its decisions. The FDA and industry officials build strong personal friendships. Naturally, the FDA has become a defender of industry power rather than a counterbalance to it. As the ineffectiveness of the FDA becomes more widely known, consumer confidence in the food supply dwindles. It would be in the interest of the consumer, the agency, the industry, and the nation if the FDA stopped apologizing for its industry friends and began to enforce the law.

6.

History That Repeats Itself

"The principle [of the Pure Food Law] that the right of the consumer is the first thing to be considered would be worth more to this country than the actual protection to health or the freedom from fraud."

—Harvey W. Wiley,
unpublished speech, 1908, in H. W.
Wiley Collection, Library of Congress

The Pure Food and Drug Act of 1906 was a climax in a long-fought campaign to purify the nation's food supply. It came at the end of a crusade for legislation against adulteration and fraud in food production and it ushered in a new campaign—the bureaucratic fight to implement the law. The first bona fide pure food bill was introduced in Congress in 1889 by A. S. Paddock of Nebraska, but Paddock's bill and others proposed in the next fifteen years met with ridicule and laughter. It was hard for anyone priding himself on having hard-headed business sense to believe that any actions taken in the effort to improve business could possibly have harmful effects.

But throughout the period, as various bills were suggested and voted down, more and more abuse and fraud were discovered in the production of food. The public began to be outraged. Watching the adulterators scurry for cover as their practices became known was more fun than turning over a log and watching the bugs uncovered try to escape, according to one participant in the battle.[1] The turning point in the campaign was the creation of what became known as the Poison Squad by the chief of the Department of Agriculture's Bureau of Chemistry, Harvey Washington Wiley. Dr. Wiley organized a group of twelve employees of the Department of Agriculture who took their meals under his direction. He carefully measured the individual

intake of various adulterants and then carefully watched
the health of the volunteers. His conclusion after five
years of controlled feeding was that many items in the
food supply were in fact dangerous. His periodic reports
on the progress of the Poison Squad experiments, more
than any other single factor, aroused public indignation
against the adulterating practices of the food industry.
With great skill, particularly in writing and public
speaking, Dr. Wiley focused this indignation on Congress. As one of Washington's most respected public
servants, he had many friends and associates both
inside and outside Congress who were moved by his
arguments and joined him in the crusade. Pressure
rose, and in 1906 the first Pure Food and Drug Act
was passed. Because of his major role in the campaign,
Wiley became known as the father of the Pure Food Act.

By every measure Harvey Washington Wiley was an
exceptional man. Mixing a quick wit and a polished
social grace with a crusader's zeal, he became the best
known and one of the most influential chemists in
America. For nine years he was professor of chemistry
at Purdue University, but he became nationally known
from his post as chief of the Bureau of Chemistry of
the United States Department of Agriculture, which
he held from April 8, 1883 to March 15, 1912. He
had accepted the position after narrowly missing promotion to the presidency of Purdue University. During
his twenty-nine years of government service, Wiley
played a central role in the development of agricultural
chemistry. He founded the Association of Official Agricultural Chemists (in September, 1884) and served two
years as President of the American Chemical Society
(1893–1894). As a medical doctor with a Ph.D. in
chemistry, Wiley brought a rare combination of scho-
lastic credentials to his books on the chemistry of foods
and to the official pamphlets of the bureau he headed,
writings which were the center of major political and
scientific debates at the turn of the century. It was from
this background of professional attainment that Harvey
Wiley fought the excesses of vested interest in the food
industry and led the campaign to establish consumer
rights.

In 1908 Dr. Wiley asked, "What is the most important task before the new Administration under President Taft?" And he answered,

Each one of course will answer this question according to his point of view. My point of view is that of pure foods and pure drugs. The establishment of the Food and Drugs Act on the principles indicated when it was discussed and enacted by Congress would do far more to this country than merely securing pure foods and drugs.

As an economic asset the actual benefit derived therefore is probably the least thing to be considered. The honor which would come to the Administration following the establishment of this law would be chiefly in the uplift of public morals. The result of the full establishment of this law would be a notice that vested interests could no longer control legislation nor execution of laws.

The principle that the right of the consumer is the first thing to be considered would be worth more to this country than the actual protection to health or the freedom from fraud. The object of all legislation of this kind is the same, no difference what its name may be, whether pure food regulation of public utilities, restraint of predatory corporations, the rights of the individual citizen against monopoly and corporation—all in principle are the same.[2]

In this manner, Harvey Wiley laid out the fundamentals of his own personal battle for the public interest.

On January 1, 1907, the Act went into effect. The first political intervention came within two months. Secretary of Agriculture James Wilson resolved a controversy about the use of sulphur in dry fruits by relying on the good will of industry and balancing industry economic interest against public health interest. As he reported it, "Well, they [the fruit dryers] said, 'We have a $15,000,000 industry here in growing and drying fruits. These dried fruits are contracted for by the big Eastern merchants. Our people borrow money from banks, etc., and when the fruit is sold everything is straightened out and things go on, but you people in Washington say that we can only use 350 milligrams of sulphur to the kilo, and the Eastern men who have contracted for our fruit will not make their contracts good; they are afraid it will not keep. . . .'

"I [Secretary Wilson] said, '. . . We have not learned quite enough in Washington to guide your business without destroying it. We will know better by and by, but I tell you what to do. Just go on as you used to go on and I will not take any action to seize your goods or let them be seized, or take any case into court, until we know more about the number of milligrams to the kilo and all that.' " [3]

The 1911 House Committee hearing testimony on the enforcement of the food law summed up this prec-edent-setting action of the Secretary. "Thus the ad-ministration of the law began with a policy of negotiation and compromise between the Secretary and the pur-veyors of our national food supplies." [4] "By and by," the Secretary said, "we will know better." Yet the 1969 cyclamates action by HEW was an almost exact replay of the 1907 sulphur action by the Department of Agri-culture. First a strong regulatory action was taken— cyclamates were banned. Within a few weeks food interests (including the California fruit interests, this time canners) complained that they would lose their entire stock of fruits and juices containing cyclamates unless the decision were reversed. The decision was then modified to extend the deadline and finally to eliminate the ban in fruits and vegetables. The most distressing fact about these decisions, both in 1907 and 1969, is that they were made behind closed doors with-out any pretense of consumer representation. Nego-tiation and compromise to suit industry's demands are still the order of the day.

Since Secretary Wilson's negotiate-and-compromise policy still prevails, a 1911 House Committee's com-ments on it are instructive:

It is a matter of common knowledge that large business concerns in this country have frequently refused to submit to the guidance of the law without a struggle, and to such of these as were engaged in the purveyance of foods the pas-sage of this law was in the nature of a challenge. It was a notice that in this country there is no question too important to be submitted to the courts for arbitrament. . . .

The standard of purity of food will never be determined with absolute finality. This standard will represent at any given moment the sum of our national knowledge on this subject, and as we extend our scientific research, and thus add to the sum of our knowledge on this subject, this stand-ard will necessarily vary; but Congress, in enacting this law, did not provide that its provisions shall remain in abeyance until we shall have completed any given course of scientific research. The problems arising under its administration today are intended to be determined according to our civilization today.

The Secretary stands on safe grounds in asserting that "we will know better by and by" but the law is in force today. . . .[5]

Four of the major struggles that Dr. Wiley directed while chief of the Bureau of Chemistry were against bleached flour, Coca-Cola, saccharin, and benzoate of soda. In each of these cases, intervention by one or another of several boards, committees, or individuals representing the Secretary of Agriculture thwarted Wiley's efforts to bring the issue to court or to enforce the ruling of the courts if finally achieved. As a result, each of these four subjects is still at issue today. President Nixon's French-born nutrition adviser, Dr. Jean Mayer, thinks that America's white bleached dough products would not even be called bread in his native land. Their food value is almost zero. White flour is preferred by food industry executives because it keeps on the shelf longer than the more nutritious whole wheat bread and because insects avoid it—it doesn't have enough food value to keep them alive.[6]

The irony of the claim that white bread is enriched is evident from the fact that twenty-two nutrients are removed from the bread in processing and only four are reinstated during the so-called enrichment process. Dr. Saul Rubin of Hoffman-La Roche has suggested that "food restoration" should be the goal and that at least three other nutrients be considered for addition to white bread. Currently, the FDA food standards for bakery products permit ninety-three different ingredients—few of them nutrients—to be added to bread products at the discretion of the processors without requiring that they be mentioned on the label. At one time the battle between makers of white breads and makers of whole wheat and other more nutritious breads was carried into the marketplace. The Ward Baking Company in 1921, committed to the arguments of Dr. Wiley, produced a highly nutritious nonwhite bread and conducted a vigorous campaign to promote it. However, in 1925 the company ran into economic difficulty and was reorganized. The new owners decided to discontinue the production of the more nutritious bread; white bread meant easier and greater profits.

Caffeine is being scrutinized as a contributing agent in heart disease,[7] and its exemption from required labeling in cola drinks and Dr. Pepper is a regulatory disgrace. Both sodium benzoate and saccharin are on the list of sixty-four "GRAS" food additives currently singled out for high-level review at the FDA.

The benzoate of soda and saccharin stories are coincidently connected at the beginning of the enforcement of the Pure Food Act. One powerful Congressman, James Sherman (soon to be Vice President of the United States), who was himself in the canning business and acted as a spokesman for the food interests opposing Wiley in Congress, asked President Roosevelt for a statement of intent on how the new food and drug law would be enforced. Roosevelt called a meeting between officials of the government and industry representatives at the White House. Sherman, of course, was there; so was Secretary of Agriculture James B. Wilson and the department's solicitor, George P. McCrab. The department's Bureau of Chemistry was represented by Dr. Wiley and his next-in-command, Associate Director Frederick L. Dunlap. Benzoate of soda, a food preservative that was a major point of contention between industry and the Bureau of Chemistry at that time, came up for discussion early in the meeting. Roosevelt told the food processors present: "Gentlemen, if this drug is injurious you shall not put it in foods." This was a victory for Wiley's side, but Roosevelt's firm stance was lost in the fray over the next item on the agenda: saccharin. Here is how Wiley's biographer described the exchange:

"But Mr. President," asked [Congressman] Sherman, "how about the saccharin? My firm saved four thousand dollars last year by using saccharin instead of sugar." Whereupon Wiley interposed, "Yes, Mr. President, and everyone who eats these products is deceived, believing he is eating sugar, and moreover the health is threatened by this drug." At this Roosevelt turned on him and hissed angrily through his teeth, "Anybody who says saccharin is injurious is an idiot. Dr. Rixby gives it to me every day."

His decision made, T.R. acted quickly. He recruited a five-man Referee Board of Consulting Scientific Experts, headed by President Ira Remsen of Johns Hopkins. . . .[8]

"Remsen himself claimed to be the discoverer of saccharin and received a medal from the Chicago section of the American Chemical Society for that accomplishment," Wiley wrote in his autobiography.[9] The purpose of the Referee Board was to "review" the work of the Bureau of Chemistry, but in effect it supplanted the Bureau. The Secretary of Agriculture followed the Board's decisions exclusively, thereby virtually eliminating the influence of Wiley's Bureau of Chemistry. To complete the squelch, the Department of Agriculture did not allow the Bureau of Chemistry to appeal the Remsen Board decisions to the courts, even though the law provided for judicial review. An administrative board appointed by executive order had usurped the judicial function assigned by an act of Congress. In 1969, when Secretary of HEW Finch sought justification for greatly modifying the ban on cyclamates, he appointed a temporary board of five scientists upon whose recommendations the roll-back of the cyclamates decision was based. Like the Remsen Board, the Finch group circumvented the procedures built into the law.

So the question of benzoate of soda safety—along with all other controversial food safety questions—was referred to the Remsen Board, which decided that the additive was safe enough to use. According to his biographer, "Wiley thought that the scientists on the Remsen Board, though honest men, had missed the spirit of the law, which had been intended to safeguard the the consumer. The act, he held, banned the addition to food not only of those substances which clearly rendered it injurious to health but of any that *might* do so." [10] Wiley's position and the publicity it generated against sodium benzoate nevertheless caused its use by manufacturers to drop, until in 1923 Wiley could write, "It is a rare thing at the present time to find benzoate of soda in catsup." [11] But Wiley continued to campaign against this particular Remsen Board decision, a campaign that critics have used to cast doubt on the activities of his last years. As his biographer says, "One wonders why he remained so disturbed about benzoate of soda when he admitted himself that very few manufacturers took advantage of the indulgence granted it." [12] In 1944, at a New York memorial of the 100th anniversary of Wiley's birth, the chemist Dr. A. L. Winton, who had worked with Wiley at the old Bureau of Chemistry, summed up his boss's career: "On the whole, I think old Doc Wiley's ideas have stood pretty well the test of time." He pointed out that benzoate of soda was still not used by most manufacturers, even though its use was legal. In other words, Wiley's publicity campaign was still effective.[13] But the Remsen Board withstood the test of time too. In 1958, when the FDA was preparing the Generally Recognized As Safe list, two Wisconsin scientists consulted complained about the inclusion of benzoic acid and sodium benzoate, on the grounds that the substances were not legal for use in food in Wisconsin. The FDA dismissed their comments, saying, "Benzoic acid limited to 0.1% and clarified by the Remsen Report." [14] For sodium benzoate, the FDA said, "Use limited and safety established"—again a reference to the nearly fifty-year-old decision of the highly controversial board. A quick label-reading trip to any food store in 1970 will reveal the addition of benzoate of soda to dozens of foods, so the residue of Wiley's personal effectiveness has faded. Voluntary action by food manufacturers is clearly not the effective food protection mechanism that officials from 1907 to 1970 have assumed.

Saccharin, too, illustrates the persistence of food regulation problems. In 1951 saccharin produced unusual combinations of cancers in a small number of test rats, indicating to the National Academy of Science at least a need for further study of the substance. Twenty years later, and sixty years after Dr. Wiley raised doubts about saccharin, the needed studies are yet to be undertaken by the FDA, and saccharin remains on the Generally Recognized As Safe list. A new study announced in early 1970 has offered new evidence of a relationship between saccharin and cancer, so the FDA has put it into the category of GRAS-list items that need review. But saccharin is still on the market, thanks at least in part to Theodore Roosevelt's prejudice in its favor.

Another board just as damaging to Dr. Wiley's work as the Remsen Referee Board was the Board of Food and Drug Inspection, appointed by Secretary of Agriculture Wilson with the support and encouragement of President Roosevelt. The Inspection Board had Wiley as chairman and included Frederick L. Dunlap and George McCrab. Wiley's two associates on the Board conspired to undermine his efforts at food protection. Having learned in advance what the Secretary wanted, they voted against Wiley whenever his scientific findings did not support the administrative decision Wilson desired.

Meanwhile, members of the Remsen Board were sent to professional meetings and court hearings around the country at Agriculture Department expense to defend department policy, while every attempt was made to prevent Dr. Wiley and his staff from presenting to the same courts and assemblies the scientific evidence they had against the department's policies. Dr. Floyd W. Robinson, a consultant to the Bureau of Chemistry who favored Dr. Wiley's positions, was dismissed from the department without a civil service hearing because, as Secretary Wilson said, he had taken "strong and public positions against the policies of this department." [15] A demoralization of scientists through administrative interference almost identical to that in the Bureau of Chemistry in 1911 existed in the FDA Bureau of Science in 1969. Scientific recommendations were routinely overruled for administrative reasons, scientific evidence that did not support current policy was ignored or suppressed, and one scientific consultant taking an outspoken position unfavorable to the administration lost his contract.

The bureaucratic maze constructed by Secretary Wilson and President Roosevelt virtually destroyed effective enforcement of the law against violators. Two thirds of the prosecutions recommended by Dr. Wiley were blocked by the Board of Food and Drug Inspection. [16] Solicitor McCrab, who served on the Board, was not satisfied with the considerable authority this position gave him, so he extended his reach by writing into the 1910 Department of Agriculture appropriation bill provisions that gave him control of all legal matters in the department, and then prepared an order (signed by the Secretary) specifically giving him direct control of the enforcement activities of the Bureau of Chemistry. The result was that the chief lawyer in the Department of Agriculture, not scientists in the Bureau of Chemistry, decided which products included ingredients not permitted under the law. In 1969 a similar situation existed with William Goodrich, assistant HEW general counsel for the FDA, exercising tremendous power over scientific decision-making at the FDA, according to the nearly unanimous opinions of persons familiar with the decisions of the FDA.

The resourcefulness and political power of Wiley's enemies also defeated his answer to the question of what whisky was and how to label it under proper food standards. Wiley thought the issue was of grave importance because "the whole subject of imitation and adulteration of foodstuffs is involved." [17] William Howard Taft, who had succeeded Roosevelt in the White House, asked the Solicitor General of the United States, Lloyd W. Bowers, to hold hearings on whisky, and Bowers decided that the definition "whisky" should not include neutral spirits unaged and artificially colored and flavored—a decision Wiley found generally acceptable from his perspective as defender of the consumer's interest. Unfortunately, the decision did not please Taft, who proceeded to hold hearings himself and ended them by ruling against Wiley. The result was that there was no way to tell from the label exactly what was in the bottle. "I felt as if I had been spanked," wrote Wiley.[18] The use of food standards to circumvent the law begun by the whisky decision continues today. Two hundred and sixty-two different ingredients are added to 541 different foods today as standard components and therefore are not named on the label.

Once the Pure Food and Drug Act had been passed, the opponents of the public's interest in pure food regulation made Harvey Wiley the focus of their attacks. In a five-year campaign of destruction, combining crude intervention with clever circumvention, the law and its chief enforcer were stripped to impotence. The final major assault of the attackers was an attempt in 1911 to have Dr. Wiley removed from government for mis-

using $1,600 in government funds. The charge origi-
nated with McCrab and Dunlap, Wiley's colleagues on
the Board of Food and Drug Inspection. They forwarded
their memo to Wilson, who passed it on to the Department of Justice. That Department officially brought
charges against Wiley. Wilson had first offered Wiley
the chance to resign quietly, but Wiley was aroused to
battle. "I would not advise anyone to wait around my
office to see me put out: there's no telling how long that
will be," he told the press.[19] The attack provided the
embattled bureau chief with the opportunity to lay before Congress and the public in detail the actions that
had eroded the effectiveness of the food law. These details and the failures they caused so closely resembled
the state of disorder at the FDA in 1970 that any assertion of progress by the agency must be greeted with
utter incredulity.

Wiley and his supporters laid out specific charges
against the Secretary of Agriculture, whose department
included Wiley's Bureau of Chemistry. (The responsibility for enforcement of the food law was transferred
to the Federal Security Administration in 1940, which
in turn became the nucleus of the new Department of
Health, Education, and Welfare in 1954.) They argued
that powerful vested interests in the food industry were
controlling the administration of the food law and block-
ing efforts to protect the public against food additives
of unproven safety, either by excluding them from the
food supply or announcing their presence on package
labels. Further, scientific judgments about food quality
and safety had been supplanted by administrative and
legal determinations which were economically and politically motivated. Enforcement of the law, they charged,
had been eroded by a policy of negotiation and compromise between government and food industry officials
and to some degree at least had been used as harassment
against companies out of favor with their politically
powerful competitors. And finally it was argued that the
opportunity to define what constituted adulterated products and thereby establish some kind of standard food
definitions as an aid to consumers had been turned into
an opportunity for the industry to avoid the effect of
the law by including misleading or dangerous practices

as standard. The uncanny similarity between these 1911 charges based on the first five years of experience with the food law and the current state of deterioration of the FDA suggests that more than the current shuffling and nudging at the FDA is needed. The situation in 1911 so resembles the situation in 1970 that it must be assumed until otherwise shown that minor organizational changes now taking place at the FDA will have no more impact than any of those in the past sixty years.

All the issues of the first controversy were argued before the House Committee on Expenditures in the Department of Agriculture. The immediate purpose of the Congressional inquiry was to investigate the charges against Wiley. Attorney General George W. Wickersham upheld the finding of an Agricultural Department investigation and ruled that Wiley should be dismissed from government for having agreed to pay a Bureau science adviser, Dr. H. H. Rusby, $1,600 for no more than eighty days' work. Wiley's plan was to get high-level scientific talent in spite of a nine-dollar-per-day limit on payments to advisers. On September 14, 1911, President Taft intervened in the case by writing directly to the Secretary of Agriculture to say that he thought the limitations on compensation were an unfair restriction on someone charged with enforcing so important a statute in the face of such a powerful industry. Relying on President Taft's letter and on extensive testimony from all parties concerned, the Congressional Committee investigating the charges exonerated Wiley. It developed later that the Attorney General himself had used almost exactly the same payment procedure to compensate George B. Kellogg for his two years' work on the Standard Oil and Union Pacific prosecutions. Kellogg received over $77,000. In much the same way, Henry L. Stimson had received over $88,000 from the Justice Department to investigate the sugar customs fraud of 1911. And there were many other such examples.[20] So amid much embarrassment to the national administration, Wiley was allowed to stay on the job. But the Committee did not stop with praising Dr. Wiley. It also exposed "a condition of discord existing in the Bureau of Chemistry which has lowered the discipline, impaired the efficiency of the service, and has added to the cost of administration." This disastrous condition, according to the Committee, was not the fault of Dr. Wiley. President Taft, the Committee pointed out, had completely exonerated the doctor. The President had, however, suggested that the "general efficiency of the department" had been brought into question and that correcting the problems caused by that inefficiency "may require much more radical action." [21] The Committee report laid the failure of the law directly at the door of the Secretary of Agriculture. The Bureau had been specifically created to enforce the food law by collecting evidence and transmitting it to the Justice Department. The Secretary of Agriculture had the single responsibility of determining whether the facts found by the Bureau were accurate. "From the beginning, however, the honorable Secretary has apparently assumed that his duties in the proper enforcement of the pure-food law are judicial in character, whereas in fact they are wholly administrative and ministerial. This misconception of the law is fundamental and has resulted in a complex organization of offices and boards to which have been given, through Executive order, power to overrule or annul the findings of the Bureau of Chemistry." [22] In 1970 HEW Secretary Finch is intervening in FDA activity in much the same way Secretary Wilson intervened against Wiley. He has muted FDA actions against cyclamates, the herbicides 2-4-5-T and 2-4-D and DDT in salmon as well as intervening in a number of important drug regulation decisions.

After being exonerated, Wiley finally left his government job in 1912 in bitter protest against the Department of Agriculture's failure to enforce the Pure Food and Drug Law and went to work as head of *Good Housekeeping* magazine's Bureau of Foods, Sanitation, and Health. By the end of 1926 Dr. Wiley, then eighty-two years old, was beginning to tire. The next year he gave up his position with *Good Housekeeping,* but he still had one more battle to fight. On November, 1, 1926, Dr. Paul B. Dunbar, Assistant Director of the Bureau of Chemistry, published "The Official Viewpoint in the Matter of the Interpretation and Application of the [Food] Law" in a trade magazine. Dunbar's official reliance on voluntary compliance, advice to industry, and education of food producers as the main tools of enforcement outraged Wiley, who responded in the next issue of the magazine. Dunbar said, "It is the Bureau's theory that more is to be accomplished by acting in an advisory capacity under such conditions as will insure legal products than by accumulating a record of successful prosecutions with attending fines turned into the Treasury of the United States."

Wiley answered, "This theory, not authorized by law, which is now fully put into practice is perhaps more than any other of the many factors in the case, the cause of the unnecessary and illegal delay in the execution of the food law as Congress intended it to be done. Last week a penniless thief was sentenced by one of the judges in Washington to ten years in the penitentiary for stealing twenty dollars. Those convicted under the food law often get by with a fine of five dollars."

Dunbar said, "Its [the Bureau's] policy, therefore, is to pursue educational methods as a preliminary to legal action where this can be done without jeopardizing the public interest or legitimate competitive conditions."

Wiley answered, "What we need is an education movement on the part of the Bureau of Chemistry not to persuade manufacturers to obey the law, but to induce the court to affix the penalties which the law provides. A few sentences of a year and a few $1,000 fines would do more than all educational endeavors with violators of the law to bring the offenders into respect and obedience of the law."

Dunbar said, "[In certain cases] it is not the practice of the bureau to institute action either by prosecution or by seizure without warning. But, instead a notice is given to the manufacturer that his product is regarded as misbranded within the meaning of the food and drug act, and he is given a hearing at which opportunity is offered him so to revise his labels as to bring the claim made within [the law]."

Wiley answered, "There is no warrant in the law, nor any suggestion of a warrant, that offenders should be called before the Bureau of Chemistry for the purpose of receiving instructions in ethics, nor that the Bureau of Chemistry should waste its energies and appropriations in trying, in a kind of ethical-Sunday-school fashion to persuade manufacturers to be good. Congress laid down the plan which was to be followed and the administrator of the law has no authority to deviate from the plain spirit and word of the law itself." [23]

Unfortunately for consumers, it was Dunbar's view that prevailed. Dunbar saw himself and his agency primarily as policy-makers, not as enforcers. He thought it was his job to get cleaner food by any means—cajoling, prodding, helping, suggesting—that would convince industry to obey the law as well as by enforcing it. The Bureau of Chemistry in his view was not supposed to root out and prosecute violators. It became the practice of the agency and its successors to hold hundreds of meetings each year with representatives of industry to discuss what co-operative efforts could be made to ensure that the provisions of the law were not violated. In these meetings much of the FDA's power has been eroded. If the Justice Department held regular meetings with the Mafia suggesting that it knew of gambling at certain addresses which if not stopped would lead to a raid of the premises, it would be following a procedure not unlike that used by the FDA to convince the food industry to obey the law. What made Dunbar's argument so important was its role in corrupting one of Dr. Wiley's most important legacies—an energetic staff committed to serving the public interest through vigorous government action. For the next thirty years men hired by Wiley but believing Dunbar's argument ran the FDA. These men had been recruited for the food protection field by Dr. Wiley in 1907, the year the food law went into effect. Until 1944 Walter Campbell served as Director of the Bureau of Chemistry and its successor agency, the Food, Drug, and Insecticide Administration (created in 1927 and renamed the Food and Drug Administration in 1931). He was singled out for stinging criticism in Wiley's 1929 book, *The History of a Crime Against the Food Law*. In 1940 the Food and Drug Administration was transferred out of the Department of Agriculture into the Federal Security Administration, and Mr. Campbell's title became Commissioner of Food and Drugs. In 1944 he was succeeded in that post by Dr. Paul Dunbar, who occupied it until 1951. The two chief inspectors under Campbell and Dunbar were Charles W.

Crawford and George P. Larrick; each was trained in the Campbell-Dunbar style of enforcement. Crawford succeeded Dunbar as Commissioner in 1951 and was himself succeeded by Larrick in 1954. Larrick served until 1966. The anti-Wiley argument has been the working standard of the FDA for over forty years.

In 1947 Commissioner Dunbar restated his friendly view of the industries he was charged to regulate in his *Creed of the Food and Drug Administration:* "Most American manufacturers of food, drugs, and cosmetics have the scientific knowledge, the technical equipment, and the will to produce articles which meet both the spirit and the letter of the law: most manufacturers recognize that consumer interest and producer interest are inseparable, and that practices adverse to consumer interest are likewise adverse to the interest of industry; and that most manufacturers make sincere efforts to meet all legal requirements not only because they are the law of the land, but because it is the right thing to do." [24] This section of the creed was quoted with approval by Fred J. Delmore, Director of the FDA Bureau of Voluntary Compliance, in the history of his bureau prepared for inclusion in the *History of the Department of Health, Education, and Welfare* during the Presidency of Lyndon Baines Johnson—prepared at the order of President Johnson and known generally as the Johnson Papers. Fred Delmore was designated by former Commissioner Ley to assume the duties as chief of all enforcement activities of the FDA just prior to the most recent agency reorganization. In commenting on the 1947 creed, Delmore said, "Enforcement officials have long recognized that at least 95 per cent compliance comes voluntarily and that this is the major source of consumer protection." [25] The same could be said about voluntary compliance with the homicide laws.

Wiley was not a saint and his adversaries were not devils. He made the mistake of allowing his feelings, hurt by the disregard with which "his" law was treated, to direct the course of his debate. He argued too much about specific problems with the law before 1912 and too little about later developments with which he was less familiar. This focus allowed Campbell and Dunbar to minimize his attack as outdated and to obscure the real problems Wiley was talking about. Although they were men of good intentions, Campbell and Dunbar were caught in a legacy of nonenforcement that severely limited their options. Within these limits they worked manfully, in part successfully, to make sense out of confusion. However, their basic commitment was to an enforcement philosophy opposed by Wiley. The old doctor described that philosophy in his 1930 autobiography, saying:

There is a distinct tendency to put regulations and rules for the enforcement of the law into the hands of the industries engaged in the food and drugs activities. I consider this one of the most pernicious threats to pure food and drugs. Business is making rapid strides in the control of all of our affairs. When we permit business in general to regulate the quality and character of our food and drug supplies, we are treading upon very dangerous ground. It is always advisable to consult business men and take such advice as they give that is unbiased, because of the intimate knowledge they have of the processes involved. It is never advisable to surrender entirely food and drug control to business interests. There is much to be done yet before we can point to a food and drug control that is wholly interested in the welfare of the consumer.[26]

In 1930 a progressive Senator from Montana, Burton K. Wheeler, entered the fray over food and drug standards by writing a magazine article extremely critical of the administration of Walter Campbell, Director of the Food, Drug, and Insecticide Administration. Shortly afterward Wheeler convened Senate committee hearings to investigate Campbell's competence, and the star witness he summoned to testify was Campbell's own former boss, Harvey Wiley. Although Wiley was eighty-six years old and not well, he was still carrying on his fight for strict enforcement of pure food and drug standards. He had just written a new book, *The History of a Crime Against the Food Law,* describing in great detail the early battles in the Bureau of Chemistry. The appearance before Burton Wheeler's committee was Wiley's last appearance in public, and it was a brief one. He scarcely had time to commend his new book to the Senators when he became too ill to testify effectively, and so his place was taken by his wife, Anna Kelton Wiley. Mrs. Wiley was thirty-three years her husband's junior and eager to stake out a claim to his legacy. Unfortunately, she did not have Wiley's understanding of law enforcement in general or the Food and Drug Law of 1906 in particular. She embraced Campbell's voluntary compliance principles, thereby effectively becoming a witness defending, rather than criticizing, the new regime at the enforcement agency that had now taken the place of her husband's old Bureau of Chemistry.

Among the Senators present at the hearings was one who did not actually have a place on the Wheeler Committee but who had been asked to sit in because of his medical and public health background. He was Dr. Royal S. Copeland, former Health Commissioner of New York City and the only physician in the United States Senate. Copeland slowly emerged at the hearings as Campbell's defender, and as Campbell gave a good accounting of himself and was exonerated of all the charges brought by Burton Wheeler, Wheeler developed considerable resentment for Copeland.

As it turned out, the hearings were not productive because they addressed themselves to side issues of little importance, but the personal feelings vented during them created an atmosphere of bitterness that haunted the greater issues of food and drug regulation throughout the decade and beyond. Wiley was bitter at the destruction of his life's work, particularly since it was being wrought by his star pupils. Commissioner Campbell remained personally loyal to Wiley although convinced that he misunderstood what was happening to the Food, Drug, and Insecticide Administration. Campbell, of course, resented Wheeler for the charges the Senator leveled at him. Senator Copeland, although he had high praise for Campbell himself, became convinced during the hearings that the weaknesses of food and drug law enforcement that emerged during the testimony required serious and immediate remedial action.

The failure of the hearing to produce the spectacular results that Senator Wheeler sought embittered him permanently, particularly on the subject of Senator Copeland. He was still incensed in 1938 when he wrote the Wheeler-Lea advertising act, which proponents of the new pure food law (passed that year) looked upon as a huge step away from consumer protection. It gave the control of food and drug advertising to the Federal Trade Commission, where it remains today. There is little doubt that Wheeler designed the act at least in part to embarrass Senator Copeland, who was the sponsor that year of what became the Food, Drug, and Cosmetic Act of 1938.

The conflicting opinions and flamboyant personalities that emerged at the 1930 Wheeler hearings set the stage for the complicated and extremely bitter controversy of the 1930's. The character of the period and of the job that needed to be done was captured by Upton Sinclair, himself famous as a pure food crusader, in his 1930 review of Dr. Wiley's book, *The History of a Crime Against the Food Law:*

Are you looking for a career? And if so, would you like to consider that of martyr? Would you like to devote thirty or forty years of your life to struggling for a great cause and almost wholly fail of success? Would you like to be met with abuse and slander all your days, and to have all the great organs of public opinion closed to your defense? . . . Dr. Harvey Wiley [is] the author of the book I am telling about. The career I am offering is the one which he will soon have to lay down, because he is an old man and needs some young martyr to come along and take up his burden. I should think this ought to prove an extremely melancholy book for those liberals who believe in present-day America, who think that day by day, in every way, it is getting better and better. For here is a man who has devoted his entire life to a most important reform, and most of the time has been on the inside, in a position to know the exact facts; he shows you that day by day, in every way, America has been getting worse and worse . . . I was moved to lay aside my own writing, and make this feeble effort to find some young martyr to take up the life-work of old Dr. Wiley.

Three years later, the perfect man for the job appeared. His name was Rexford G. Tugwell.

The Pure Food Law of 1906 lay in tatters as the Administration of Franklin D. Roosevelt took office in March, 1933. Rexford G. Tugwell, one of the original three Brain Trusters and a chief adviser to Roosevelt on farm policy, took the government position of Assistant Secretary in the Department of Agriculture, which had responsibility for control of the Food and Drug Administration. As early as February 17, 1933, two weeks before the Roosevelt Administration took control of the government, Tugwell wrote in his diary that the FDA would be one of his first problems in the Department of Agriculture. "I'll do the best I can for the consumer regardless of politics; I won't compromise on this." [27]

Tugwell's battle began when upon assuming office he found a routine policy letter for his signature which expressed the Agriculture Department's concern about the effect of "certain poisonous insecticides," saying, "the Department is devoting a very material proportion of its available funds and personnel to this problem in the interest of public health and the welfare of the fruit and vegetable producing industry." [28] In the Assistant Secretary's view the food law was intended to protect the consumer, not the producer, and he said so to Mr. Campbell. After a long discussion in which the FDA chief pointed out the natural conflict between the Agriculture Department's dual roles of encouraging agricultural production and protecting food consumers, Tugwell signed the letter but vowed his support for efforts to reform the law. The day after the letter was sent Mr. Campbell filed a memorandum saying, "I am making this memorandum note to be attached to this file to record what to me is a development of extreme significance. From the assurances which I received from the Assistant Secretary, it can be definitely forecast that the effort which we have made in our service for the protection of the consumer will receive from the Secretary's office much more sympathy than has been the case in the past. I confidently hope, and definitely believe, that in the future less effort will be required in preventing reversals of our decisions by appeal to higher Departmental authority." [29]

Without knowing it, Tugwell was stumbling into a thicket of cross purposes and hurt pride, with only his strong sense of justice to defend him against one of the most vicious smear campaigns ever waged by vested financial interests against a government official. He would find his allies as divided as his enemies were determined.

The battle began quietly enough. After his long March conversation with Campbell, Assistant Secretary

Tugwell issued an administrative order lowering the amount of poisonous arsenate lead residue allowed to remain on fruit after spraying with insecticide. The new level was still above that regarded as safe by the British Royal Commission on Arsenical Poisoning, but it had been lowered enough to enrage the International Apple Association. This organization, led by Raymond G. Phillips and Samuel Fraser, was affiliated with the National League of Commission Merchants of the United States, the National Fruit and Vegetable Exchange, and the Western Fruit Jobbers Association of America, with a combined membership of twenty-four thousand. Within hours after publication of the order two Washington State progressive politicians representing apple-growing interests were in Tugwell's office asking that the new regulation be rescinded. Tugwell was amazed, as he described thirty-five years later: "If anyone would be offended, he [the Assistant Secretary] expected it would be his own Congressman and Senators; he had an especially wary eye on Senator Royal S. Copeland, whose Senatorship was combined with his occupation as a Hearst columnist. But instead, here were far westerners with tempers out of control." [30]

Coincidentally, the initial erosion of the first Food and Drug Act had come in 1907 when Far Westerners, enraged about regulations to control chemical residue on fruit, persuaded Agriculture Secretary Wilson to rescind his administrative order. And as if to maintain a kind of precise historical symmetry, on July 3, 1968, the Department of Agriculture announced tests to establish the safety of a chemical used to control apple scald, a condition making apples less salable, the use of which had caused a number of foreign countries to exclude from importation American apples on which it had been used. [31] Chemicals on Western fruit seem to be an eternal problem.

Tugwell rejected the Westerners' angry demands and began to plan the campaign which was swiftly becoming a cause to him. He relied for support on public indignation, which was being fanned by a book on the deterioration of food, *100,000,000 Guinea Pigs* by Arthur Kallet and F. J. Schlink, which went through twenty-seven printings, and on FDR's desire to outdo his cousin TR, who had taken a good deal of credit for the 1906 law. The object of Tugwell's campaign was to pass a new law. As soon as the apple growers were out of his office, he arranged for the drafting to be begun. Campbell and two administrative lawyers, David Cavers and Milton Handler, had the job of drafting. Senator Royal Copeland became the bill's chief sponsor in Congress.

To prepare the draft's reception in Congress, Tugwell decided to marshal all the means he could to drum up public interest. He approved the preparation of a large display of fraudulent, harmful, and misleading food, drug, and cosmetic products and their advertisements. The display, called the Chamber of Horrors, received wide publicity and soon became as well known as the most controversial pieces of New Deal legislation—the Agricultural Adjustment Act and the National Recovery Act. Tugwell approached Thomas Beck of *Collier's* magazine, who had been very effective in publicizing Dr. Wiley's earlier fight; he contacted Father Coughlin, who had the most popular radio program in America, and he sought the aid of the public information staff of the Department of Agriculture (led by Milton Eisenhower) to publicize the fight. But Beck was not interested, Coughlin refused to help unless Tugwell would work to ban contraceptives, and Eisenhower's efforts were not enough to counter the massive attacks of most of the American press which, concerned about the possible loss of advertising revenue, attacked Tugwell and the bill. Even the public response stirred up by *100,- 000,000 Guinea Pigs* and the Chamber of Horrors was too diffuse and disorganized to be of significant help.

The proposed law had seven major objectives, according to the letter of transmittal from Secretary of Agriculture Henry Wallace to the Chairman of the Senate and House Agriculture Committees. Four of the seven objectives dealt directly with foods—the prevention of false advertising; the limitation of added poisons in foods; the authority for the Secretary to establish for foods definitions and standards that would have the force of law; and the requirement of informative labels. The other three objectives were to bring cosmetics under the control of the law, require certain manufacturers of dangerous products to obtain Federal permits, and to restrict the claims for drugs to those agreed to by medical opinion.[32] Of the three objectives unrelated to food protection two lie at the center of major controversies still raging at the FDA in 1970. Cosmetics are still not adequately tested before going on the market, and the same kinds of abuses that outraged the public in 1933 can still occur. One of the major exhibits of the FDA's Chamber of Horrors concerned a woman who had been blinded by the application of eyelash make-up at her beauty parlor. There is today no pretesting provision for cosmetics in the Food, Drug, and Cosmetics Act. As a result, the second largest group of personal-injury claims to American insurance companies, according to the Product Safety Commission, results from injuries caused by cosmetics. While the FDA can now move against the cosmetic agent causing an injury, there is no way to block its original marketing. In the drug area expert committees of the National Academy of Sciences have declared a significant number of antibiotic combination drugs either unsafe or ineffective in carrying out the claims made for them in labeling and advertising, but the offending items are still being widely marketed across the country.

A book called *The American Chamber of Horrors,* written by Ruth De Forest Lamb in 1938, detailed the food problems that Tugwell aimed his bill at. Three of the most important loopholes in the existing law were the "distinctive name" provision, the failure to require an indication of quality on labels, and the failure to require that food products clearly identify their contents on the labels. The "distinctive name" provision in the 1906 act meant that if a manufacturer was clever enough to think up a distinctive designation for his product, it would not have to meet standards for similar products under the law. One such item was Kraft's Miracle Whip, which appeared to be a salad dressing but did not have to meet dressing standards because it was designated a "whip." Kraft and Borden used the distinctive name clause of the law to escape the requirements for process cheese. These cheeses gave Kraft and Borden a way of using up unsalable cheeses. The low quality, hard and moldy cheeses that the public will not buy could be conditioned, ground up, heated, and combined with salt, water, and an emulsifying agent, then poured into packages ready for sale. Velveeta and Borden's Chateau were similar to process cheeses and avoided standardization. Another famous product that escaped regulation was Ovaltine, essentially a chocolate malted milk drink advertised as a miracle cure-all. In 1970 this gaping loophole in the law is still substantially available to manufacturers, allowing products such as Gatorade, the "thirst-quencher," on the market. Since the law has no standards for "thirst quenchers," Gatorade can legally contain whatever the manufacturer chooses, although now he must list the ingredients on the label.

The second major loophole in the 1906 law that Tugwell aimed to close was the failure to require grade labeling. Tugwell's draft act was designed to require all products to be labeled Grades A, B, or C. The alternative proposed by the food industry was that a standard of quality be promulgated and that foods be labeled either as complying with the standard or as substandard. This industry alternative was designed to increase industry profits. Grade labeling, which would allow consumers to pick products by quality rather than brand name, would undermine the huge efforts undertaken by companies to build brand identity in preference to stressing quality. In 1966 the President's Commission on Food Marketing estimated that the average consumer food bill could be raised by as much as 20 per cent by the purchase of nationally known brands rather than high-quality local brands. Unable to tell the quality of what he was buying, the consumer was thus forced to assume that the more expensive brand names were better.

The third major issue in Tugwell's pure food fight was his attempt to obtain more accurate labeling of food products. The idea was that each consumer should be able to tell what he is buying by reading the label. The major reason cited for making information available was the widespread incidence of allergic response to various ingredients. The industry's counterproposal, again designed to protect industry profits, was that a list of the ingredients should be filed with the FDA—inaccessible to the public—so that any hazards might be ferreted out by the agency. But the file at the FDA could not help susceptible people to avoid irritants.

Two of the prime leaders of the industry's right to maintain the three loopholes Tugwell wanted to close were Charles W. Dunn, counsel for the Associated Grocery Manufacturers of America, and H. Thomas Austern, counsel for the National Canners Association. Mr. Austern rallied his organization to the fight against grade labeling, saying, "Every canner should leave this meeting ready to sell the idea to other canners and to his representatives in Congress that this bill should not be permitted to pass. Don't try to do this by writing letters. It is a selling job that you have on your hands. You must go out and talk to people." [33]

No grade labeling was adopted. Today Austern is senior partner in the Washington law firm of Covington and Burling, general counsel for the National Canners. The canners are still taking the lead in opposing full information for the consumer. At its sixty-third annual convention in January, 1970, the association took a strong stand against the proposal of President Nixon's consumer adviser Virginia Knauer that her office prepare and disseminate an easy-to-read guide to government action. The canners argued, "The government should not use its prestige and power to interfere with the competitive process by seeking to persuade or guide the public." [34]

Mr. Dunn was able to persuade Congress that labels should not carry complete lists of ingredients because allergies could be protected if ingredients were filed with the FDA. As a result, nearly two thirds of all chemicals now placed in foods do not appear on the labels, in spite of the fact that there are at least forty-nine known conditions and innumerable allergies that may require a special diet. Dunn was also able to win a partial victory on the "distinctive name" issue. While the version of Tugwell's proposed bill that finally became law in 1938 did require that all ingredients of a "distinctive name" product be labeled, there was no requirement that products which bore a strong resemblance to standardized foods and were marketed to compete with them meet the standards for those foods.

The result of these industry victories is revealed by a careful analysis of the food standards that have developed under the law since 1938. Many ingredients may be added to a food substance and need not appear on the label. There are ninety-three such permissible ingredients for bakery products, seventy-six for nonalcoholic beverages, fifty-eight for frozen desserts, thirty-three for fruit butters, and thirty-one for cheese. In short, without grade labeling, without a complete listing of additives present in a food, and without some regulation of the quality of foods, the consumer gets little or no useful information about the nature of the food he eats.

In Tugwell's mind the protection of consumer rights and the development of consumer power were an integral part of badly needed economic redevelopment in the 1930's. In pursuing these goals, Tugwell not only sought reform of the Food and Drug Law, but as a principal draftsman of both the Agricultural Adjustment Act and the National Industrial Recovery Act he was instrumental in the creation of the Office of Consumer Counsel in the Agriculture Adjustment Administration and of the Consumers Advisory Board in the National Recovery Administration.

The Agriculture Department's consumer counsel, Frederick C. Howe, worked to ensure that the expected rise in farm prices would not gouge the consumer. The Consumer's Advisory Board, led by W. Averell Harriman's sister, Mary Rumsey, had the task of resisting industry efforts to keep production and prices up. Like Tugwell in his efforts to reform the food law, neither agency was particularly successful at its task. The New Deal was not a time for the consumer. Arthur Schlesinger described the theory of consumerism as stated by economist Gardiner Means:

The question now was whether consumers could develop enough strength to restrain the producer from succumbing to the temptation to raise prices and limit output. If so, the organized consumer could become the key to increased production and thus to the restoration of economic balance. Still, as Means carefully warned, wishing would not make it so, nor would even the ritual of appointing consumer representatives to it. "The consumer will get nothing for which he does not fight, however socially minded the agents of Government may be. . . . If there is no pressure on Government from people as consumers, there is little likelihood that their interests as consumers will be effectively represented." [35]

The pressure did not come. All the New Deal consumer efforts were, as Tugwell described the members of the Consumers Advisory Board, "spearheads without shafts." [36] Many who saw consumerism as the peculiar American answer to economic distress that would cause the nation to avoid the extremes of fascism and communism watched with the rest of the nation as the NRA failed. That failure, according to Schlesinger, resulted from the inability of New Deal and NRA leadership to understand the importance of strengthening government, labor, and consumer representation as a countervailing power to business in the operation of the NRA—and, for that matter, the whole New Deal.[37] According to Robert S. Lynd, who served for a time on the Consumers Advisory Board, "It was an afterthought —a gesture to the women of the country that was never intended by General Johnson [NRA Administrator] to work." [38]

Tugwell revealed his despair at the failure of his consumer protection activities in a 1934 speech to the Consumers League of Ohio where he said, "Perhaps the efforts which went into the building of these governmental consumers' agencies will prove not to have been justified by results; certainly they have not been up to now in spite of some lesser achievements and in spite of an excellent record of criticism and protest which came to very little." [39] The most dramatic and crippling attack on the consumer interest was waged against Tugwell's Food and Drug Law. It set the tone, and was a major cause of the New Deal's failure to develop consumer power and protect consumer interests. While the consumer activities of the NRA and the AAA were carried on in relative obscurity, the vicious attack on Tugwell and the Food and Drug Law was conducted in, and by, the overwhelming majority of the nation's newspapers, supported by their advertiser allies. The heart of the opposition, as Senator Copeland termed it, to Tugwell's bill in Congress, lay chiefly in the attempt to substitute the more lenient Federal Trade Commission for the Food and Drug Administration as the agency that would control food, drug, and cosmetic advertising. The attempt was successful and its sponsor was Senator

Burton K. Wheeler, still eager to get credit for pure food legislation despite his earlier failure.

Rexford Tugwell asked for Presidential intervention to solve the conflict between the FDA and the FTC. "The [Federal Trade] Commission is not empowered to penalize offenders," he wrote to the National Emergency Council. "As one authority puts it, 'through its cease and desist' order it can merely direct the offender to go and sin no more." [40]

Roosevelt supported this view. "Frankly, I do not approve the proposal that provisions against false advertising be enforced by the cease and desist order procedure of the Federal Trade Commission. This procedure is time consuming. It carries no penalty and has no deterrent effect on the evader and chiseler." [41] Senator Wheeler insisted on proving himself after his first failure. He was supported by the food and drug advertising lobby and the FTC. ("Nobody," according to Sam Rayburn, "has lobbied around this Capitol on any bill in the twenty-three years I have been in Congress more than the members of the Federal Trade Commission have lobbied on this bill.") [42] Together they pushed the bill through.

Even though Wheeler's act included limited criminal sanctions, it was such a blow to food and drug regulation that FDA officials hoped Roosevelt would veto it. He did not. The Wheeler act is still in effect and still greatly limits the FDA's food protection effectiveness. In fact, it was one of the major problems pointed out to President John F. Kennedy by Judge James Landis in his 1960 report on regulatory agencies.

With the advertising sections of the original bill destroyed, the opponents of effective food and drug regulation set about passing the other gutted sections of Tugwell's original plan. The unqualified prohibition against added poisonous or deleterious substances in food was modified to allow such substances when they were required in food production or crept in under "good manufacturing practices." The abuses that grew up under these exceptions were so outrageous that twenty years later, after extensive Congressional hearings and another great public outcry, the law was amended in an attempt to control the addition of chemicals to foods.

The original section authorizing food standards was also mutilated. The grade labeling provision was deleted; the standards of quality, identity, and package fill were reworded to reflect the concerns of various industries, containing language that allowed manufacturers to include in food products chemicals which did not need to be declared on the labels. The modified food standards provision destroyed the final objective of the original bill by providing a major loophole in requirements for informative labels. In the words of Tugwell, the bill was a "discredit to everyone concerned with it." [43] To be sure, Food and Drug Commissioner Campbell found many provisions of the new law helpful to his embattled agency. Labeling would be a bit more informative, standards, however defective, could finally be issued, and there was a provision for injunctions. In a narrow bureaucratic sense the law was something, but the few advances it made were meager compared to the needs it left unanswered.

Publishers and advertisers were "up and roaring" against Tugwell from the minute he mentioned food and drug legislation, Russell Lord remarked, and some of the most powerful among them openly threatened to "cut him down." The basic tactic of their attack was to connect the food and drug bill with Tugwell and discredit him in the eyes of the public. As an economic historian put it, they "ascertained that the bill was sponsored by Rexford Tugwell; Tugwell was a 'brain truster'; brains were a dangerous commodity in any government; hence the bill was anti-American, revolutionary, bolshevistic, and to be reviled by all good 200 per cent Americans." [44]

Before the ink had dried on the proposed legislation the New York *Sun* began referring to Tugwell as "Rex the Red." [45] Tugwell had made a trip to Russia, and that was enough for the advertisers. Newspapers across the country took up the cry against him, spurred on by not-too-veiled threats against their advertising revenue if they wavered on the attack. The Associated Grocery Manufacturers of America, on the advice of their general counsel, Charles Wesley Dunn, wired all newspapers that had a Washington correspondent: "May we respectfully call your attention to revised Tugwell-

Copeland Bill Senate 2800 as a measure that may seriously affect future newspaper advertising volume."

The whole show was a repeat of 1906. Ruth De Forest Lamb wrote: "But opponents of the proposed legislation did not need to know what was in it in order to criticize it. They simply dusted off the same old arguments they had used in 1906, substituted the names 'Campbell' or 'Tugwell' for 'Wiley,' changed 'czar' to 'dictator' (in making invidious comparisons between the Secretary of Agriculture and the head of the Russian Government), and had their propaganda circulating in no time." [46] The attacks on Tugwell not only resulted in the destruction of the Food and Drug Law he had helped to create but they also destroyed his reputation and undermined the effectiveness of his activities in government. As a result the Resettlement Administration, which he headed, was severely handicapped and never achieved what was hoped for it. Equally important, Tugwell's role as a leading, if not *the* leading, advocate of consumer power within the New Deal tied the effectiveness of consumer activities to his reputation. As his reputation declined under constant attack from irresponsible newspapers and advertising agencies, hopes for the consumer dwindled. As people lost confidence in Tugwell, his arguments became less convincing and his power dwindled. Sumner Welles, Under Secretary of State under Roosevelt during the Second World War, described what happened to Tugwell in a review of the former Brain Truster's book *The Stricken Land:* "No member of President Roosevelt's earlier administration was more bitterly derided and more unjustly pilloried as a strange amalgam of a Fascist, a Communist and a menace to the liberties of the American People than Rexford Guy Tugwell. . . . Those of his fellow citizens—and I fear there are many of them who, as a result of one of the most vicious and effective campaigns of character assassination in history, have been deluded into believing that Rex Tugwell was a Communist or an authoritarian bent upon depriving them of their rights and liberties, and who are willing to read this book with an open mind, will find conclusive proof to the contrary on every page." [47]

Tugwell left the government before his law was passed in 1938. He felt little had been accomplished for the consumer even after passage of the act. The 1938 act, still the nation's basic food protection law, has not been successful in providing the safe, wholesome, and inexpensive food consumers need and deserve. Among the recommendations of the December, 1969, White House Conference on Food, Nutrition and Health were proposals for various kinds of grade labeling, the elimination of loopholes in food standards leading to uninformative labeling, and a more vigorous control over misleading advertising. These proposals were just what Rexford Tugwell hoped to achieve when he began planning in 1933.

7.

Destruction of the Food Protection Amendments

"I am not going to tell you that FDA has devised the perfect system for keeping hazardous chemicals out of our foods . . . you'll simply have to live with it."

—FDA Commissioner Herbert L. Ley, Jr.
12th Annual Food and Drug Law Institute-
FDA Educational Conference
December 3, 1968, p. 4

In August, 1969, Dr. D. A. Hillman and Dr. F. C. Fraser reported in *Pediatrics* that two women living in the same upper New York State township each gave birth to a baby with unusual deformities—one on December 25, 1967, the other on March 5, 1968. Each child had a lobster claw deformity (the fusing together of the toes or fingers) and a cleft lip (the fusion of the upper lip to the gum). This combination is rare. It would probably not occur by chance as often as once in 100 million births. The reporting doctors concluded:

The occurrence of such unusual malformations in two infants born in the same district within a period of approximately two months suggests the possibility of an environmental teratogen [a chemical that causes birth deformity]. In spite of repeated questioning of the parents of these children, we have not been able to identify any pharmacological, genetical or other agent common to both histories that could be implicated as a teratogen, with the possible exception of the artificial sweeteners used in low calorie foods, or as additives. Since these compounds have been widely used by pregnant women for some years, without any noticeable increase in the malformation rate, it seems unlikely they are relevant here.[1]

This letter presents but one example of a growing concern about the hazards presented by the increasing use of chemicals in the environment. Other scientists are also concerned. The use of nitrate fertilizers building up large residues in stored green vegetables, especially spinach, celery, and green salad may possibly be related to cancer in animals and men.[2] In 1968 Dr. James Crow of the University of Wisconsin, Chairman of the National Institute of Health's Genetic Study Section, reported on the possible genetic effects of chemicals in the environment. *Medical World News* summarized the report, saying: "Potentially irrevocable [genetic] damage might be done without immediate warning by some of the more than 10,000 natural and synthetic chemical agents now produced commercially or by the million or more additional agents that have been isolated or synthesized by man, most in recent decades. Fewer than 200 of these suspected mutagens have been systematically assayed." [3] The potential hazards from chemicals in the environment are staggering: these present three kinds of danger about which we have only limited knowledge. First, some chemicals have the ability to cause teratogenic deformities—the kind of deformities, like those produced by thalidomide, which affect individuals in the current generation but are not passed on from one generation to the next. When a child deformed by his mother's ingestion of thalidomide reaches adulthood and has a child of his own, the deformity probably will not be passed on. Second, many chemicals can cause cancer. Third, and most disturbing, is the possibility that some chemicals can cause mutations that will be irrevocably engraved upon the genetic code and passed on from generation to generation. Some of the mutagenic changes are so subtle ("A ten-point change in IQ, perhaps," says FDA biochemist Dr. Marvin Legator) that they might go completely undetected for several generations. Under the Food, Drug, and Cosmetic Act, the Food and Drug Administration is given the responsibility of protecting consumers from these potential chemical hazards when they are related to chemicals in food.

In 1950 Congressman James Delaney of New York, serving as Chairman of the House Select Committee on Chemicals in Foods and Cosmetics, began extensive hearings into the effects of chemicals in and on food. The major legislative results of these hearings, which lasted for three years, were three amendments to the Food, Drug, and Cosmetic Act: (1) The Pesticide Amendment of 1954, (2) the Food Additives Amendment of 1958, and (3) the Color Additives Amendment of 1960. Each was designed to place the chemicals in and around food under stricter control. They are all important pieces of legislation which should be rigorously applied. However, knowledge about potential chemical hazards has developed more rapidly than the FDA's ability to control the spreading use of food chemicals.

The complexity of hazards presented by the chemical environment has become a matter of grave concern to many thoughtful scientists. Several thousands of the people who used the sedative thalidomide between 1954 and 1962 were pregnant women (nearly all were Europeans), who because of the drug's effect bore cruelly deformed children lacking useful arms or legs. The incident dramatically alerted the world to the danger of everyday chemicals. The thalidomide deformities were gross, clearly noticeable to all who saw them. Yet it took five years of piecing together the scattered reports of occurrence of the deformity before the cause was isolated and the use of thalidomide stopped. What troubles many scientists is that if it took five years to track down the cause of deformities such as stumps of children's arms and legs, how much longer will it take to stop the possibly hundreds of more subtle deformities that potentially can be caused by chemicals in the environment? At a spring, 1968, conference held in Bar Harbor, Maine, reported by *Medical World News,* a group of National Institute of Health scientists led by Dr. James F. Crow spelled out the dangers:

Dr. Crow's report lists two ways a mutagenic chemical could affect exposed populations. The more likely is a mild increase in the mutation rate through exposure of a few individuals to a powerful agent, or of many to a weak one. Especially threatening in this type of slow contamination of the gene pool would be the introduction of a mildly mutagenic substance, such as an additive into a food or beverage that is mass produced for wide consumption . . . such a silent increase in man's quotient of bad seed could not in any way . . . be detected.

The first warning of such an event might be an increase in the number, incidence, or severity of genetic illnesses; marked changes in the birth ratio of men to women; or an almost imperceptible loss of vigor and vitality, progressing from generation to generation. . . .

The chemicals that most concern the Bar Harbor conferees as potential mutagens include chemosterilants, and other pesticides, food additives, cosmetics, air pollutants, herbicides, known carcinogens, industrial chemicals, drugs, vaccines and contraceptives.[4]

The bad seeds may have already begun. Victor Cohn, reporting the conference in the Washington *Post,* said, "The effect may be showing up in some unknown share of the 20 to 30 per cent of all conceptions (a conservative estimate) that fail to produce live babies. It may be showing up in an unknown share of the 7 per cent of all live babies born with some birth defect." [5]

No one knows how much of this genetic damage is caused by chemicals; the source of only 5 per cent of it (from X rays and viruses) has been identified.

In the 1950's, when the current laws controlling the use of chemicals in and on food were passed, little was known about chemical hazards. But the law did specifically recognize the fact that hazards existed, and it established procedures to isolate them and protect the public against them. The first major amendment to the Food, Drug, and Cosmetic Act of 1938 gave the FDA the authority to set and enforce safe tolerances for pesticide residues remaining on food after harvest. The amendment, passed in 1954, was designed to protect the general public from the harm of poisonous residue without banning the use of pesticides completely. The law supplemented the Federal Insecticide, Fungicide, and Rodenticide Act (FIFRA), which requires that the Agriculture Department certify pesticides for use, by requiring that the FDA give an advisory opinion on the safety of the proposed use of any pesticide being considered for certification.

Once a pesticide is certified for use, the FDA is authorized to allow a certain amount of residue on various agricultural commodities. The allowance, called a tolerance, is granted (or set) by the FDA which, in a reverse of the certification process, considers the opinion of the Secretary of Agriculture about the usefulness of the pesticide. The FDA then polices the marketplace to insure that no food contains more than the allowed amount of pesticide.

Thus the FDA has three major pesticide responsibilities: (1) to set and enforce tolerances, (2) to advise the Department of Agriculture on the safety of pesticide products proposed for registration, and (3) to monitor pesticide levels. There are plenty of pesticides to keep the FDA busy in this job. The Department of Agriculture register files show more than forty-five thousand individual pesticide product formulations. They are made of nine hundred separate pesticide chemicals.

Pesticides are chemicals that will kill insect and plant pests; the problem is that chemicals that kill pests can also have an effect on animals and humans. In setting tolerances, the FDA tries to establish a level that is greatly below that which causes observable damage in animals. But the agency does not routinely consider indications that a pesticide may cause mutations, birth defects, or chromosome breaks when it sets a tolerance. Even though a number of pesticides have been shown to produce these kinds of effects in animals, it is the agency's position that they do not know enough about how these agents will act in people to be able to say for sure that they will cause harm. In the case of pesticides, as in the case of many chemicals added to food products, the consumer is taking the unknown risk that limited and developing science is unable to make precise. This is true in spite of the fact that many scientists are convinced that chemicals producing abnormalities in animals are likely to produce some kind of problem in people even though they don't know exactly what it will be.

The FDA sets pesticide tolerances on vegetables, fruits, meats, and other foods. But it is never sure how much of the residue a given individual will ingest if he eats vegetables, fruits, meats, and other foods at one meal. In addition, he is likely to ingest the same chemical residue in the water he drinks and even in the air he breathes. At best, then, the tolerance is a crude measure of safety. The precision of animal tests themselves is so crude that they often raise more doubts than they answer. A fifty-rat study is a major study in most research laboratories. If one rat shows a sign of hazard, it is not always considered significant. However, if the population of the United States were subjected to an analogous dosage and the chemical had the same effect on humans as it did on the rats, it would affect four million people. The point is that talk about setting tolerances at seven parts per million of food is reassuring, but the data used to arrive at that amount are very crude.

In her well-known book of 1962, *Silent Spring,* Rachel Carson analyzed the way the FDA decides how much poison is safe. She wrote:

The system by which the Food and Drug Administration establishes maximum permissible limits of contamination, called "tolerances," has obvious defects. Under the conditions prevailing it provides mere paper security and promotes a completely unjustified impression that safe limits have been established and are being adhered to.

. . . In setting a tolerance level the Food and Drug Administration reviews tests on the poison in laboratory animals and then establishes maximum levels of contamination that is much less than required to produce symptoms in the test animals. This system, which is supposed to insure safety, ignores a number of important facts.[6]

First, Miss Carson points out that the very idea of setting a tolerance for chemicals known to be harmful is questionable. She suggests that the system of "deliberately poisoning our food, then policing the result" is reminiscent of Lewis Carroll's White Knight, who thought of "a plan to dye one's whiskers green, and always use so large a fan that they could not be seen." She points out that a number of chemicals less toxic than currently used pesticides, chemicals such as pyrethrins, rotenone, ryania, and others derived from plant substances, already exist.[7] Neither the argument nor the alternatives presented in Miss Carson's book have been pursued with vigor.

In 1969 Secretary Finch appointed a commission, chaired by Emil Mrak, Chancellor Emeritus of the University of California at Davis, to study and make recommendations on pesticides and their relationship to environmental health. The Mrak Commission's report urged the elimination of all nonessential uses of DDT, thus recognizing the cogency of *Silent Spring*'s argument—

seven years after the book was published. Unfortunately, this delay has cost valuable time in the effort to find nonpoisonous methods of pest control. The FDA reported in 1969 that "conventional insecticides are needed to control 80 to 90 per cent of insect problems affecting agriculture and public health." [8] According to Edward F. Knipling of the Department of Agriculture, the reason for the delay is that "a single insecticide that may with minor modification control a hundred different kinds of harmful insects, can be developed at a far lower cost than the research needed to develop biological or selective chemical methods of insect control." [9] By dismissing the strong arguments for alternatives to commonly used chemical pesticides and concentrating on the development of pesticide products that would return fast, large profits, the chemical industry has created the massive pollution problem caused by pesticide residue.

As environmental deterioration begins to mount, long-forgotten alternatives look more and more appealing and dramatic. Texas cotton, threatened by insects, was saved without the use of chemicals through rigorous crop rotation, timed planting, and tillage procedures designed to eliminate insect reproduction. The screwworm, which used to kill or maim millions of dollars worth of Florida livestock each year, was eliminated through the breeding of sterile strains of the insect that prevented reproduction. The cottony-cushion scale, a pest that once plagued California citrus, has been brought under control without the use of chemicals. Lures have been effectively used to combat various insects, and a new strain of alfalfa was developed to resist the spotted alfalfa aphid, which at one time nearly destroyed the entire alfalfa industry. These various biological, environmental and other nonchemical means of insect control date as far back as the 1890's but still account for only 10 to 20 per cent of insect control activities. Chemical pesticides are cheaper to produce and therefore more desirable to corporations looking for large profits.

The governing principle for the development of chemical pesticides seems to be selling pesticides rather than controlling insects. In 1965 nearly one billion dollars' worth of pesticide chemicals were used on agricultural and forest products. But studies conducted by University of Georgia entomologist Dr. Chester Himel "show that up to 99 per cent of pesticide sprayed with current equipment is wasted, because only from one to 10 per cent of spray droplets are small enough to be effective." [10] The Department of Agriculture is currently working on a chemical which can control certain insects when as little as one-fourteenth of an ounce per acre is used. The drama of this breakthrough is suggested when the quantities are compared with the 87 pounds per acre of 2-4-D used in some areas to get effects on certain pests.

A more conservative tolerance-setting program in the FDA could be an essential force in bringing the kind of pressure that would cause development of alternative means of pest control. While complete elimination of pesticide residue in food is not necessarily practicable, that fact should not be used, as it is now being used, to allow a wide range of tolerances whose safety has not been definitely established.

Once set, tolerances are not properly enforced by the FDA. Its stated method for enforcement is to collect samples of produce for evaluation of pesticide residue. In 1963 the FDA reported that it expected to inspect twenty-five thousand shipments of produce entering interstate commerce. This figure was admitted to be less than one per cent of the total shipments. In 1967, the agency reported that it had actually conducted only 49,044 inspections between July 1, 1963, and June 30, 1966—significantly fewer than even the modest projection. This record of inspection, covering approximately 0.7 per cent of the total number of shipments, is hardly as reassuring as the FDA's glowing reports sound. With over 99 per cent chance of going undetected, there is little incentive provided by this program to apply pesticides sparingly.

Three per cent of the FDA's collected samples violate tolerances. These are not purely random samples. Many inspections are conducted by FDA inspectors only after they have received information that a given shipment is likely to contain an excessive amount of pesticides. Such a program does not provide a truly nationwide surveillance. By the FDA's own statistics, which it claims reflect the general situation in the country, at least seventy-five thousand interstate shipments between 1963 and 1966 had residues in excess of set tolerances but went undetected. In fact, it is not clear that the FDA has any accurate idea of how much food has pesticide residues that exceed established tolerances.

A second breakdown of the FDA's pesticide responsibilities has resulted from a running battle between the FDA's Division of Pesticide Registration (formerly in the Public Health Service) and the Pesticide Regulation Division of the Department of Agriculture. The conflict was revealed in spring, 1969, hearings on the Federal Insecticide, Fungicide, and Rodenticide Act. The FDA division was assigned to advise the Agriculture Department on the safety of pesticides proposed for registration; however, its recommendations have been disregarded virtually 100 per cent of the time. For instance, the FDA objected to the use of poisonous rodent baits made from human food because of the hazard they present to children; Agriculture's Pesticide Regulation Division dismissed the warning. The FDA urged regulations to prevent the use of highly toxic chemicals around the home and was ignored by the Department of Agriculture. The FDA objected to Vapona Strips for use in closets or homes, recommending that they be used in garbage cans or tight metal boxes; this objection was resolved by a compromise label warning. The FDA objected to Agriculture's failure to extend its policy of dyeing seeds treated with pesticide. It also objected to rat poison that had to be put on bread, to cancer-causing substances, and to many insect control items. The resolution of nearly every objection was unsatisfactory to the FDA.

The overwhelming use of pesticides by volume is made by farmers. However, of the forty-five thousand pesticide products registered with the U.S. Department of Agriculture, about half are for use in and around the home. This fact is largely responsible for the FDA attempts to make more precise the use and direction for various pesticides. In 1969 alone, the FDA recommended 5,052 label changes. Not one was adopted.

Another phase of the FDA's pesticide control efforts is its "Total Diet Study" program, which is designed to monitor the amount of pesticide residue in the entire food supply. The FDA periodically purchases the amount and type of food that the average nineteen-year-old (the nation's biggest eater) eats in a two-week period and subjects this "market basket" to detailed analysis to determine how much of various pesticides it contains. FDA officials regard the program as one of the most important programs—perhaps the single most important one—in protecting the public from the hazards of unacceptably high pesticide residues. Dr. Leo Duggan of the FDA, before a recent promotion by Commissioner Charles Edwards, had responsibility for the program. He said, "Several investigators have stated that foods are the major sources of pesticide chemicals in man. There has been relatively little information concerning the kind and amounts of residues in foods as they are eaten. The 'market basket' or 'total diet' studies by the Food and Drug Administration provide the most reliable index of the residues being consumed in the diet in the United States."

Dr. G. Q. Lipscomb was even more explicit about the importance of the program. "The efforts of the FDA have been a major factor in contributing to what little information we now have on man's total exposure to pesticide chemicals." In March, 1969, he said, "The importance of the Total Diet Program cannot be overemphasized. It has, I believe, at least equal value, if not more than, the regulatory program to the FDA. It is the international standard program of this type and is being copied by at least five other countries that we are aware of. . . . Let me repeat, this is one of the most important programs of those which FDA is now carrying on." [11]

One month after Dr. Lipscomb made this statement, Dr. William C. Purdy, the FDA science adviser in the Baltimore district, attacked the Total Diet Study in a detailed memorandum sent directly, outside official channels, to an Assistant Administrator in the FDA's parent organization within HEW, the Consumer Protection and Environmental Health Service. The substance of his charges was that the Total Diet Study program was chemically irrelevant (i.e. based on unsound scientific procedures) and that an impartial study conducted by persons outside the FDA should be convened to re-evaluate and reorient it. He said the program reports were deficient in that they claimed to find residues at levels lower than the methods used could detect. In one case it was reported that a certain pesticide was discovered at a level ten times smaller than the amount of error in the method used for detection. Another distortion occurred in verifying the methods used to detect pesticides. It is the accepted scientific practice to add a known amount of a given pesticide to a sample of food and to then try to recover it from the sample by a chemical method. In this way, the recovery method can be verified for accuracy. In one case the FDA claimed that the average recovery figures ranged between 85 per cent and 115 per cent, which allowing for error is considered acceptable by scientists. But these averages were based on figures which varied tremendously, in one case from 0 to 188 per cent. This is like taking a man with $200 in his pocket and one with no money and saying they are both pretty well off because they have an average of $100 each. The program had no mechanism to review and verify the work done in each of the five district laboratories. The methods for conducting the study had not been verified by the Association of Official Agricultural Chemists, which establishes the official test methods used by FDA. In at least one district, residue reports were made even though they did not have the equipment necessary to do the studies reported. Most important, not only were the American people being misled by the program but many observers were coming to this country from abroad to observe it and, according to Dr. Purdy, "The competent analysts among them can only leave in a state of shock when they find out about our Total Diet Program." [12] In sum, he said, "The tragedy about this entire program is that the data are presented in a manner that suggests that our food contains no harmful residues. In actuality . . . the citizens of this country are not being protected. Furthermore, they are being led to believe that there is no cause for worry." [13]

Five months after Dr. Purdy sent his letter, and after considerable maneuvering and attempts to suppress the charge, the FDA finally agreed to meet with him. In the FDA's summary of the meeting, officials tried to minimize the importance of the program and its effect on public awareness:

He [Dr. Purdy] said the articles [on the Total Diet Program] were now misleading the public into thinking that they were being protected and he wasn't sure this was the case. It was explained by the FDA officials that it was the FDA's Pesticide Regulatory Program that actually protected the consumer from excessive residues and that the Total Diet Program was intended as a fact-finding study to determine trends in pesticide residue.[14]

In a few short months the program had gone from being called perhaps the most important pesticide program in the FDA to being called merely a fact-finding survey of trends. Purdy's detailed charges against the program had shaken a number of government officials out of their lethargy and a review of the program was ordered. The agency even expressed its willingness to have its own investigation joined by an evaluation conducted by a group of outside pesticide experts. What was revealed about the program brings into doubt all of the reassurance about pesticide residue circulated by the FDA over the past few years.

Another FDA science adviser to whom the charges against the program were circulated told Purdy: "Obviously you have raised many valid criticisms concerning the Total Diet Program and many of the District chemists would agree with you, at least in principle, if not in every detail. Perhaps even Duggan would agree that improvements are desirable if not mandatory. The program does need a hard look, but the FDA is doing all that can be expected with the resources available. Whether or not Duggan has overstated the validity of the results and conclusions is certainly open to question."[15] If the best that can be said for a program is that it is doing well given the restricted resources applied to it, it should not be used to reassure the American people.

What happened next in the controversy over the Total Diet Program makes even the slight excuse of limited resources lose all credibility. Without advance warning, Dr. Purdy's contract as a science adviser to the FDA was terminated or, as the FDA would describe it, simply not renewed. Shortly afterward, the FDA sent a car to its district headquarters in Baltimore and removed all the raw data laboratory sheets related to the Total Diet Study program, ostensibly for the purpose of a more detailed study at the central office. Whether it was incidental or central to this action, the effect was to remove some of the major evidence supporting charges against the program from the reach of persons who might be critical of it.

The FDA is quick to reassure the population about pesticide use. However, the three pesticide programs of the agency do not reassure, they raise doubts. The tolerance-setting program does not consider serious threats such as genetic damage or birth defects possibly posed by pesticide residue. Even when a tolerance is set it is virtually impossible for the agency to enforce it. And when a pesticide residue is found that exceeds the set tolerance, the tolerance is sometimes raised to correspond to the residue level found. The FDA's recommendations about safety to the Agriculture Department go almost completely ignored, removing another important protection from the American public. Its food monitoring program, used to justify optimism, is found to be in need of complete overhaul. Faced with this, the agency chooses to terminate the services of one scientist who shows both the willingness to help solve the problem and a detailed knowledge of it. That the FDA can assume such postures in a program so central to the protection of public health reveals an agency which has shockingly abused its statutory mission.

In enforcing the law against pesticide residue, the FDA is required to use "official" analytical methods approved by the Association of Official Agricultural Chemists. The AOAC is supposed to provide a kind of professional check or balance for the FDA. Astonishingly enough, for an organization performing such a function, its leadership is made up of FDA officials. In effect, the pesticide control officials of the FDA are checking on themselves through the AOAC. Another area of expertise in the pesticide field is provided by the National Academy of Sciences-National Research Council pesticide committee. FDA pesticide officials are members of this committee and crucial to its operation. One member who is not from the FDA claims that he was never notified of committee meetings, finding out about them only when he received minutes after the meetings had taken place. Thus, whether by accident or design, effective control over pesticide information has been placed in the hands of a small, select group of people who are constantly asked to check on, evaluate, and approve themselves. The FDA is proud of its monopoly and says so:

The scientists of the Food and Drug Administration, both in the field and in Washington, have been instrumental in developing the multi-residue methodology which is used throughout the world by regulatory agencies. The Food and Drug Administration is recognized as the leader in this area and as having the expert knowledge. It would be difficult to staff a committee with competent people in the field of residue analysis who are not using the same methodology which has been developed by FDA.[16]

A self-contained, unscrutinized, scientific-regulatory community tends to get complacent and incompetent. The self-satisfied attitude of the FDA has destroyed its ability to meet pesticide problems effectively. According to an aide to Senator Gaylord Nelson of Wisconsin, the FDA's constant reassurance that there is no real danger from pesticides is the most important single factor in preventing Congress from undertaking serious efforts to control the increasing danger of pesticide residue. The unfortunate effect of the FDA's public posture on pesticides is to undercut the popular and widely based public concern necessary to support a searching and thorough re-evaluation of American pesticide use. In short, the FDA is deliberately keeping people unnecessarily ignorant.

Of course, contrary to the FDA's assertion, there are a number of well-established institutions that could, if invited, provide well-qualified people to evaluate and upgrade the FDA's program. The University of California at Riverside, Cornell University, the University of Florida, the University of Missouri, and New York State University at Stonybrook, for example, as well as the state governments of Wisconsin and California, have many people well trained in how to detect and control pesticides, what to do about their residue, and in analyzing their effect on the environment. An immediate and rapid effort should be undertaken by the FDA to seek professional help and evaluation for its pesticide program—not only the Total Diet Program but also the residue program and the advisory program to the Department of Agriculture. Such a review could only help the general public and the agency. It is a discredit to the FDA that it finds itself constantly reassuring the public while the same public is being constantly warned by other scientists.

Once an independent evaluation is undertaken and some measure of credibility is restored to the FDA, some structural changes in the law should be considered. First, since it is clear that safety from pesticides has become more important than their effectiveness in controlling pests, Congress should consider eliminating the role of the Department of Agriculture in certifying pesticides. Instead of giving advisory opinions on safety, the FDA should have the power to certify pesticides after receiving an advisory opinion on their usefulness from the Department of Agriculture. Second, Congress should consider making the Delaney Clause clearly applicable to pesticides. Consideration should also be given to extending the clause to include banning from the food supply chemicals that cause birth defects, hereditary changes, and chromosome breaks, not just chemicals that cause cancer. No tolerances should be allowed for such substances. When they cannot be used without leaving a residue they should be barred from use. Such a program should be viewed as a major spur to pursuing the development of alternative methods of pest control. Third, detailed legal methods should be designed to relieve the Secretary of Health, Education, and Welfare of discretionary powers and duties in regulating pesticides and other chemicals. Cabinet secretaries charged with enforcing the laws protecting the food supply from 1907 to 1970 have found the pressure against taking strong action in the public interest impossible to resist. They must be relieved of this burden. Requirements for setting tolerances or setting standards must be tightly drawn so that, as nearly as possible, factual and not political questions are being resolved by government agencies.

The Pesticide Amendment of 1954 has had no significant effect in stemming the tide of environmental contamination resulting from pesticide use in the United States. In such impotence, it resembles the other major food protection amendments passed in the 1950's. The Food Additives Amendment of 1958 was intended to regulate the addition of chemicals such as preservatives and flavors to the food supply. A total of 842 chemicals had found their way into the food supply at one time or another before 1958. In 1958, 704 chemicals were in use in the food supply (a number having ceased to be used) of which only 428 were definitely known to be safe. This meant that 276 chemicals used in food in 1958 had not been proven safe. The Surgeon General of the United States testified that food chemicals could have adverse effects on human health since many of their toxic effects were unknown and because there was lack of adequate information about their long-term impact. The American Public Health Association similarly warned that the increasing use of chemicals in food was a potential health hazard which might become one of the greatest problems the food industry has ever had to face.[17] Because of this concern, vigorous legislative action was taken, leading to the passage of the Food Additives Amendment.

In accordance with the Additives Amendment chemicals added to food are to be treated in one of three ways. They are to be: (1) excluded from food if they cause cancer when ingested by man or animals (the Delaney Clause), (2) not subject to any restriction if considered generally recognized as safe (GRAS), or (3) subject to intensive testing by manufacturers and excluded from food until proven safe. The job assigned to the FDA is difficult and complicated—too difficult, it appears, for the agency with all its weaknesses to perform.

The first step in administering the Food Additives Amendment was to determine which chemicals should be subject to extensive testing and which were generally recognized as safe. To begin this task, the FDA established the Generally Recognized As Safe (GRAS) list in 1958 and 1959. According to the law, an item went on the list only if it was "generally recognized, among experts qualified by scientific training and experience to evaluate safety, as having been adequately shown through scientific procedures . . . to be safe," [18] or if it had been generally used prior to January 1, 1958. Safety established by either "scientific procedures or experience based on common use in food" [19] could qualify an additive. All three guidelines, as well as the concept of expert scientific evaluation, either proved to be unworkable or were ignored as the GRAS list was actually prepared.

To begin the process of preparing the list, the FDA sent the names of 189 substances to 900 selected scientific experts across the country. The 900 were asked to comment on the safety of listed items not on whether they had been tested or used as the law required. Of the 900, only 350 replied and only 194 (21 per cent of the scientists contacted) responded favorably or without comment on the list. The remainder of the 350 criticized various parts of the list. On September 2, 1959, after all responses had been evaluated, the food and pharmacology divisions of the FDA prepared a joint memorandum called "Defense of the White List"—the list of 189 GRAS chemicals. It said in part:

In our final evaluation of the safety of a substance we have taken cognizance of the fact that all opinions are not of equal value, and thus have weighed most heavily the opinions of scientifically recognized and often world-renowned experts. Common sense as well as scientific principle requires us to accept the opinions of some and to reject the opinions of others. The Administration has long recognized the validity of this policy with respect to scientific matters and employs it in our day-to-day operations. [20]

Using this policy, the FDA dismissed statement after statement of concern about various substances on the list. The only comment about cyclamates, a critical one, was dismissed; "safety established," said the FDA. Henry M. Burlage of the University of Texas questioned the safety of ammonium carbonate. The FDA dismissed the question tersely, saying, "Henry M. Burlage is not qualified to discuss the safety of ammonium carbonate." (But the FDA had thought enough of him to solicit his opinion.) Henry Scott, Chairman of the Wisconsin State Food Standards Advisory Committee questioned the safety of benzoic acid, pointing out that benzoates and benzoic acid are illegal in many foods in Wisconsin, such as sauerkraut and dairy products. He was dismissed with this line: "Benzoic acid limited to 0.1 per cent and clarified by the Remsen Report." Now the FDA is finally re-examining sodium benzoate. Ammonium hydroxide was questioned by T. H. Jukes of American Cyanamid Company and others as too strong; it might be dangerous in the hands of persons not trained in chemistry. The FDA passed it as safe, saying, "Ammonium hydroxide does not exist as such in the food or at most as a very limited amount." This list of critical comments rejected is long and discouraging.

The chemical NDGA was questioned by Dr. W. F. von Oettingmen, M.D., who wondered if enough toxological information was available to warrant its use. The FDA replied, "We have information to show safety and this has been published." Eight years later, the FDA removed NDGA from the GRAS list after it caused damage to rats. A 1968 revelation led to the removal of all brominated vegetable oils from the GRAS list. Twelve scientists objected to the listing of vitamin D—many because it might cause hypercalcemia in infants, a condition which in its severe form involves changes in the bony structure of the face, effects upon the aortic valve of the heart, and mental abnormalities. The FDA confidently said, "Nutrient levels of vitamin D will not produce hypercalcemia effects," [21] and its unlimited use was permitted, particularly in milk. In 1965, six years later, FDA lowered the amount of vitamin D that could be added to food products "to prevent possible injury to infants. Excessive amounts of vitamin D was a possible cause of infantile hypercalcemia." [22] Now that the FDA has undertaken a review of the GRAS list, it is likely that there will be others.

This selective acceptance of expertise deprived the creation of the GRAS list of any respectability as a scientific endeavor. The FDA picked the answers it wanted according to unspecified criteria. The vigor with which the FDA announced that it had consulted nine hundred scientists about the list suggests that the consultation was done for public relations and not scientific reasons. Public relations at the expense of public health is indefensible.

The use made of the experts was not only scientifically

unsound, it was logically unsound as well. The FDA is also authorized to apply the concept of generally recognized as safe in its drug regulation activities, and when the agency wishes to establish that a drug is *not* generally recognized as safe, it relies on the opinion of *one* established expert to prove its point. But the word of a single authority speaking against a food additive has little weight. While drugs are more dramatically dangerous to their individual users, the widespread use of food additives makes the GRAS-list double standard undesirable.

A more important mistake distorting the intention of the law was made, however, when the experts were asked to perform a task not authorized by law. The law exempts only those chemicals "generally recognized, among experts qualified by scientific training and experience to evaluate its safety, *as having been adequately shown through scientific procedures* . . . to be safe." (Italics added.)[23] Or if the chemical was in use prior to January 1, 1958, safety could be shown by "experience based on common use in food." The FDA did not ask its chosen experts consulted about the proposed GRAS list if the listed chemicals had been widely used or tested. They asked if they were safe. There was no indication in the response how the few experts who did so arrived at their appraisal of a chemical's safety. Their answers did not fulfill the requirements of the law. In fact, the reference to nine hundred experts was unrelated to GRAS-list preparation; the FDA established the list by itself and for all practical purposes unaided by so-called experts.

In an interview on September 9, 1968, the FDA's Associate Commissioner for Enforcement, Kenneth Kirk, gave an idea of how some of the GRAS-list decisions had been made. He told how Dr. Barbara Moulton came into his office "hopping mad" about seeing folic acid on the proposed GRAS list. Later she testified before the Kefauver Committee about the inclusion of folic acid on the GRAS list. But what she didn't know, according to Kirk, was that after she left his office, "I took out a red pencil and crossed through folic acid and it never appeared on the list." This won Kirk a debating point before Congress, but it is just one more illustration of the arbitrariness that governed selections for the GRAS list.

Dr. Moulton was not the only person in the Bureau of Medicine to be upset by the way in which the GRAS list was prepared. While the FDA was publicly justifying the means by which it had arrived at the list, the Bureau of Medicine wrote:

We have reviewed the list with an assumption (but not a conviction) that the proscription against poor manufacturing practices will prove adequate in a general way to prevent harmful concentrations. . . .

As a single example, we do not actually recognize calcium phytate as necessarily safe used as a sequestrant, but without more details of its customary use and of its pharmacology and without more insight into the expected interpretation of the paragraph introducing the list (i.e., good manufacturing practices and conditions of intended use) we have no actual opinion of its propriety on the list.

In addition we have considered the list with an attitude consistent with the assumption apparently held in its preparation—namely that the substances will meet necessary standards of identity, quality and purity even though specifications are not stated. At least, it leaves unanswered the questions of just what allowances of impurities will constitute good manufacturing practice when substances are used for the purposes specified.[24]

When the original list was approved it included 182 items, seven of the original items having been deleted because of unfavorable comments from various sources. But in spite of internal criticism, the list continued to grow. From time to time, announcements were made in the *Federal Register,* without the pretense of scientific consultation, which expanded the list until it finally reached approximately 700 chemicals. FDA policy has made it virtually impossible to tell which chemicals are food additives, how many of them there are, and who, if anyone, has tested and evaluated them. In 1961 Commissioner George P. Larrick told a Congressional committee that there were 718 chemicals on the list.[25] The FDA 1964 annual report, the first annual report to mention the subject, claimed that the FDA had recognized only 575 GRAS items. Neither the report nor the records of the FDA reveals any effort to remove items from the GRAS list. Subsequent FDA annual reports repeat the number 575. In 1969 Dr. Robert Byck, M.D., and Dr. Herbert H. Schaumberg, M.D., of the Albert Einstein College of Medicine, concerned about the use of monosodium glutamate in food, "became embroiled in sort of a federal nightmare trying to find out about the GRAS list." [26] Newspapers following up the testimony of the two scientists before a Senate select committee were told by the FDA that the list contained 680 items. [27] If simple counting is this difficult, regulating is impossible. In addition, according to Winton B. Rankin, Assistant to the Commissioner, the FDA sent out letters to various manufacturers indicating certain additional GRAS items:

It must be kept in mind that these are only the figures of items published in the *Federal Register*. In correspondence, we have agreed that others are, in our opinion, generally recognized as safe and we expect to propose further lists to be published in this category as soon as the press of other urgent matters permits. [28]

Many of these items (estimated to number between one thousand and ten thousand), although treated as safe by the FDA, have never been added to the published *Federal Register* list. HEW Assistant General Counsel William Goodrich complained about this kind of procedure in a January, 1961, memorandum to Assistant Commissioner Kenneth Kirk. He said, "Sooner or later these . . . letters are bound to get us into trouble."

The time has come for an accounting. More incredible even than this chemical-by-chemical deception practiced by FDA officials was the agency's total acquiescence to industry's interpretation of the law. In March, 1961, the trade magazine *Food Processing* laid out the industry position on the GRAS list: "Contrary to the opinion held by many people in the food industry, the law confers no special authority on the FDA for deciding that an ingredient is GRAS. If experts who are qualified to evaluate the safety of a particular ingredient generally recognize it as safe under the conditions of its intended use, then according to the language of the law itself . . . it is not subject to the provisions of the Additive Law."

The law, of course, says nothing of the kind. It says that the determination to be made by experts is not that an item is safe but rather that it has "been adequately shown through scientific procedures to be safe," or that its common use in foods has established safety. Scientific fact, not the opinion of experts, is what the law called for. Not even scientific opinion, let alone the required facts, was sought in the vast majority of cases. The FDA sent letters directly to manufacturers, saying, for example, "It is our belief that . . ." certain chemicals are GRAS. Or, "It is our belief that qualified experts would consider . . ." certain chemicals GRAS.[29]

The FDA's procedure on deciding what chemicals were safe so distorted the law that nothing practical was left of its provisions. After the 1960 list was published in the *Federal Register,* the Flavor Extracts Manufacturers Association prepared a list of one thousand items. Following an intense internal struggle, the FDA issued a regulation allowing the vast majority of chemicals on the list into the food supply under conditions nearly the same as GRAS-list items. In this way, they retained a certain kind of shadowy legal control over the items, while in practice they were treated as GRAS. Even this small attempt at some kind of control was soon abandoned, as described almost ten years later by Deputy Commissioner Rankin. "The manufacturer is entitled to reach his own conclusions, based on his scientific evidence that a subject is, in fact, generally recognized as safe. And he is not required to come to us then and get the material added to the list." [30] This interpretation totally destroyed the Food Additives Amendment of 1958. The burden of establishing that an item considered safe by industry is not in fact safe falls on the government, and industry is absolved of its responsibility under the law. Since, in Rankin's words, the industry is not required even to tell the FDA which items it is assuming are safe, there is no possibility of systematically checking the safety of these items. For all practical purposes, the FDA has relinquished the control of food additives to industry.

The same disorder exists in the supposedly more carefully controlled program to evaluate and approve petitions for the use of additives tested by manufacturers.

In the first ten months after the Additives Amendment went into effect, only twenty-six food additives petitions were filed with the FDA. Either the additive manufacturers had not conducted any safety tests before the act was passed—a fact contrary to their claims—or they were withholding their tests from the government. When the time allowed for testing currently used additives had passed—thirty months after enactment of the law—the FDA had granted three thousand extensions of the deadline and requested and got authority to grant additional delays, dragging out the process even longer. The purpose of a food additive petition is to present to the FDA the evidence that the additive concerned has been proven safe. The law required all food petitions to contain "full reports of investigations made with respect to the safety for use of such additives, including full information as to the methods and controls used in conducting such investigation." [31]

In the overwhelming majority of cases, the FDA does not test the additives themselves when approving their safety. But more basic than that, in most cases the FDA does not even receive the complete reports of tests run on additives. Instead it receives *summaries of these reports*. During the hearings on irradiated foods Kenneth Kirk was asked:

Don't you normally ask for the supporting evidence, the raw material in the case, or do you accept conclusions that other people give you?
MR. KIRK: As time goes on, I find our scientists are asking for the raw data more and more than they used to.[32]

It is on the basis of this rickety system that the FDA certifies the safety of food additives. Manufacturers are well satisfied with the way it operates.

The FDA's approval and subsequent disapproval of the use of atomic radiation to preserve foods gives a glimpse of the potential tragedy that lies at the heart of this patchwork system of law enforcement. On February 15, 1963, the FDA approved bacon preserved with atomic radiation for unrestricted public consumption. Since radiation is defined as a food additive under the Food, Drug, and Cosmetic Act, the FDA processed it through its additive petition procedures. The FDA neither conducted its own research on radiation and food nor reviewed the actual research data of others. Instead, it approved the process based solely on summaries of the research conducted. Officials of the agency were pleased to have helped make a major "breakthrough . . . in food preservation with promise of new convenience and economic benefit." [33]

Dr. Daniel Banes, the FDA Assistant Commissioner for Science, testified before the Joint Committee on Atomic Energy that when the original petition for irradiation of food, that for bacon, was submitted to the FDA, "There was an indication of hazard. There certainly was no proof of safety." [34] In spite of the indicated hazard, the FDA allowed irradiated bacon to be cleared for public sale in 1963. (The treated bacon actually was never produced for general public consumption because of marketing problems.) Fortunately, the same FDA scientists who had warned of hazards in irradiated bacon were able to get the ear of the Commissioner, Dr. Goddard, when the Army sought to place irradiated ham on the market in the summer of 1968. The FDA moved to stop it because the original raw data on bacon showed that test animals had been fed in a way that masked nutritional difficulties. A 25 per cent reduction in live rat births and 25 per cent rat and 32 per cent dog death rate increase between birth and weaning had been dismissed as insignificant by testers. The testers had failed to check all animals for tumors, in spite of the fact that the Food, Drug, and Cosmetic Act expressly forbids treating foods with any additive that can cause cancer. In addition, the testers dismissed findings that suggested that irradiated food could damage vision and blood, and depressed body weight. [35] It has also been revealed that the experiments indicate the possibility that radiation creates a substance in meat that destroys certain vitamins even when they are taken in supplemental form apart from the meat. [36] The disapproval came in the nick of time. Over twenty other foods were slated for radiation treatment and a huge combine of companies including Alpo Dog Food and Uniroyal Tires had signed contracts to construct a major irradiation plant in Allentown, Pennsylvania. In commenting on the incident afterward, Dr. Goddard pronounced what must, if FDA hopes to function at all effectively, become the first goal of agency reform. "The lesson of the irradiated ham incident, as far as I am concerned, is that the men and women responsible for administering any consumer protection program anywhere—public or private—must be true to the disciplines of science."

Radiation is not the only food additive that has had to be withdrawn after having its safety certified by FDA. In addition to cyclamates, Saforale (for years the chief flavoring constituent of root beer), folic acid (the vitamin), Nordihydroguaiaretic Acid or NDGA (used for twenty years as an antioxidant in fatty foods), and oil of calamus (used to flavor candy, baked goods, bitters, liquors, and beverages), are all substances which had first been approved for use by the FDA under the 1958 law and then withdrawn for various reasons. NDGA caused mesenteric cysts and kidney lesions in rats fed over a two-year period. Research on the whole class of brominated vegetable oils followed this study. It has led to the quietly announced order that all brominated oils, now used largely in citrus fruit drinks, be removed from the GRAS list by summer, 1970. BHT and BHA, two widely used antioxidants, have been the focus of considerable controversy for a number of years, leading to the heavy restrictions of BHT use in Britain. Following the cyclamates ban, Nobel Prize-winning geneticist Joshua Lederberg prepared a list of nineteen substances used that he "idiosyncratically selected" as needing further study and evaluation because their chemical make-up suggested that they might have a negative chemical effect on those who consume them. The FDA itself has prepared a list of sixty-four additives currently recognized as safe which it feels are in need of further study.

As important as removing unsafe additives from the food supply is the need for fundamental reorganization of the system that permitted them to get there. The petition review system used by the FDA rests primarily on luck. The main reason that more mistakes have not been discovered is because they have not been looked for.

The FDA's treatment of what it calls "indirect additives" demonstrates the weakness of its additive control program. Indirect additives are chemicals used in packaging or manufacturing which are not intended to become part of the food but which end up there by accident. The difficulty for the FDA was in deciding how the hundreds of such accidental additives should be treated under the law, and the agency's attitude is suggested by a 1961 letter from the FDA's legal adviser, William W. Goodrich, HEW Assistant General Counsel, about one indirect additive:

The only way we can cancel these notices [the FDA's permission to industry to use indirect additives] without their being withdrawn by the petitioners is to rule that the substances are not food additives. This would involve stating in the notice cancelling the previous notice that the articles are not food additives, and why they are not.

It could be very much wiser to ask the firms to withdraw the petitions and to cancel the notices on that basis. By this method, you would be ruling on the food additive question only in the letter to the firm, and not in a publication in the *Federal Register*.

Sooner or later these letters which remove products from the scope of the food additives amendment are bound to get us into trouble. . . .

I see no reason why we should not issue a regulation. . . . We would then be on the road to proper control, rather than creating a very large no-man's land where a chelating [combining] agent made by a certain firm, used in a specified way, and which meets identity specifications is not a food additive, while it is a food additive if made in another way or used in another state.[37]

The FDA's idea was that if a manufacturing chemical found its way into food but was not harmful in that food it should not be called an additive, it should instead go onto the GRAS list. The FDA apparently felt it did not have the resources to conduct or review the thousands of tests that would be required to establish the safety of all these items. Mr. Goodrich was complaining about that policy because it made legal action based on new scientific information almost impossible because it would probably require court action for the FDA to get an item off the GRAS list. The FDA followed the policy Goodrich recommended when the Flavor Extracts Manufacturers Association presented the agency with its list of one thousand items considered safe. The FDA conducted a specific evaluation of just over one hundred of the items, but it promulgated two regulations allowing the use of the vast majority of the others in food even though there was no evidence that they had been tested. The effect was to allow most of the thousand into the food supply without thorough FDA screening. It is not clear today how many of the over 1,600 indirect additives acknowledged by the FDA get into food but are not considered additives.

The one section of the Food Additives Amendment that has provided some slight measure of protection is the so-called Delaney Clause against the use of cancer-causing chemicals in the food supply. Even it has been greatly subverted in practice. The clause itself states: "That no additive shall be deemed to be safe if it is found to induce cancer when ingested by man or animal, or if it is found, after tests that are appropriate for the evaluation of the safety of food additives, to induce cancer in man or animal." [38] The FDA has in effect disregarded the second half of this provision because it has not undertaken to develop any methods for detecting cancer-causing properties of chemicals by tests other than those requiring ingestion. FDA policy is never to remove an item from the market unless it causes cancer when ingested.

Even the strict prohibition of the first half of the Delaney Clause has not been vigorously applied. Substances such as saccharin and cyclamates are still sold on the market in spite of the fact that both caused cancerous tumors when ingested by animals in 1950. Even if, as some scientists argue, those tests were not conclusive, there is no excuse for not having followed up the preliminary indications for nearly twenty years. HEW Secretary Finch's attacks on this clause show an unfortunate lack of understanding about how badly food additive regulation is being conducted. In a November, 1969, interview on National Educational Television, he suggested that the FDA be allowed to set tolerances for cancer-causing chemicals.[39] If this suggestion, which dismayed a number of HEW officials, were followed, the last shred of protection of food against the hazards of chemical additives would be eliminated. The irresponsible lack of restraint of industry in its use of cyclamates in spite of repeated warnings, combined with repeated inability of the FDA to use discretionary authority to protect the consumer, would turn repeal of the Delaney Clause into a monumental disaster. In fact, the strict limitations contained in the Delaney Clause should be extended to other hazards of the chemical environment. The hazards of these additives to consumers far outweigh their benefits to industry. The primary purpose of food additives to industry is to increase profits. Coloring, tenderizing, or extending the shelf life of food products to grind out more millions of dollars should not be tolerated if there is the slightest indication that a hazard to consumers might exist.

The Color Additives Amendment, designed to control the large group of color chemicals added to food, has received the same treatment as the Food Additives Amendment. First, it was subjected to massive delays that kept it from even appearing to function for almost ten years after its passage. Second, it has been sabotaged by the same kinds of cowardly bureaucratic backsliding that destroyed the Food Additives Amendment. In 1965, the FDA announced that the food coloring called Red 4, widely in use in foods and drugs, would be eliminated in six months. The Food and Agricultural Organization-World Health Organization (FAO-WHO) joint committee on color had called this color "harmful . . . should not be used in food." [40] Before the ban could take effect the maraschino cherry producers convinced the FDA to allow the dangerous chemical color in its products. The argument was that very few maraschino cherries are ever actually eaten by one person so that they really didn't present much of a hazard.

The same FAO-WHO joint committee said that another FDA color, Violet No. 1, showed the "possibility of harmful effects." This the FDA felt was a warning to be ignored since the tumors caused by the color occurred only after injection of the chemicals under the skin of rats. World Health Organization scientists felt this fact should cause concern; FDA scientists did not. Taken together, the various FDA programs designed to control chemical additives to food have subverted the law and left the consumer without protection.

The tragedy of this fact is that the chemical problems faced in the 1950's and 1960's were a picnic compared to the problems now developing. The use of food chemicals is a result of and a contributor to the fact that there is less and less distinction between the foods consumed by various individuals. The dwindling variety in the marketplace is an important effect of a nationwide mass-marketing food industry. However, this trend is coming at a time when medical science is beginning to isolate more and more kinds of individual susceptibility to environmental contaminants. For example, there are now close to fifty different diseases that, like diabetes, may require special dietary intakes, including the exclusion of various chemicals now routinely added to food. Allergy problems complicate the problem even more. Two prominent California doctors wrote in 1963: "The practical applicability of this knowledge concerning food additives and contaminants should alert all physicians to maintain a critical and sober attitude to the potential hazard of these agents. An increasing number of patients have been observed in clinical practice with diffuse hair fall, chronic urticaria [red patched skin], toxic epidermal necrolysis, pemphigoil [spotted skin], and other such illnesses in which ingested drugs or predisposing factors can be excluded in the etiologic investigation. It is common practice to consign these diseases to causes unknown or to classify them as idiosyncratic." [41]

Many individuals know from their physicians that they have adverse reactions to certain substances added to food, but they find it is almost impossible to avoid them because of their widespread use (such as MSG) or the failure of labels to announce their presence—the fact in the case of several hundred chemicals.

Industry has reaped millions in profit from this total breakdown in food additives control, and they have been pleased to acknowledge publicly the assist they received from the FDA. In a two-part 1966 series on food additives, *Chemical and Engineering News,* the most prominent chemical trade publication, presented industry's view of chemical additives use and their control by the FDA. "The most frequently heard comment today about FDA's handling of the law is that it has been 'entirely reasonable.' Many of the companies praise FDA for its 'able handling of a difficult set of regulations.' 'The provisions,' says one industry man, 'could have been hideously misapplied. They have not been. Much of the original anxiety was simply fear of the unknown.' " [42]

The only opposition to this point of view mentioned by the magazine comes from a small portion of the population, less than 5 per cent, identified as "the people whom industry men frequently classify as crackpots, faddists, food quacks or well-meaning but pitifully misinformed people." No mention is made of the large number of public officials, scientists, and members of the general public who are highly critical of the FDA's public protection efforts. In fact, confidence in the FDA was and is so low outside the industries it regulates that four separate men have served as FDA Commissioner between January 1, 1955, and January 1, 1970—as many as occupied the office in the FDA and its predecessor agencies between January 1, 1907, and January 1, 1950. Confidence in the agency is so low that it has just completed its fifth major reorganization in five years. It has been the subject of fourteen critical management reports in the past fourteen years. Through all of the criticisms the food and chemical industries have treated the FDA with a pleasant tolerance, calling it "entirely reasonable."

It is easy to understand industry's friendly feelings toward its regulator. The FDA has allowed a massive market in food additives to develop with no significant regulation. Foods packaged for ease and speed of preparation lie at the heart of the problem. They mean more profits but require more additives. *Chemical and Engineering News* says:

Partly because of her greater buying power, she [the housewife of today] is quite willing to pay the extra price for what food companies elegantly call "foods with built-in maid service." . . .

Expressing the views of many leaders in the food additives field, Joseph G. Jarrell, industry manager of the cellulose land protein products departments of Hercules says, "Our optimism about the use of chemical additives in the food industry is based largely on the sensational growth of convenience foods."

Such foods usually require more additives than conventionally cooked foods because in many cases they are prepared under more severe conditions of temperature, pressure or agitation. Therefore, they may require special flavorings, flavor enhancers, colors, and other additives to make up for the partial loss of flavor, color, texture, and other properties caused by processing.[43]

The FDA has not exerted any control over this rapidly developing market. Since 1958 the situation has deteriorated. Now fewer than half of the 2,500 additives in use have actually been tested for safety. According to the FDA's 1970 operating plan:

The use of direct food additives in food manufacture will have approximately doubled by 1974 from the level of use prior to the passage of the Food Additives Amendment to the Food, Drug, and Cosmetic Act. Over 1,000,000,000 pounds of 2,500 food additives chemicals will be consumed. Both the methodology for their detection and their long-term toxicological significance require an expansion of research activities by the FDA. Unknown alterations of products further complicate attaining the necessary security in the safety of the food supply. The primary need at present is for the development of multi-additive detection methods to facilitate surveillance and measurement of actual additive intake levels. The needs are similar in the area of natural poisons such as mycotoxins.[44]

This tremendous rise in use of food additives, coupled with increasingly difficult regulatory problems, came *after* passage of the Food Additives Amendment of 1958. Unless this law is enforced as intended, far more stringent laws will be required.

The Kinslow
Report Fraud

*"The thing that bugs me is that the
people think the FDA is protecting them
—it isn't. What the FDA is doing
and what the public thinks it's doing
are as different as night and day."*

—*Dr. Herbert L. Ley, Jr.,*
Former FDA Commissioner
New York Times, *December 31, 1969*

In the summer of 1969 a Ralph Nader Summer Study
Group consisting of sixteen students from law schools,
medical schools, and other graduate programs, spent
three and a half months doing research on the food
protection aspects of the Food and Drug Administration. The study, done with the co-operation of the
agency, relied upon an extensive review of the FDA's
files and on interviews with past and present members
of the agency's staff and with scientists in the food
protection field.

After the Nader Study was planned, but before the
students arrived at the FDA's offices, the agency under-
took a study of its own, and on August 7, two months
after the student group began work, the FDA released
its report, which appeared to be highly critical of its
own consumer protection activities. In reality, the
substance of the report whitewashed the agency leadership by laying the blame for its poor decisions on
Congressional failure to provide enough "legislation,
manpower, and money." The entire report was an
exercise in public relations led by the FDA's Baltimore
District Director, Maurice D. Kinslow. It was designed
to win public sympathy for an underfunded, under-
staffed, but honest regulatory agency harassed by
Congress.

Like rangers preparing for an oncoming forest fire,
the FDA was setting a backfire to strip a narrow area

of the woods and thereby stop the holocaust. The report humbly confessed the FDA's difficulties:

Our responsibility is simply stated. The consumer has virtually no control over the quality of vital products which he uses every day. When industry fails to exercise adequate control, he must rely on regulatory agencies such as the FDA.

The problem is simply stated. Increasing volume and sophistication in types, production and marketing of consumer goods under our jurisdiction has outstripped our ability to assure the public that all is well with respect to these products.

The result is simply stated. We are forced into reacting to meet individual problems rather than acting to head off impending crises.

Beyond this, very little else is simple.[1]

In spite of this strong confession of failure contained in the report's introduction, the report itself was a mild rehash of relatively minor problems. Before its release, FDA Deputy Commissioner Winton B. Rankin held two closed-door sessions with Maurice Kinslow to edit the rough draft of Kinslow's report. The idea was to give Congress and the public the impression that the FDA was well aware of all its weaknesses, knew how to correct them and, with the proper support from Congress, would do so splendidly. The second step in the program was to leak the "confidential" report to the press. This was done with the tacit if not the explicit support of FDA Commissioner Herbert Ley. Once a public stir had been created, Ley's HEW superior, Charles C. Johnson, directed him to find and discipline the individual responsible for the leak. In a private interview with a Nader team member, Ley said he had no intention of carrying out the directive, even though he was pretty sure who had leaked the report, because "on the whole it has not been particularly damaging."

As a public-relations tactic, the report succeeded. Walter Cronkite reported on CBS News: "The American consumer is surrounded by an arsenal of products which can kill or maim him, and the Food and Drug Administration has neither the money nor the authority to do much about it. That's the gist of a confidential report prepared by seven senior members of the FDA and submitted last month to the Administration's Commissioner, Herbert Ley. A copy was obtained today by UPI." [2] Other news outlets made similar reports. Newspapers across the country reported on FDA failures as if all the agency needed was a good shot of funds, a little more authority, and some additional inspectors and investigators to supplement the admirable work being done by agency leaders under deplorable conditions.

The report and the picture of the FDA it created were false. On August 8, 1969, the day after the study was leaked to the press, Representative L. H. Fountain, whose House Intergovernmental Relations Subcommittee has been the Congressional committee most actively concerned about FDA's regulatory failures, issued a rebuttal to the FDA study:

I think it is commendable that the report frankly acknowledges inadequacies in the agency's consumer protection program. However I cannot agree with the clear implications of the report that the inadequacies are due largely to insufficient money, personnel and legal authority.

I have always been quick to recognize the limited resources with which the agency has had to work in relation to its overall responsibilities. However, when I have questioned the Commissioners of FDA about their appropriations, they have invariably responded that the Congress has granted most of their requests, at least in the period since 1962. . . .

With respect to the agency's legal authority . . . the question must be asked whether the agency has actively sought and been denied such authority by the Congress. I do not believe there are many such cases, if any.

Finally, I would note that . . . it appears to me that frequently FDA has not utilized to the best advantage resources which have been available to it.

Even Dr. Ley, who for all intents and purposes accepted full responsibility for the release of the confidential report, gave a quite different assessment of the agency once he had been removed as Commissioner. In an interview with *The New York Times* printed on December 31, 1969, two weeks after he left the FDA, Ley said:

A majority of the medical staff people are retreads, persons who have suffered coronaries or who have personality problems; at the moment they're the only people that FDA can get.

Merely putting more money into the agency will not change it. A more highly motivated staff and better administration of it also is needed.

If the Administration really wants to get better scientific people into FDA, the time is now because the squeeze on university research funds has made talent available.

We also need to sit down and find out what the gaps are in the consumer protection that the FDA is responsible for, then what the needs are, then what can be done.

The FDA also has to be raised to the status of a policeman-type activity.

None of these weaknesses was recognized in the supposedly searching, confidential Kinslow Report. When Ley told the *Times* that the gaps in the FDA's consumer protection had to be identified, he was virtually quoting his own directions to Kinslow eight months before. On May 1, 1969, he had asked the Kinslow group to undertake four tasks: " (1) define the consumer protection objectives of the Food and Drug Administration; (2) analyze and compare the agency's present programs in light of these objectives; (3) identify existing or anticipated problem areas resulting from gaps between defined objectives and current programs; and (4) suggest changes in programs to meet our objectives more completely." But ignoring the Commissioner's orders has been honed to a fine art at the FDA. None of these tasks was completed. Instead, the report was turned into an opportunity for entrenched FDA leadership to restate its own pet theories about the agency's role. The sum total of the Kinslow Report was to recommend weakening not strengthening the protection the FDA provides the consumer. The study group failed largely because it set out to fail. It never consulted the dozens of critics inside the FDA who had on numerous occasions raised serious questions about the agency's commitment to consumer protection.

The Bureau of Regulatory Compliance, the enforcement arm of the agency and therefore the branch most directly aware of its consumer protection failures, contains some of the most critical and dissatisfied of the FDA's personnel. The Kinslow group consulted only one person from this bureau—on a minor regulatory point. The failure appears to have been entirely intentional. The committee also avoided the numerous scientists critical of the agency's science policy, all public information personnel, consumer specialists employed by the agency, and the large community of former FDA employees who had left the agency because of its consumer protection failures. To put it bluntly, no known critic of the agency's policies was consulted by the committee. Instead, Kinslow's group talked with seventeen highly placed FDA officials, many of whom had previously been singled out by critics as responsible for the FDA's failure to protect consumers. Given that background, it is remarkable that the report went as far as it did in recommending changes in what little protection the agency was already giving.

In his cover letter transmitting the report to Dr. Ley, on July 14, 1969, Kinslow said, "You will find in reviewing our recommendations that many of them call for the Food and Drug Administration to exert greater efforts to provide industry as much guidance and information as possible to facilitate compliance with the law. We feel this would contribute materially to consumer protection. The responsibility for producing legal products, however, still rests with the industry." The committee assigned to come up with an imaginative approach to consumer protection simply reiterated the principle responsible for sixty years of failure.

The December 10, 1969, report of HEW Secretary Robert Finch's own FDA review committee headed by HEW Deputy Undersecretary Frederick V. Malec casts grave doubt on Kinslow's findings. In the Malec Committee's view, internal organizational problems and incompetence of the FDA were a major cause of agency failure that could not be blamed solely on the lack of "legislation, manpower, and money." If a competent, responsible FDA official had conducted a thorough and internal report of the agency which was accurate, it would be assumed that he would have included all the major problems facing the agency in that report. In fact, the press treated the Kinslow Report as if that is what it did. But the supposedly thorough and searching Kinslow Report had not, for example, even mentioned the Generally Recognized As Safe list, cyclamates, monosodium glutamate, or any other safety problem related to current FDA food additive programs, so the report did nothing to prevent Secretary Finch from being caught off guard when food additive safety became a national issue. The Kinslow Committee could only have avoided mentioning the problems of food additives through incompetence or design.

An analysis of the report's recommendations in the food field illustrates what a shoddy and treacherous document Kinslow prepared. The analysis is of crucial importance, since Kinslow has emerged as the single most important adviser to the new FDA Commissioner, Charles C. Edwards, during the period of transition and reorganization. The most striking character of the recommendations is their general amorphous nature. Of the twenty-seven recommendations directly related to food protection, thirteen are couched in general terms such as "develop a program" or "undertake research" or "explore means" which suggest that there are problems which someone should look at but give no indication of what the goals of such research, programs, or means should be, even in broad terms.

After making very general comments suggesting grave problems, the report often recommends actions that can seriously damage the consumer interest. An example is the recommendations in the veterinary drugs section of the report. This section deals with drugs administered to food-producing animals. The recommendations raise major questions about food safety and then—as though forgetting what was just said— suggest relaxing what little protection already exists. The report says that more research on veterinary drugs should be undertaken to determine the "long-term ecological impact of drug residues in animal tissues and the effect of developing resistance [by animals to the drugs] on human health." It suggests that at present no "objective surveillance system . . . to determine the incidence of drug residues and drug-resistant microorganisms in food of animal origin" exists and that one should be developed. It recommends filling another void by establishing "residue-monitoring and adequate follow-up programs." And it recommends that a "system to identify all marketed veterinary drug products" be developed. It would seem from these recommendations that the report is acknowledging that veterinary drugs need serious regulation they are not now receiving: there is no system to identify and keep track of the use of veterinary drugs; there is no residue-monitoring program, so there is no adequate indication of drug residues in meats destined for human consumption; and there is no accurate information about how much of a health hazard such residue might present. Further support for these somewhat vague criticisms is given by Great Britain's action in late 1969 to restrict the use of a number of veterinary drugs because they presented a serious health hazard which they felt might have already resulted in the death of a small number of people. But the Kinslow Report's response to the dismal picture drawn in its own pages was to talk in terms of expanding research, gathering information, and re-evaluating its program—all rather vague antidotes. When the report gets down to specifics, it is to recommend weakened regulation of veterinary drugs. The recommendations say: " (30) Establish provisional approval for certain veterinary drugs so that efficacy can be established on basis of field use. (31) Provide financial assistance to the states so that a fully adequate joint surveillance and compliance program between FDA and the states can be developed. (32) In view of the need for an increasing world food supply, the FDA should re-evaluate its conservative drug residue policy and develop objective criteria for evaluating the benefit-risk ratio of new veterinary drugs."

These three recommendations add up to a systematic abdication of FDA responsibility in the veterinary drug field. First, it will consider the industry position that more drugs should be used; second, it will turn over a major portion of its regulatory authority to state governments; and, third, it will allow certain drugs to be registered on a temporary basis so that their effects can be tested under actual conditions of use. All of this is to be undertaken at a time when Britain has sounded a strong warning against the expanding use of animal drugs by withdrawing a number from the market; at a time when state governments have been roundly criticized by the Department of Agriculture and state officials for their general failure to conduct proper inspection of meat in every area where they have authority. Basically, the three enforcement recommendations presented in the Kinslow Report are exactly what the animal drug industry needs to continue its profitable expansion. Put into effect, they would lead to wider and less regulated use of the drugs at a time when Kinslow himself admits that FDA surveillance of animal drugs is seriously lacking.

Five of the Kinslow Report's recommendations deal with the FDA's scientific capability. Two of these are the vaguest in the entire report: to "stimulate research" and "strengthen capabilities" in scientific areas. Two others, while a bit more specific, do not include suggestions for implementation. One of these is for the development of a system to collect all information on products regulated by FDA that have caused injury. The other is the use of Federal grants to universities to discover long-range research goals. The report does not even consider how, once discovered, the long-range goals are to be met, paid for, or enforced. There is no mention of specific budgets for the recommendations or of what legal sanctions are available. The apparent assumption is that once the goals are known they can be met. The final pure science recommendation has a very familiar ring. "Undertake research in process technology to provide guidance to industry." This attitude toward science, which fundamentally minimizes its importance at the agency, except as a tool to "provide guidance to industry," is an important part of Maurice Kinslow's approach to regulatory action, and not just in the report that bears his name. As Director of the Baltimore District, he refused to renew the contract of Dr. William Purdy, his science adviser, in July, 1969, and nine months later had not hired a replacement.

Purdy was released just when he submitted a detailed critique of the FDA's efforts at pesticide control. In spite of his full knowledge of the heated debate over the quality of the FDA pesticide program, Kinslow included only nine innocuous lines about the program in his detailed report:

There is a need for better coordination of pesticide programs both in FDA and among other Federal and State
agencies having responsibilities in this field.

RECOMMENDATIONS: Develop within the FDA a centralized
coordination point for pesticide activities to work with Federal committees on Pest Control, Environmental Control
Administration, National Air Pollution Control Administration, and other Federal, State and local agencies to develop
a national program for safe pesticide use.

Kinslow did not mention that the whole monitoring
program needs serious review, or that the Department
of Agriculture consistently rejects virtually all of the
recommendations the FDA makes against the use of
specific pesticide products, or that less than 1 per cent
of all interstate shipments of raw agricultural commodities are inspected for pesticide residue by the FDA.
The recommendation assumed that the FDA was doing
quite well; all it needed was a little better co-ordination
with the rest of the government. Kinslow himself was
thoroughly familiar with the serious problems related
to pesticide control, but he overlooked them to make
this casual appraisal.

The Kinslow Report's remaining food recommendations continue in the same generalized way or else
recommend further reductions of FDA authority. The
only recommendation addressed primarily to food additives said: "Develop the necessary capability to undertake long range ecological studies to assure that chemical
and other environmental contaminants will not adversely affect our future food supply." There was no
mention of the GRAS list, of cyclamates, of inability
to monitor additives in food, or the many other problems of food chemicals which have since emerged and
seriously undermined the FDA's public credibility. Two
recommendations on food standards called for re-evaluation of the standards program to see if it was meeting
consumer needs, particularly nutritional needs, and
calling for informative labeling. Neither recommendation suggested how their goals of better nutrition
standards or labeling could be met. Neither mentioned
the fact that several hundred chemical additives are
now allowed in foods without informative labeling, or
that hundreds of products are allowed on the market

without any standardization. In fact, Mr. Frank Mc-Gloughlin, formerly of the FDA and the FTC and now on the staff of President Nixon's consumer adviser Mrs. Virginia Knauer, is concerned that the food industry will seize on the argument that better nutritional food manufacturing requires the elimination of the entire food standards program, resulting in the elimination of a major source of consumer protection. Kinslow's recommendation does not exclude that possibility. In the area of compliance the report recommends that more state and local food control activities be funded by FDA, that criteria for measuring compliance be developed, that all administrative guidelines be published, and that imported products be more closely monitored. This set of recommendations illustrates the tendency of the report and the agency generally to focus on peripheral matters. The idea of strengthening state and local regulations when Federal regulation is abysmal, or increasing the monitoring of imported goods when monitoring of domestic products is almost nil, seems like a disingenuous effort. That an agency has to recommend to itself so basic a change as the development of criteria to measure compliance suggests that it has not been attending to even its most fundamental duties. Publishing all administrative guidelines is a positive and direct recommendation to ensure that industry will know more exactly what an FDA inspector is looking for when he enters a plant. While this may be a desirable goal, it is a controversial enough point to have received more than the five lines of explanation devoted to it by the report, particularly when it is placed in a context generally recommending ways to relax rather than tighten the regulation of industry.

The report's general attitude on encouraging compliance in place of regulation is illustrated (in the drug section of the report) by its recommendation for control of insulin and antibiotics:

In the 1969 fiscal year, only 0.3 per cent of insulin samples and 1 per cent of antibiotic batches were rejected as not meeting specified standards. The Study Group believes FDA may be expending more resources in assuring the quality of antibiotics and insulin by batch certification than the problem dictates. The need for this level of control was certainly necessary when antibiotics were first marketed. We are not sure if it is necessary today.

RECOMMENDATION: 26. Consider a program of statistical sampling for antibiotics and insulin rather than batch-by-batch certification.

The reasoning supporting this recommendation would undermine any effective FDA program that might develop. Basically, it says there is a program that has been effective in insuring the quality of all insulin and antibiotics that reach the market. It has been so effective, in fact, that it should be discontinued. Actually, the effectiveness of this batch-by-batch testing program should suggest that the principle be extended to more products. In the case of the batch-tested drugs, removal of the program could be dangerous. The agency has been able to remove a small percentage of drugs that violated FDA standards. Some of them might have been seriously inferior—enough to have caused harm to persons who used them. In addition, because of the fact that the FDA does test each batch of drugs, the industry also tests each batch prior to FDA evaluation. There is no indication of how much of each batch tested by industry is returned because it would not pass FDA inspection. Under the statistical sampling program suggested by Kinslow it would be possible to allow on the market much of the insulin and many of the antibiotic drugs currently being rejected. For this reason Commissioner Ley repudiated the recommendation. But the importance of this particular recommendation is that it reveals that Kinslow and the report are committed to the idea that industry does not need regulation to perform adequately. It is this conviction that has led the FDA to failure in the past and, if continued, will lead the FDA to failure in the future.

The remaining food recommendations deal with food and nutrition-related diseases and consumer involvement in FDA decisions. The disease-related recommendations call for more accurate labeling of health claims for food, expansion and co-ordination of nutritional research activities to be directed by a Bureau of Food in the FDA, and the treatment of poor sanitation in food plants as a health problem.

There is no mention of the FDA's position that the

food supply provides all needed nutrients, nor that a re-evaluation of this position is needed. There is no recommendation to divert resources away from unnecessary health food prosecutions toward the pressing need for research on nutrition. The report proposes creating a Bureau of Foods (which has since been done) as a means of improving nutrition, but it does not deal with the possible fragmentation of the FDA's most vital scientific work that might be produced by such a division between foods and other products that the agency regulates. In the 1970's the FDA's paramount responsibilities are to a co-ordinated regulation and control of the vast and largely unknown dangers in the chemical environment, whether they appear in drugs, cosmetics, pesticides, or food additives. Any bureaucratic restructuring tending to divide the agency's scientific research into tests relevant to food and tests relevant to drugs, for example, would be an unnecessary blow to unified thinking and action on subjects of prime importance to American health and safety.

The Kinslow Report's recommendations on nutrition are vague and could lead to a serious undermining of the limited protection provided by the current food standards program. It is important that this program be strengthened while including nutritional consideration within it.

The consumer-participation recommendations of the report also are too general. One suggests the development of a program that would inform consumers and allow more consumer influence on FDA activities, but it gives no indication as to how this should be carried out. The other recommendation talks of consumer participation in priority-setting at the agency, but it also fails to indicate how such participation would be organized. In fact, the use of the word "consumer" throughout the report has no substance and appears to be merely a sop to current agitation over consumer protection.

Maurice Kinslow and the members of his committee were unable to carry out the direction of the Commissioner to look imaginatively at FDA consumer protection. Instead of a thoughtful report, outlining the hundreds of major agency failures, the group produced a routine appraisal of general difficulty that could not cause any embarrassment for any individual bureaucrat. The fixing of responsibility for failure, the analysis of major breakdown in specific programs, the raising of questions which might have been embarrassing to the bureaucracy, were all scrupulously avoided. Unfortunately, the sloppy and superficial nature of the report escaped the notice of the press in its report of the spectacular quality of failure to which the FDA admitted. Until cyclamates were removed from the market, MSG was voluntarily taken out of baby food, and controversy began to build over a series of unfortunate drug regulation decisions, no one really asked the agency to account for its failures.

Because of the general impression created by the press about the report, Kinslow became something of a hero in the FDA bureaucracy. When Commissioner Edwards took over the agency he immediately moved Kinslow to Washington as his temporary special assistant. Kinslow was able to use a shoddy and superficial report to build a major career advancement. He has been picked to remain as a key adviser to the new Commissioner. His kind of mediocrity has been the key to advancement at FDA for so long that the overwhelming majority of crucial decision-making positions are occupied by people like those Dr. Ley called "retreads."

The failure of the Kinslow Report and the subsequent elevation of its prime author also represent a kind of bureaucratic failure common at the FDA. As a former adviser to Dr. James Goddard, Dr. Ley's predecessor, put it, "We were constantly being sandbagged from inside the agency." What is most important about the sandbagging is that it is never apparent until too late. Dr. Ley was unable to see the inadequacies of the Kinslow Committee until the report was completed. By that time, two months had elapsed and the Commissioner still did not know what FDA weaknesses existed in the consumer protection field. Within three weeks of completion, the report had been leaked to the public, which immediately gave Kinslow an identity in the bureaucracy.

The Commissioner's reliance on Kinslow for advice is particularly unfortunate since other and better guides to action were available. President Nixon, in his October 30, 1969, consumer message to Congress, Deputy Undersecretary Malec in his December 10, 1969, report to Secretary Finch, and Dr. Jean Mayer, in his report on the White House Conference on Food, Nutrition, and Health, all gave specific and important suggestions for the improvement and reorganization of the FDA that could have been easily followed by the new Commissioner. These sources certainly had no more knowledge or access to information about the FDA than the Kinslow Committee did. But the recommendations their separate efforts produced should serve as a good set of goals for the new Commissioner.

Dr. Mayer's report contains the most important consumer protection guidelines. As a basic principle it states: "Inasmuch as the consumer is the primary consideration in deliberations on the safety and adequacy of the food supply, the consumer must be represented on panels convened to examine these problems." President Nixon's consumer message highlighted the most important single area in which this principle must be rigorously applied. He said, "I have already asked the Secretary of Health, Education, and Welfare to initiate a full review of food additives. This investigation should move as fast as our resources permit, re-examining the safety of substances which are now described by the phrase, generally recognized as safe."

A full review of food additives cannot hope to dispel consumer doubts about the food supply unless it is an effort conducted openly and with the participation of consumer representatives; that is, people who are not related to either the FDA or the food industry, and who have the confidence of the consuming public. The Mayer report outlines two important changes for the food additive policy of the FDA:

In view of the fact that it is not possible to determine with absolute certainty the safety of the ever-increasing number of chemicals added to or present in our foods and taking in account the possible interaction of these chemicals with each other or natural food constituents, no additional chemicals should be permitted in or on foods unless they have been shown with reasonable certainty to be safe on the basis of the best scientific procedures available for the evaluation of safety and meet one or more of the following criteria:

1. They have been shown to be significantly less toxic by appropriate test than food additives curently employed for the same purpose.
2. They significantly improve the quality or acceptability of the food.
3. Their use results in a significant increase in the food supply.
4. They improve the nutritive value of the food.
5. Their use results in a decrease in the cost of food to the consumer.

It is essential that the chemical environment be controlled as completely as possible. Traditional or long-continued use of any additive can no longer be considered to be sufficient evidence of safety. Thus, it is necessary that a continuing re-evaluation be maintained of all compounds whose use in foods is relatively freely allowed. This re-evaluation must be based upon objective investigation under controlled conditions. A mechanism must be provided by which these goals may be attained.

RECOMMENDATION: Since there is a need for better control of the chemical environment, it is recommended that the list of substances known as GRAS be systematically reviewed for safety in the light of new knowledge, experience, new levels and new categories of food use.

None of these recommendations was part of the Kinslow Report. Commissioner Edwards has said that he plans to review (not necessarily implement) the recommendations of the White House Panel. If he implements them it will be an important step forward for food protection in America.

The Mayer report also recommended more detailed and informative labeling, specifically saying that all chemicals added to a food should be listed on its label. This recommendation, if put into force, will require a complete rewriting of the labeling section of nearly all food standards to insure proper and complete information for the consumer. It is an excellent suggestion. An example of complete and detailed labeling already exists on dog and cat food.

President Nixon asked in his consumer message, "Are [FDA] laboratory findings communicated as promptly and fully as is desirable to high Administration officials and the public?" The Malec Committee of HEW answered no, pinpointing what it considered were the reasons and suggesting these remedies:

Implement a planning and control system through which the Commissioner can direct (according to his set of priorities) and monitor key research and investigative activities.

Install a simple procedure by which anyone in FDA can initiate a "critical problem report" to go immediately to the Commissioner.

Designate, for each new application or marketed product to be investigated, a "product manager" who will be held responsible for all activities relating to that application or product, including final recommendation to management.

Expand the concept of using part-time science advisors from the private sector (now in each District Office) as "ombudsmen." Each headquarters bureau should have both a science and medical advisor.

Adopt the proposal to set up public forums on specific problem areas through the NAS, with representation from industry, consumer groups, universities, and interested government agencies.

These five procedures represent an important beginning point for a reorganization effort at FDA. They are much more specific than the recommendations of the Kinslow Report. They are also directed to FDA internal organizational problems, which go almost completely unmentioned in the FDA report.

9. Misused Professionals

> *"It is very hard to work here and have other scientists respect you."*
>
> —*M. J. Nelson*
> *FDA researcher,*
> *August, 1969*

For fifteen years the FDA has been criticized for its lack of scientific research ability. In 1955 Secretary of Health, Education, and Welfare Oveta Culp Hobby convened what has come to be known as the First Citizens Advisory Committee on the Food and Drug Administration, which, among other recommendations, called for a reorientation in FDA philosophy and an upgrading of the scientific research capability of the agency. "Research is the heart of any scientific operation. Although the FDA is primarily a regulatory agency, it must engage in research of the sort that leads to more accurate scientific methods of determining whether a food or drug is safe. Such research in scientific methodology, and perhaps a limited amount of what might be termed 'random' research, can do much to upgrade the professional competence, elevate the morale of the scientific workers, and contribute to the general effectiveness of the FDA." [1]

Other important review bodies made the same recommendation. In 1956 the National Academy of Sciences-National Research Council *ad hoc* committee on coal-tar dyes urged the FDA to strengthen its review of the dyes by expanding its research and hiring more scientists. In 1958 a special team of consultants retained to evaluate the FDA's education programs wrote:

. . . a vigorous research effort is critically important to the effective performance of the statutory responsibilities of the FDA. Clinical investigations, research on improved analytical and testing methods, toxicological research, and observations of the effects of antibiotics over long periods of time must be carried on with well-qualified personnel, having adequate equipment, funds, and facilities at their disposal.

One hundred and twenty-two professional scientists are a woefully small group with which to resolve the manifold complex problems arising in the food, drug and cosmetic areas. In recent years the meager research resources of the FDA have been swung from one emergency to another. Sufficient staffing and space have not been available to permit the "follow through" on long-range programs nor the proper expansion in relevant new scientific fields.[2]

In January, 1959, in response to the pressure for scientific improvement, the agency obtained the full-time services of Dr. Paul L. Day, installed him as Scientific Director of the FDA (at a civil-service rank second only to that of the Commissioner) and asked him to build a science arm for the FDA. Six months later Dr. Day prepared a detailed report on the conditions of science at the FDA and provided a set of recommendations to improve that condition. He repeated the recommendations of each of the scientific review committees and cited the result of his own six-month day-to-day observation of FDA scientists. He said, "I have been repeatedly amazed by evidence of scientific 'provincialism'—seeming competence in the narrow speciality but abysmal ignorance of closely related scientific fields." He singled out a major part of the problem saying, "When a project requiring a new basic approach is attacked, it is often to meet an immediate regulatory problem and a quick answer is needed. There is little opportunity for careful planning. As one person has phrased it: 'We are so busy putting out fires that we don't have time to do any fire prevention.' " Among his recommendations Dr. Day included "the appointment of a Scientific Advisory Board of distinguished scientists from universities, foundations, industry, and other Governmental laboratories."[3]

No effective action was taken on the report for the next fifteen months, and so on October 12, 1960, before a meeting of the Animal Nutrition Research Council, Dr. Day publicly presented his views of the FDA's deficient scientific policies and how he thought they should be improved. In the meantime a committee of the National Academy of Sciences-National Research Council, asked to prepare "recommendations it might consider desirable for the protection of the public health through the functions of the FDA" by HEW Secretary Flemming, said, "The Committee urges the Commissioner to seek such authorization as may be necessary to establish an advisory organization of scientific and technical experts as a recognized resource for advice on criteria, procedures and policies for the execution of the responsibilities." [4]

In spite of constant warnings, the FDA allowed its scientific capability to deteriorate so badly by 1962 that a Second Citizens Advisory Committee was convened to evaluate its failings and recommend improvements. The Committee reported, "Analysis of the testimony of FDA representatives before congressional committees in recent years reveals that their emphasis has been upon the first Citizen Advisory Committee's recommendations for increases in FDA resources; less has been said about the views of the first CAC concerning the philosophy of FDA. . . ." [5] Specifically, the second CAC concluded that "The scientific functions of FDA should be upgraded." [6] The Committee explained the effect of FDA's interpretation of the original recommendations. "In the status report on progress in implementing the first Committee's recommendations which the Commissioner of FDA has submitted to the Secretary of the Department of Health, Education, and Welfare, there is a tendency to evaluate implementation primarily in terms of quantitative measurement, usually equating progress with increase in staff. These reports contain only limited information regarding program content or trends in compliance with the recommendations." [7] In his October 12, 1960, speech, Dr. Day cited the same problem in the science programs of FDA. "From the sharp upturn in appropriations . . . and in manpower, one would suppose that scientific work in FDA has prospered in very recent years. Actually the reverse seems to be the case; there are many more scientists in FDA laboratories than at any time in the past, but there is good evidence that imaginative scientific work is at a low ebb. At a time when scientific research is recognized as the open sesame to progress in any field—whether the purpose is profit, prestige or survival—FDA's research productiveness has been, in recent years, near an all-time low." [8]

One bright spot in the efforts to upgrade FDA science at the beginning of the 1960's was the fact that the FDA official responsible for its scientific capability, Dr. Day, was acutely aware of the problem and specific about ways to eliminate it. Unfortunately, the FDA failed to act on his internal recommendations and viewed his public statements as a failure of his loyalty to the agency. Shortly after the October 12 speech, Dr. Day left the FDA amid accusations and counteraccusations. It appears that he had not received official clearance for release of the substance of his memo, even though the Commissioner had referred to it in Congressional testimony. Instead of seizing on the opportunity to begin eliminating its scientific problems, presented by the clear and detailed criticism of its scientific adviser, the agency chose to sever its relationship with the critic. The result was more delay in improving the quality of FDA's scientific research—a failure which in part caused the convening of the Second Citizens Advisory Committee.

The Second CAC's recommendations caused no more improvements in the FDA's methods than the first had. In 1966, after ten years of controversy that began with the First Citizens Advisory Committee Report in 1955, the agency was still being told it should attempt to upgrade its scientific competence. To help accomplish the task, Secretary of Health, Education, and Welfare John Gardner broke with the tradition of appointing career bureaucrats as Commissioner and instead selected James Goddard, a medical doctor, to replace George Larrick, who had no formal professional education but had worked himself into the Commissioner's office through the ranks as an FDA inspector. In one of his first acts, Commissioner Goddard retained a group of science advisers—on a part-time basis—to improve the quality of FDA research in its district offices. The hope was that regular interaction between FDA and university scientists would improve the agency and inform the teachers. The program was never the success it could have been. Annual meetings in Washington were held by the science advisers. However, the minutes of these meetings, prepared by FDA officials, always omitted references to scientific shortcomings in the FDA's work and failed to mention recommendations for improvement. The Deputy Commissioner, the man most responsible for internal FDA activities, did not even know that these annual meetings were being held. Science advisers found it difficult to communicate their concerns to their district directors or Washington officials. Frustrated in what they thought they had been hired to do, some simply allowed their association with the agency to end. Others more vigorously pressed their ideas. A particularly striking case was that of Dr. William C. Purdy, professor of chemistry at the University of Maryland.

In February, 1967, Dr. Purdy signed a contract to advise the Baltimore District of the Food and Drug Administration on scientific matters. He and sixteen other scientists (one in each FDA district across the country) contracted to spend one day a week reviewing test methods, evaluating research techniques, and attempting to upgrade the scientific quality of the scientific staff's work in the district offices. Purdy carried out his weekly duties without particular incident until April, 1969, when he discovered what he considered to be serious flaws in the FDA pesticide-residue monitoring program. He prepared a detailed memorandum outlining them, which the FDA answered in equal detail, explaining— or denying outright—each of the weaknesses Dr. Purdy had cited. Purdy replied immediately, restating each of his original comments and outlining the ways in which they had not been answered. In response the FDA suggested that he seek a meeting with the FDA's Baltimore District Director, Maurice Kinslow, which he did. Another FDA science adviser who had followed the Purdy-FDA exchanges expressed the hope that the agency would not fire Dr. Purdy. "This would imply that FDA hired science advisers to solicit their advice only if it were complimentary. I do not believe this to be the case," he wrote.[9] But when Purdy returned from a meeting with Kinslow's deputy on July 2, 1969, he found another letter, this one from Maurice Kinslow, the FDA District Director, saying, "Now that your appointment as Science Advisor to the Baltimore District has terminated, I want to thank you for your contributions to the District research program. I trust your association with the Baltimore District scientists has been rewarding."

Six weeks later Kinslow and Winton B. Rankin, the FDA's Deputy Commissioner, answered questions about Dr. Purdy's charges before the House Subcommittee on Public Health and Welfare. Asked if the pesticide residue program had been criticized, Deputy Commissioner Rankin answered, "There has been some criticism from one scientist about the way we conduct these tests. We have invited him to come in and talk to us and tell us what he believes is wrong. He has not seen fit to come forward yet and give us the details of his criticism." [10] At the time this statement was uttered, the FDA not only had Purdy's detailed memoranda in its files, but in response to outside pressure the agency had set up a meeting between Dr. Purdy and the administrators of the monitoring program. (The meeting was held September 25 and led to a review of the program.)

Later the same day, Committee Chairman Paul G. Rogers (Democrat from Florida) asked Mr. Kinslow about the status of his science adviser in Baltimore:

MR. KINSLOW: We do not have a science adviser at present. We are currently attempting to get one. These gentlemen are on a "when actually employed contract" that runs from year to year and we are in the process at this time of attempting to locate some.

MR. ROGERS: What happened to your science adviser?

MR. KINSLOW: His contract expired at the end of the last fiscal year, June 30, and I did not renew it.

MR. ROGERS: Was he not a good adviser?

MR. KINSLOW: I felt that he had contributed in the past, but I felt that I wished to have an opportunity to change in this area and since it is just a year-to-year basis, I concluded that I would let it expire.

MR. ROGERS: Is this the man who disagrees with the handling of the pesticides?

MR. KINSLOW: Yes sir, it is.

MR. ROGERS: When do you plan to hire one?

MR. KINSLOW: As soon as I can locate a man that is suitable. I have not been able to turn my attention to this recently.

MR. ROGERS: Thank you.[11]

As of March 1, 1970, the Baltimore District still had no science adviser.

In February, 1970, Dr. Purdy was invited by the newly appointed Commissioner of FDA, Dr. Charles Edwards, to present his observation of the state of science at the FDA. Dr. Purdy presented his information. In response, Commissioner Edwards assigned Sam Fine, the newly appointed Associate Commissioner for Compliance, to answer—not investigate and correct, but answer—the charges. One week later Mr. Fine presented the answer to James Turner of the Nader summer task force. He read verbatim from notes prepared for him by his deputy Reo Duggan—the man most responsible for the confusion in the FDA pesticide program—the very same comments that had been presented to Dr. Purdy more than six months earlier. He apparently felt there was no contradiction in his repeating these remarks even though the FDA had officially undertaken a review of the pesticide monitoring program based on Dr. Purdy's criticism. It appears that the familiar FDA policy of subordinating science to administrative needs still dominates thinking at the FDA.

The failure to renew Dr. Purdy's contract is not an isolated example of administrative interference with scientific research at FDA. On April 30, 1970, the Associated Press reported that scientific distortion was so serious a problem at FDA that the agency had retained a special consultant to investigate the situation and answer charges of long standing interference made by one highly respected scientist. Dozens of interviews with FDA scientists between June and September of 1969 suggest that the conclusions of a study of employee attitudes conducted in 1960 by Dr. Charles Goodman of the Department of Psychology at American University would be the same if the study were run again in 1970. FDA scientists have not been and are not now happy. Dr. Goodman concluded, "Scientists by and large do not look upon FDA as providing the kind of environment ordinarily sought by scientists or believed to be associated with maximum creative productivity." [12]

Several researchers interviewed read from "atrocity logs" in which they kept a detailed and regular account of assaults on their scientific integrity. For example, some individuals in a supervisory capacity routinely sign their names to research work they have not conducted; in one division, invitations to attend scientific meetings were dispensed not routinely but to reward what were variously referred to as "yes men," "pets," and "stooges" of the supervisor; another supervisor was credited with saying that the mediocre researchers should be promoted because they need more help than good researchers do. Some of the FDA scientists complain of being kept from using equipment, or of having to begin work at five in the morning because they have no lab assistants and must raise, slaughter, section, prepare, and clean up after lab animals. One researcher who was a civil rights activist was asked if there was any racial discrimination in his division. "No," he said, "they treat us all badly here." The most often repeated comment from dissatisfied scientists was that the FDA constantly interferes with medium and long-range research projects, making it almost impossible to complete them. At least part of the reason, they assert, is that certain results might embarrass the agency either by showing a lack of scientifiç support for an already established regulatory policy, or, conversely, establishing scientific evidence of a hazard which there is no legal authority to bring under control.

On October 17, 1969, after Food and Drug Administration scientists had presented a strong argument against the safety of cyclamates to the NAS-NRC committee evaluating the sweetener, Dr. Keith Lewis, chief of the agency's Bureau of Science, surprised the committee members and angered his FDA colleagues by asserting that the committee should remember, while considering the scientific evidence of cyclamate hazard, that the FDA's legal authority to take action against the chemical was severely limited. (Two days later, with its so-called severely limited authority, the FDA removed cyclamates from the food market without even falling back upon its basic legal powers to do so, using instead the Delaney Clause on cancer.) Such an overt assertion of the proposition that scientific evidence should be subordinated in advance to legal restrictions confirmed the fears of FDA scientists that their laboratory research serves primarily as window-dressing for already arrived at administrative decisions. Several scientists in FDA prepared a confrontation with Dr. Lewis over his statement but called it off as unnecessary when cyclamates were removed from the market two days later, after being shown to cause cancer in rats. Nevertheless, the episode did not improve the morale of FDA scientists.

FDA attorneys at public hearings, trying to support the agency assertion that vitamin supplements are unnecessary for the average American, were embarrassed by the meagerness of the scientific support for the position. FDA scientists were unable to provide significant facts to support the regulatory decision already arrived at by FDA administrators. On at least four occasions within the past ten years, scientists who disagreed with an administrative decision and felt compelled to bring forward evidence that tended to discredit rather than support the policy consulted private attorneys because they feared that taking this kind of independent line would endanger their jobs.

At his October 18, 1969, press conference announcing the cyclamates ban, even Commissioner Herbert Ley had to admit that the FDA had some problems with its method of handling research information and recommendations. He said, "I have become convinced within the past few weeks that we do have communications difficulties within FDA, as any organization has. These disturb me greatly. I am taking steps to solve problems that exist. Some of the problems have been blown up beyond their real status and some have not been known to me before. I will solve the problems." [13]

What Dr. Ley described as a "communication breakdown" was really a more basic failure: it is too simple to say that the problem at the FDA is that scientific facts do not routinely reach the Commissioner. The psychological atmosphere created by placing administrative choices before scientific facts tends to filter out and reject evidence that does not support the administrative position already taken, and to elevate even the most flimsy information that does support the administrative position. A striking example of this effect had come to light shortly before Dr. Ley referred to the communication breakdown. It occurred in the FDA's handling of evidence related to the use of monosodium glutamate in baby food.

In mid-July of 1969 the Senate Select Committee on Food Nutrition and Health, under Senator George Mc-

Govern, heard testimony on MSG. The first witness to testify was Ralph Nader, who said that serious questions about the use of MSG in baby food were being raised by nutritionists. Why, he asked, when MSG has no nutritional value and babies cannot distinguish between tastes, take the risk of adding it to baby food without studying the effects first? Dr. John W. Olney, a psychiatrist at the Washington University School of Medicine in St. Louis, followed Nader with testimony that he had fed MSG to rats in doses comparable to the amounts that babies would consume in baby food, and that the rats he had fed suffered brain and eye damage from the chemical.

MSG had been singled out by the FDA as one of the safest chemicals used in foods. Undeterred by the questions raised about MSG safety, the agency set out to defend its regulatory position. Believing firmly that there was no problem with MSG, FDA administrators reviewed the evidence in their files and concluded that it supported the belief that MSG was safe for use in baby food. In this firm belief they prepared a staff paper for presentation to the McGovern Committee by Commissioner Herbert Ley, specifically citing four "refined toxicological" tests which they said supported their position.

On July 22, 1969, Commissioner Ley read this detailed staff paper as part of his testimony, concluding unequivocally, "We have seen no convincing evidence of a significant health problem in this area." But the paper he relied upon subordinated science to the agency's administrative position. The four tests Ley cited as the major evidence of safety had been seriously distorted. The first study cited in the staff paper stated: "When MSG was injected into fertilized eggs it caused no adverse effect on the embryo." In fact, two months earlier the staff that conducted the test mentioned held a meeting at which it was pointed out that only a limited number of eggs had been used in the test and "these results, based on such a limited number of eggs, are too preliminary for any conclusions to be drawn." [14] Amazed to see this extremely preliminary test cited by the Commissioner to support his position, the investigators who conducted the test wrote to Dr. Edwin L. Hove, the

Acting Director of the Division of Nutrition. "Positive statement on findings with the chick embryo may not be warranted at this time. The investigators have requested that appropriate modification of this statement by the Commissioner be made." The test if anything suggested some slight possibility of a problem with MSG.*

The second study cited by the Commissioner did not take place until eight days after the Commissioner cited it. The staff paper states: "Another of the new tests has to do with cytogenic abnormalities, primarily in the indication of chromosome breaks in the cells of treated animals or bacteria. When MSG was subjected to these highly critical tests, no adverse reactions were noted." According to Dr. Marvin Legator (FDA cell biologist and expert on chromosome breakage) no FDA studies on MSG chromosome damage had been conducted.

The third study cited in the paper states, "When fed to rats at levels of 30 per cent of the diet, MSG has produced no adverse effects on growth." Dr. Hove later notified the Commissioner that the actual figure should have been 30 per cent of the protein in the diet, not 30 per cent of the entire diet. More disturbing, when questioned, no FDA investigators in the protein field could recall that such a study had even been done by the FDA.

The fourth study cited in the staff paper was incomplete at the time of the testimony. The paper states: "When fed to pregnant rats at a level of 10 per cent of the diet (equivalent to 20 grams of MSG per kilogram of body weight) no adverse effect on the pregnancy occurred. The young born from those mothers were normal and developed normally." Had the report of this experiment been accurate, it would have said the rats "*are developing* normally," since the rats had not yet grown to maturity and since no rats had yet been sacrificed and autopsied. Dr. J. S. Adkins, FDA protein expert, was surprised to see his study mentioned, since

* While the FDA was publicly using the chick embryo test on fewer than 200 eggs to suggest the safety of MSG, it was ignoring the fact that the very same test carried out to completion on over ten thousand eggs had shown significant hazards from cyclamates. This is another example of the way in which the FDA tailors its scientific information to support its administrative decisions.

the data was preliminary and in parallel MSG tests preliminary data showed that some rats fed MSG did show a significant loss of weight when compared to controls.

These four tests were relied upon by FDA officials to convince the Committee of the safety of MSG. Two of the tests had apparently not been conducted at all and the other two were preliminary in nature. None had shown safety.

In his zeal to defend the administrative decision of his agency Ley also misrepresented the nature of Dr. Olney's tests on MSG by greatly exaggerating the amounts of MSG used and by asserting that MSG had been *injected* into rats when in fact it had been administered orally. The effect of both distortions was to minimize the value and importance of Dr. Olney's tests and to enhance the FDA's defense of MSG. When these distortions were pointed out, Dr. Ley wrote a letter to the McGovern Committee apologizing for misrepresenting the amount of MSG used in the Olney experiments. A later FDA document presented to the committee acknowledged that MSG had been administered orally in the Olney tests. Concerning the four misrepresented FDA tests, members of the Nader Summer Study Group mentioned the distortions to the FDA officials responsible. When the FDA took no action to correct the testimony, Ralph Nader wrote a letter to the McGovern Committee pointing out the distortions. The Committee asked the FDA to respond. The same official who had drafted the original FDA position on MSG for Dr. Ley prevailed upon him to send McGovern a second staff memo that further distorted the facts on MSG. Dr. Ley's cover letter apologized for citing a test that had not been conducted until eight days after the testimony, but this was the only apology he made. The new staff paper that he attached acknowledged that the investigator who conducted the study on chick embryos said it could not be cited for any purpose in relation to MSG except as a preliminary test. In regard to the feeding test on rats, the new paper reiterated the conclusion that it indicated MSG had no ill effects; however, it included a new citation from FDA experiments indicating that "L-glutamic acid [similar to MSG] fed to young rats at 25 per cent of the total diet resulted in a reduction of growth rate of about 50 per cent as compared with controls." [15]

Dr. Ley's response to the charge that the fourth test was nonexistent was the most grossly distorted. He said, "The reference for this 'non-existent study' is: Hepburn, F. N. and Bradley, W. B. 'The Glutamic Acid and Arginine Requirements for High Growth Rate of Rats Fed Amino Acid Diets,' *Journal of Nutrition* 84:305–312 (1964). FDA scientists were the source of my information about the study which is why I cited it in testimony. Neither I nor Dr. Hove were aware of any error in reporting the level of feeding until Mr. Nader stated that the reference should have been feeding levels of 30 per cent of protein in the diet, instead of '30 per cent of the diet.' Since the study does exist, apparently Mr. Nader was able to check it and bring this error to our attention. Moreover, studies of this same general nature were in progress at FDA at least a month before I testified and are continuing now." [16] Seven months earlier Dr. Edwin Hove, a key adviser to Ley in the preparation of his MSG testimony, had singled out the Hepburn-Bradley study as a test suggesting potential problems related to MSG saying, "When monosodium glutamate was fed to growing rats at 6 per cent of diet . . . (Hepburn & Bradley; *Nutrition* 84:305, 1964) it reduced growth rate by 16 per cent; glutamic acid or glutamine had no effect. At 2 per cent of the diet, the salt was without adverse effect." [17] Convincing evidence that the test referred to by Dr. Ley does in fact exist is still missing.

There are other examples of major scientific failure at the FDA. The same subordination of scientific fact to other regulatory considerations has resulted in reduced health protection for the American consumer in the case of the cyclamates hazard, pesticide monitoring, the establishment of food standards such as fat labeling, and the establishment of regulations to control vitamin use. When an organization is known by scientists to be repressive and unresponsive to scientific information, they tend to censor themselves. As a result important scientific questions are never asked out of the fear that the unwanted answer will bring down the wrath of the administration on the researcher. The researcher who failed to report the 1950 indications that cyclamates are said to have caused cancer told the Commissioner in 1969, "I didn't want to make any trouble." The same attitude may explain the agency's failure to follow up the important possibility that saccharin might cause cancer.

In 1951 three FDA scientists reported that at certain levels saccharin might be implicated as a cause of cancer. They said:

Saccharin—no pathological effect whatever could be attributed to saccharin at levels of 1.0% or less. At 5% only one effect was noted, in the latter part of the experiment, namely an increased incidence of the ordinarily uncommon condition of abdominal lymphosarcoma. In the 5% group, there were seven animals with lymphosarcoma; this number is not out of line with the incidence in comparable groups of rats, but the fact that in four of the seven rats abdominal as well as thoracic lymphosarcomas were present is unusual, since ordinarily the ratio is about 1 to 15–20.[18]

It would not seem unreasonable that an agency charged with the responsibility for insuring the safety of food additives would follow results it considered "unusual" with tests to demonstrate more exactly the safety of the sweetener. However, the FDA did no such thing. In a 1968 report on artificial sweeteners the NAS-NRC committee reviewing cyclamates and saccharin referred to the *1951* FDA study: "Administration of saccharin at levels up to and including 5 per cent of the diet was continued for 24 months. No pathological effects were observed with levels of 1 per cent or less. In the group given 5 per cent of the diet, Fitzhugh et al., observed seven animals with abdominal lymphosarcomas. . . . In view of the small number of tumors this incidence cannot be considered significant without additional experiments." [19]

An agency that takes more than eighteen years to follow up "unusual" findings in its field of responsibility —particularly on a widely distributed food additive— cannot be regarded as effectively scientific.

Science is best served when ideas and information circulate freely within the scientific community. Scientists at the FDA should be allowed to publish their findings in appropriate journals without administrative restraint, but they are not. All writings done by FDA scientists must be reviewed and approved for publication by the agency's writing review committee. As a result of this procedure, several scientists have been unable to publish important scientific discoveries; others have published their articles without agency sanction. The agency rationale for the writing review board is to review the quality of the writing and the research, but the editors of scientific journals are better equipped to do this job.

In addition, FDA policy keeps certain important information within the agency when it should be made public. Its internal publication, called "Interbureau By Lines," has a restricted circulation, as it declares proudly on the cover: "Copies of By Lines and reprints of articles are not available to the public." From time to time the publication contains information of great importance to the scientific community, the interested public, and regulated industries. For example, a recent issue included a complete annotated bibliography on cyclamate research that could have been of great value in sharpening comment on the additive but which was locked away from the public because of FDA policy. Another example is a very important speech given to FDA scientists in 1963 by Nobel Prize-winner Hermann Muller about the genetic effects of chemicals. The speech was printed in the November, 1964, issue of "By Lines," but public mention of it was withheld until the July–August, 1969, issue of the publicly circulated agency magazine, "FDA Papers," carried a summary of the speech. The FDA still has not printed the full text of the speech for public consumption. The failure to release this speech may have contributed to the situation one expert described in 1968 when he said, "Well planned systematic investigations on existing or newly introduced chemical agents in our environment that could produce adverse genetic effects are almost non-existent." [20] A widely circulated call to work by a Nobel Prize winner usually creates dynamic scientific exchange, but the FDA apparently did not feel inspired to publish the remarks that might have occasioned the exchange.

Year after year since 1955 the weak, distorted and uncritical scientific review given by FDA to important public health problems has been singled out as a failing in need of immediate effective solution if the FDA is to function properly. Reforms have been clearly spelled out: HEW Assistant Secretary Malec's reorganization committee recommended hiring more science advisers and turning them into an ombudsman (complaint-investigating) group to inform the Commissioner directly of scientific breakdown when it occurred. HEW has prepared a detailed report, "Improving the Environment for Science in HEW" (December 23, 1968), which sets out detailed recommendations that must be adopted if the FDA's use of science is to improve. Basic to this report's recommendation is this point: "More than any other incentive or form of recognition, the opportunity for the scientist to have a voice in the conduct or kind of research in which he is involved is of primary importance to his professional status and feeling of involvement." [21]

Besides first opening up internal communications between FDA scientists and the Commissioner and, second, giving the scientists a vote in planning research, the third FDA reform needed to upgrade science at the agency is creating more opportunities for FDA scientists to communicate their findings to other scientists and the public.

So far in the new regime of Commissioner Charles Edwards there has been no noticeable change in the handling of important scientific questions by the agency. Instead of adopting the science adviser recommendation of the Malec report, Commissioner Charles Edwards has appointed an in-house supervisory committee for science. The purpose of this committee may be suggested by its deliberations on the Delaney Clause. This clause of the Food Additives Amendment of 1958 is crucial to consumer protection because it *prohibits* the use as a food additive of any chemical that causes cancer in animals that ingest it. It is the only section of the law that has been at all effective in removing potentially hazardous chemicals from the food supply. Secretary Finch and Commissioner Edwards are both on record as desiring a change in the clause. Secretary Finch clearly desires to soften it while Commissioner Edwards has not specified the nature of the changes he favors. When the new FDA co-ordinating committee for science met to discuss the clause they were presented with an argument justifying softening the clause. There was opposition to that position by FDA scientists present, and the issue was dropped. But the committee did not make a recommendation to the Commissioner that the clause be retained; nor did it consider strengthening it. When the committee met to discuss the problems surrounding the use of the pesticides 2-4-D and 2-4-5-T they were joined by representatives of Dow, Hercules, and Monsanto to discuss regulation. The result was postponement of any government action on the pesticides for three months in the hopes that industry itself could solve the problem. The participants in the meeting were directed to keep the discussion secret. Clearly this kind of procedure does not encourage the uninhibited exercise of scientific judgment. The FDA remains a scientifically unsophisticated organization. In spite of an engaging manner, Dr. Charles Edwards has not yet taken control of the agency.

10.

FDA Mythology

"The great enemy of the truth is very often not the lie—deliberate, contrived and dishonest—but the myth—persistent, persuasive and unrealistic. Too often we hold fast to the clichés of our forebears."

—President John F. Kennedy,
Yale University Commencement,
1962

"If FDA is not careful, if it moves too fast, it might have its budget Taberized." In FDA jargon, this statement made to a student interviewer by an official of the Bureau of Medicine summarized one of the great myths of the FDA—the Taber beet incident. John Taber, upstate New York Congressman and Chairman of the House Appropriations Committee in 1953, disliked the FDA. "I have had a lot of trouble with the Food and Drug Administration and they have not acted in the interest of obtaining good food many times . . . I felt they were the biggest menace to the food industry and the getting of pure food into the people," he told FDA Commissioner C. W. Crawford in a telephone conversation on February 5, 1953.[1] Three and one half months later he led a successful fight on the floor of Congress to eliminate $648,000 (over 10 per cent of the total) from the FDA operating budget.

The FDA's view of the incident was set forth by Wallace Janssen, historian of the Food and Drug Administration, who wrote, "Conscientious officials adopted attitudes and policies designed to produce maximum results from minimum funds. . . . In fact, the attitude of firm adherence to principle, necessary in effective law enforcement, on more than one occasion led to appropriation cuts." [2] The facts surrounding the Taber incident make the FDA interpretation suspect.

Congressman Taber's dissatisfaction with the FDA began on April 19, 1948, when a man named Schuyler Hibbard of Macedon, New York, asked him for help in a controversy with the FDA. Two years earlier Hibbard had patented a machine that could cut a beet into small round spheres and had sought direction from FDA on how the resulting product should be labeled. The official FDA opinion, that small round beets would be inherently deceptive and therefore under the deceptive packaging section of the Food and Drug Law could not be marketed, was difficult to defend. Without supporting evidence other than "viewing the submitted glass jar of the product," [3] the FDA concluded that consumers would be misled by the product even if labeled "imitation baby beets" because restaurant patrons don't see the labels and that manufacturers would not be interested in the machine in any case because it wasted too much of the beet in its trimming operation.

Congressman Taber arranged for Hibbard and an FDA representative, J. Kenneth Kirk, to meet on March 24, 1948, at which time Kirk presented the FDA's position as inflexible. During the next five years the FDA position continued to be attacked. First the State of New York allowed distribution of the beet product under properly informative labeling. Then the Federal District Court in New Mexico ruled that products simulating other products could be marketed if labeled "imitation." Finally, on March 31, 1953, John Harvey of the FDA, when asked by district officials if the FDA should proceed against the manufacturers of Hibbard's "beet balls," ruled no,[4] saying the FDA did not have the authority to do so.

Two months after Harvey's ruling Congressman Taber successfully cut the FDA's budget. His pique at the agency came from the fact that the FDA had exceeded its authority on a number of occasions and he erroneously cited the baby beets incident as an example. The FDA responded by adopting Taber's mistaken view of the incident. Winton B. Rankin circulated a memorandum of Taber's comments on the beet situation to all district chiefs, thus establishing the FDA's version of the story—that a vigorous and justifiable regulatory action had led to the cutting of FDA appropriations by 10 per cent.

While Congressional retaliation against a regulatory agency through restricting its budget can be an offensive procedure, the FDA was at least as much at fault in the Taber incident as the Congressman. During over five hundred interviews with members of the Nader Summer Study Group, many present and former FDA personnel and observers mentioned the Taber beet incident and concluded that whatever the law might say the FDA had to move cautiously against violators who might have powerful political allies. No one cited the incident as a reason for moving cautiously and carefully in areas where the FDA's legal authority was not clear or its factual evidence not strong. The Taber beet myth has worked its way into FDA mythology, allowing officials at every level of the organization to justify lethargy. Unfortunately, the facts cited to support the myth are a complete fabrication. In every year of the decade from 1960 to 1969, the FDA failed to use all the money Congress appropriated for it. In that period a total of $7 million went unused—over $1 million in 1963, and nearly $3 million in 1966, much of which reverted to the U.S. Treasury.

The "Trade Secret Syndrome"—the most common way in which FDA officials suppress or withhold information—is a second self-justifying deception used by FDA staff to explain doing a poor job. A "trade secret" is a plan, process, or other important part of a manufacturer's operation which is not patented but which receives limited legal protection, including the protection from being released by a government official. Government officials who let out a trade secret, whether intentionally or inadvertently, are subject to a fine of $1,000 or a year's imprisonment. FDA regulations state: "Manufacturers *may regard* some of the data in such files [kept by FDA on products it regulates] as trade secrets and request the Food and Drug Administration to treat such information as confidential. The Food and Drug Administration will preserve the confidentiality of such data to the extent that it may properly do so." (Emphasis added.) [5] The problem is that nobody really knows what a trade secret is, so the tendency on the part of the FDA is to treat as much information as possible as trade secrets. Theodore Cron, former FDA Assistant Commissioner for Education and Information, described how the trade secret protection worked to suppress information: "To sum up, then, the Food, Drug, and Cosmetic Act says that I should do whatever I can to tell things to the consumer, but I should do all this mindful of the fact that a year in jail and a thousand-dollar fine may be my reward. This produces the so-called 'Trade Secret Syndrome' among some government information fellows. Suspecting that a fact just might turn out to be a trade secret, the information officer examines the matter in painful detail, ultimately proving that—indeed—it *is* a kind of trade secret after all and then files it in an irretrievable folder." [6]

FDA's withholding of information during the 1969 MSG controversy illustrates what this attitude means to the public. On January 31, 1969, Dr. Marion J. Finkel, chief of the FDA's Division of Metabolism and Endocrine Drugs, answered a request on MSG from Dr. Robert Byck of the Albert Einstein College of Medicine. Dr. Byck was trying to evaluate possible negative side effects of the additive, which is also used in certain drugs. Dr. Finkel replied to his inquiry saying, "The safety studies [on MSG] submitted to FDA in support of these applications [for the drug use of MSG] are confidential information. . . . During the nine years since the approval of Glutavine, the FDA has not received any information regarding safety that would cause it to withdraw approval of this application." [7] The FDA files are filled with information on the safety and quality of food additives, pesticides, drugs, and other chemicals that is withheld from the public because it is believed to contain trade secrets.

In all its information-handling the FDA runs on the premise that the agency staff and those they choose to consult are the only people who have any information of value about food safety. Naturally, this makes it privileged information, and the agency goes through great contortions to insure that the information is not freely shared.

Two students from the Nader Summer Study Group investigating food additives at the FDA in 1969 obtained a list of the brand names of all foods containing cyclamates and the amounts they contained. Shortly afterward a third student asked for the same information but did not identify herself as a member of the summer student project. The FDA spokesman she talked to denied that any such list existed.

In a case tried against the FDA under the Freedom of Information Act the plaintiff sought to obtain the names of certain scientists who had recommended to the FDA that certain vitamins were not safe. The FDA avoided releasing the information because they claimed not to know the names of the scientists. It seems unlikely that the agency would rely on the recommendations of individuals whose names it did not know.

A disturbing tendency to dismiss the opinions of individuals who disagree with official FDA policy no matter what their credentials or their arguments crops up repeatedly in the conversation of agency officials. In 1958 Dr. W. C. Hueper, chief of the Environmental Cancer Section, National Cancer Institute, alerted the scientific world and the public to the fact that a number of chemicals long used in food could be the cause of cancer in men. His statements, which had been made to a specialized scientific meeting in Rome, received wide press coverage in the United States in papers ranging from *The New York Times* to *Police Gazette,* which ran a sensationalized analysis of Hueper's remarks in several consecutive issues. Dr. Hueper is generally credited with having alerted scientists to the possibility that environmental chemicals, such as food additives, could be a cause of cancer. His book, *Occupational and Environmental Cancers of the Urinary System,* published by Yale University Press in 1969, raised serious questions about the danger of various food and other environmental chemicals. According to Dr. Hueper, at least one article he prepared while a government official was blocked from publication by the FDA. In a June, 1968, interview with James Turner and Robert Rideout, an FDA press officer, referred to Dr. Hueper as "the man who writes in *Police Gazette.*" It is not unusual for FDA officials to call critics "quacks."

In preparing the Generally Recognized As Safe list, the FDA dismissed most of the critical remarks received from scientists on the grounds that "common sense as well as scientific principle requires us to accept the opinions of some and reject the opinions of others." [9]

The treatment the FDA gives the press is not much better than what it gives to other interested observers. All FDA scientists have been cautioned not to discuss their work with anyone outside the agency until discussing it has been approved internally. On August 12, 1969, the Commissioner ordered all employees to "report all policy conversations with communications media representatives." The vigorous efforts of Louis Rothschild, editor and publisher of *Food Chemical News,* who wrote to Herbert Klein, Nixon's Director of Communications for the Executive branch and to Congressman John Moss, author of the Freedom of Information Act, brought enough pressure against the order to cause it finally to be rescinded. Unfortunately, the new FDA administration under the leadership of Dr. Charles C. Edwards seems to be anxious to continue restricted information policies. When a reorganization of the FDA was announced in 1969, HEW spokesmen said that it had been based on consultation with many consumer representatives. Asked which consumer representatives, they were reluctant to say. Not until Mal Schechter, Washington editor of *Hospital Practice* magazine, and other journalists telegrammed HEW asking who had been consulted was any information made available. It was so scant that Schechter and his associates concluded that little if any consumer consultation had been demonstrated. When Commissioner Charles Edwards held his first staff meeting, he invited selected members of the press to receive a press briefing on the subjects of the meeting. Again, it took an official letter of protest, this time from Stanley Cohen of *Advertising Age,* to call attention to the fact that news is not a commodity to bargain with for favors. As yet it is not clear that the new FDA administration under Edwards intends to avoid the news management habits of its predecessors.

Although heart disease, cancer, stroke, infant mortality, and hunger are all national health problems related to the fact that large numbers of Americans do not get enough wholesome food, the FDA persists in maintaining that there is little wrong with the American food production and distribution system. In its effort to regulate vitamin and mineral supplements, the FDA sought to have all such products labeled: "Vitamins and minerals are supplied in abundant amounts by the food we eat. The Food and Nutrition Board of the National Research Council recommends that dietary needs be satisfied by foods. Except for persons with special needs, there is no scientific basis for recommending routine use of dietary supplements." This label declaration, first required in 1966, represented the FDA's optimistic view of the American food supply. In May, 1967, the FDA issued a fact sheet that said:

FACT: Chemical fertilizers are not poisoning our soil. Modern fertilizers are needed to produce enough food for our increasing population.

FACT: When pesticides on food crops leave a residue, FDA makes sure the amount will be safe for consumers.

FACT: Dr. Goddard has often stated his view . . . "There are some food faddists and quacks who would have you believe the wildest stories about the depletion of our soil, the loss of food values because of modern processing techniques, and a lot of other nonsense. Frankly, it is time we faced facts about our American diet. Our soil is naturally rich and the envy of every nation. Our ability to grow, pack, ship and sell food is a modern marvel because the natural value of the food is not lost in the process. In fact, the reverse is true: foods can get better in the process.

FACT: Dangerous food preservatives were a major concern of the Food and Drug Administration when it began operations on January 1, 1907. Today's scientific knowledge, working through good laws to protect consumers, assures the safety and the wholesomeness of every component of our food supply.[10]

This positive opinion of the American food supply undermines the FDA's regulatory position. It is difficult for the agency to correct a problem that it claims does not exist.

Responsible scientists have criticized every point of the FDA's view of American food. Dr. Barry Commoner, Washington University, St. Louis, has warned that the vast overuse of artificial nitrogen fertilizers may be leading the country into serious health dangers particularly for infants who are highly sensitive to poisoning from nitrogen by-products.[11] Dr. W. H. Sebrell, Chairman of the National Academy of Sciences-National Research Council Committee on Nutrition, demanded that the name of his organization be removed from the vitamin regulations because they distorted the academy's view of the supplement problem. Dr. George Mehren of the Department of Agriculture attacked the assertion that the average American gets all the vitamins and minerals he needs from the food he eats, saying it was not supported by Agriculture Department surveys showing a distinct deterioration in the American diet.[12] Dr. William C. Purdy of the University of Maryland Department of Chemistry has raised serious doubts about the FDA pesticide monitoring program, suggesting that the FDA has little knowledge about how serious the situation may be. Dr. Jean Mayer has said, "We can live perfectly well without additives." [13] The American Medical Association in a joint statement with the National Academy of Sciences suggested that processing was not as positive a procedure as the FDA argues. It recommended that education and research be developed to improve food production, processing, storage, and distribution in order to retain food's essential nutrients and suggested the addition of nutrients to foods ". . . which have a diminished nutritive content as a result of loss in refining or other processing." [14]

The FDA denies that its positions or regulations are controversial. This denial not only undermines the vigor of the agency's regulatory action, but also reveals the agency's attitude that the public is primarily an ignorant and hysterical mob from whom any suggestions of danger must be kept at all cost. Not only does the practice of avoiding bad news as long as possible lull the public into a false sense of confidence, it leads to outraged reactions when the facts about danger finally do become public knowledge. The FDA was unwilling to inform the public clearly about potential dangers from cyclamates as they developed. (At one point in 1965 the director of the FDA's Bureau of Medicine refused to release information on cyclamate danger to a reporter, and in 1968, when the agency warned the public against the excessive use of the additive, it listed the daily recommended intake levels in terms of grams per kilo-gram of body weight, which was of little use to the average citizen.) As a result, the 1969 ban came as a shock to the public and cost millions of dollars to the unprepared food industry. If the public and the food industry are to be spared future shocks, the FDA will have to repudiate its current posture of putting a good face on all potential dangers. It will have to take the public into its confidence in deliberation of pending problems and publicly declare how limited science is in insuring the safety of chemicals.

One of the most enduring charades played by the FDA is its conduct of public hearings. Allegedly called to protect the public interest by allowing controversial questions of food regulation to be resolved by careful public fact-finding procedures, the public hearings have become a gigantic maze through which the FDA tries to sneak its predetermined set of facts unscathed. Rather than using the public hearing to try to determine the magnitude of a possible problem and then propose a method for solving it, the FDA arrives at its conclusions behind closed doors and then convenes a public hearing only when forced to seek endorsement for its position. No public hearing was called when over seventy persons sought to oppose the promulgation of the regulation allowing Coca-Cola, other cola drink manufacturers, and Dr. Pepper to add caffeine to their products without declaring the fact on the label. The FDA dismissed the several correspondents' requests for a public hearing because they were not couched in the proper form. Thus the FDA quietly promulgated, against the desires of a large segment of the public, a regulation allowing deceptive labeling.

An almost incredible sample of FDA bungling began in 1962 when the FDA decided that vitamin supplements and health foods cost the American people an un-necessary $300 million each year. The agency then issued regulations to suppress the "fraud." The most significant item in the regulations was a requirement that each bottle of vitamins be labeled to "inform" Americans that they got all the vitamins they needed from the food they ate. Over fifty thousand people sent cards and letters to the FDA protesting the regulation. The vast

majority of these communications were dismissed by the
FDA Commissioner James Goddard as the work of
"food faddists" and "health food" promoters. As a
result, FDA, after going through various legal maneu-
vers, began hearings on the regulations in the summer
of 1968, in which the FDA took a position opposed by
both representatives of the public and of industry. The
vitamin hearings have become one of the notorious
boondoggles of bureaucratic Washington. With twenty
months of hearings, over twenty-five thousand pages of
testimony, and with almost no scientific support the
FDA moves stoically ahead with its effort to put the
so-called "crepe label" on each bottle of vitamin supplements.

The FDA's vitamin regulations rested on the major
premise that the FDA knows best what is needed for
the country. In this case the FDA was basing its assumptions that the food supply in the United States provided
more than enough of the food value for an average
American on twenty-five-year-old scientific data. The
FDA also claimed to have the support of the National
Academy of Sciences-National Research Council although it had changed the amounts of various vitamins
recommendd by the NAS-NRC. Dr. William Sebrell, the
chairman of the NAS-NRC committee that had made the
recommendation concerning vitamins, denounced the
vitamin regulations. In fact, FDA scientists who were
themselves highly qualified in the field of nutrition found
themselves in opposition to major portions of the regulations. The situation was so seriously distorted that FDA
Commissioner Dr. James Goddard said in recalling it,
"It shook me up that we didn't have enough know-how
to prevent the mistakes that became apparent in the
dietary supplement regulations." [15] He had tried to
track down the man who had changed the NAS-NRC
recommended amounts only to find that immediately
upon filing the report he had left the agency. By this time
the agency was so far down the path of pushing the
regulations that it could not change course.

As the issues developed, the "crepe label" denouncing
the value of supplemental vitamins emerged as the most
important point of controversy. Industry and consumer
representatives wanted it off the label and the FDA

wanted it on. It is striking that Dr. Goddard later said that he "never expected the crepe label to go through" but rather intended it as a "trading point" with industry.[16] Not only were the FDA's scientific contentions over vitamins shoddy but its strategy became distorted. As a result the agency has turned a "trading point" into a major cause, spending over two hundred thousand dollars on it without hesitating to continue complaining about a lack of funds. Unfortunately the FDA is caught in the myth that unless it wins the vitamin fight it will lose face and thereby cause all its other regulatory positions to fall like dominoes. The FDA's mishandling of the vitamin hearings is unusual in that it alienated both the consuming public and a segment of the food industry. Usually FDA positions are worked out enough in advance so that industry is not subjected to excessive hardship. Official explanation for regulatory action from both industry and the FDA often sound exactly alike—that is they are based on the same myths.

Both the FDA and the food industry argue strongly that their efforts are in the public interest. In answer to all critics the FDA and industry present a predictable set of responses. First they argue that the issue of food safety should be left to scientists. This overlooks the very important fact that, as the White House Conference on Food, Nutrition and Health pointed out, "It is not possible to determine with absolute certainty the safety of the ever-increasing number of chemicals added to or present in food." Even the best scientific study will not establish perfect safety. Therefore the issue facing the public and Congress is how much risk the public should be subjected to. This is not a determination to be left to scientists; scientists have only the responsibility to point out the degree of risk that a substance might present. The people of the country speaking through Congress define whether that risk is acceptable or not. It is irresponsible to confuse the debate on the safety of individual chemicals with the question of how much risk is acceptable. Recognizing this fact, the White House Conference Panel on Food Safety urged that consumers not be excluded from deliberations on food safety.

In most cases, once official spokesmen for industry and the FDA do admit that there is a risk in dealing with a particular food chemical, they argue that the benefit of the chemical outweighs the risk. But again they are anxious to keep that judgment within the confines of science. Scientists will judge the ratio and make the decision. Often the public is not even informed that there has been any weighing of risks. Dr. Frederick J. Stare, Chairman of the Department of Nutrition at Harvard University, is one of the leading apologists for the food industry and puts the best possible construction on the use of any food chemical. In his February 8, 1970, column in the Washington *Post* he wrote of cyclamates and monosodium glutamate in terms of the risk-benefit doctrine. Speaking of MSG, Stare said, "Although there are indications that some people may have transient allergic reactions after eating food heavily seasoned with MSG, there is as yet no indication such reactions are widespread. . . . FDA has no intention of banning MSG or restricting the labeling of foods containing the substance. . . . If action is warranted in the future it will come only when and if more definitive scientific evidence becomes available." [17] Stare admits that there may be some problem with MSG but dismisses its importance because there is little to show that the problem would be great. Actually, there is little evidence either way; MSG may be harmful or it may not; nobody knows. Several researchers, including Dr. John Olney of Washington University in St. Louis, Dr. Robert Byck of the Albert Einstein School of Medicine, and Dr. James Adkins of the Food and Drug Administration, have raised serious questions about MSG safety which must be answered if widespread use is to continue. Government investigators have found that Chinese restaurants often use nearly five times as much MSG as necessary to obtain the desired flavor-enhancing effects. In 1969 New York City officially ordered all restaurants to cut down on the amounts of MSG used in food. But Frederick Stare concludes that since we don't know either way we should go ahead and use it until we find out that there is a problem. He takes the position that the slight allergic reaction of a few people is a risk worth taking for the benefit of MSG. There is no indication that those affected would agree, nor is the benefit of MSG spelled out.

It is important to remember that Dr. Stare's argument for continuing the present treatment of MSG means that he believes that the substance is generally recognized as safe and need not go through the official testing procedure required for substances that might cause harm. Like most industry apologists, Stare relies on the fact that the FDA has not moved against a substance as proof of its safety. This is either cynical or naïve. When the FDA says a substance is safe it merely means that for its own reasons—usually not explained—it has chosen to take no action against the substance. A perfect example of the confusion generated by FDA safety determinations was the press reaction to a September, 1969, study by the FDA advisory committee on birth-control pills. On September 5, 1969, the Baltimore *Sun, The New York Times,* and the Washington *Post* all reported the release of the study. The *Post*'s headline said, "Pills Called Safe, More Study Urged." The *Times* said, "Birth Control Pills 'Safe,' Drug Agency Report Says." And the *Sun* said, "U.S. Study Confirms Pill Danger." FDA determinations of safety are legal conclusions, meaning that within the agency's budget, manpower, and priorities it does not consider court action against a substance warranted. Such a determination does not mean that a substance is necessarily free of harm to some individuals. Stare's reliance on the FDA ruling in the MSG case is also misplaced when he argues that no labeling restrictions are being considered by FDA. Currently, MSG can be added to mayonnaise, salad dressing, and French dressing without any label indications. This means those people who may be affected by the substance are unable to know what dressings to avoid. In addition more and more foods now contain MSG.

Dr. Stare is concerned that studies suggesting that MSG causes brain damage in infant rats will undermine confidence in the food supply. Rather than trying to appraise the new test result thoughtfully (no test of MSG on rats between birth and twenty days had been conducted before those in 1968 which showed the damage), Dr. Stare suggests that the evidence from them be withheld from the public. This kind of protectionism actually does more to undermine confidence in the food industry than a frank discussion of the real possibility of danger. When the public discovers, as it inevitably does, that doubts have been raised privately about components of the food supply, it begins to doubt all assertions of safety. A frank recognition of a serious issue when it comes up would be the best way to restore confidence in the many components of the food supply that are actually safe.

The food additive apologists and food industry spokesmen argue that only scientists should be allowed to decide safety and risk-benefit ratio and that the public should have confidence in the FDA's rulings. They attack the scientific methods used in tests that raise doubts about an additive's safety, even though these are the same tests the industry relied on to establish safety.

One major industry attack on tests with displeasing results is that the tests are unrealistic because the doses given are massive. Food industry spokesmen argue that any substance given in large enough doses can cause cancer. This is not true. In a recent study on pesticides, over 120 different pesticide chemicals were injected into infant mice in massive doses and only about 10 per cent caused cancer. HEW Secretary Finch, who is not a scientist himself, repeated the argument when he said that even salt injected into eggs in high enough dosages will cause damage. But eggs injected with salt have not produced embryos with teratogenic—or birth—deformities. At high enough doses, salt can cause irritation to the embryos but not the kind of backbone deformity, change in leg length, or rotating of legs in chickens caused by cyclamates. Even if the food industry's arguments against tests were valid, which they are not, they would only point up the important fact that science is limited. Whatever drawbacks tests for cancer or birth defects might have are strong arguments for limiting reliance on food additives which cannot be adequately tested. Thomas Whiteside, writing on pesticide testing in *The New Yorker* magazine, expressed the situation precisely: "The very coarseness of the screen used in all these tests—that is, the relatively small number of animals involved—means that the bad news that shows up in the data has to be taken with particular seriousness, because lesser effects tend not to be demonstrable at all." [18] To the extent that industry spokesmen are correct in doubting the validity of animal testing, they are also bringing into question all the tests that show the *safety* of additives and are thus contributing to the argument for drastically cutting down on the use of additives.

Taken together, food industry and FDA distortions make accurate public information on food safety, quality, and cost a rare commodity. The keystone myth that ties the FDA and the food industry together is the FDA assertion that the food industry is primarily concerned with advancing the interest of the food consumer. This assertion has been raised to the level of an article of faith as part of the official creed of the FDA. The agency believes that the overwhelming majority of the food producers in the country will voluntarily and without regulation insure that the quality, safety, and cost of the food supply are set at the level most advantageous to the consumer. It assumes that everything is going pretty well in the food industry. The only problems the agency feels it has are generated by an insensitive Congress trying to protect the few small companies that do violate the food law. These myths, largely composed of disjointed and inaccurate fragments of scientific research and regulatory history, are cited in office after office of the FDA as justification for the lack of vigorous protection of the public interest.

11.

Self-Defense

"The FDA has been under continuous investigation by the Congress for almost a decade, and this continuous and contemporaneous surveillance, this Congressional 'oversight' of the FDA goes on, by and large, with little pretense to legislative purpose."

—R. Berles, "The FDA and Congress, 1958–1965," staff report to the Commissioner, October 29, 1965

Shortly after assuming his duties as Secretary of Health, Education, and Welfare in January, 1969, Robert H. Finch sought advice from several of his predecessors. "What did you do for problems before HEW had such a large responsibility for civil rights activity?" he asked. "Well," several answered, "we always had the FDA." The FDA was criticized almost constantly from 1955 onward. Between 1955 and 1970, fourteen major studies of FDA were conducted by citizens' committees, department task forces, and commissioner-appointed FDA evaluation groups. Between 1963 and 1968, the Food and Drug Commissioner or his selected representative was required to appear on the average of once every three weeks before one of sixteen different Congressional committees (excluding appropriations committees) investigating the FDA's involvement in thirty-seven different problem areas. All of the major studies and nearly all of the Congressional investigation focused on one or more of the FDA's failures or weaknesses. The FDA's response to this massive body of criticism—defense and self-justification rather than re-evaluation and reform—has increased the pace of the agency's disintegration.

The first major trauma the FDA suffered at the hands

of Congress was the revelation of a highly questionable
financial conflict of interest involving an important
FDA official. Between 1953 and 1960, while serving as
director of the FDA Antibiotics Division, Henry Welch
edited two private drug journals financially supported by
antibiotic drug manufacturers like Charles Pfizer, Up-
john, Smith, Kline and French, and Abbott Laboratories.
A third journal designed to be edited by Welch failed,
but not until Parke, Davis and Company had spent
$100,000 financing it. In 1959 John Lear of the *Saturday
Review* called attention to the conflict of interest inherent in a situation that allowed a regulatory official to
be financially related to the producers of the product
he was supposed to regulate. FDA officials and the
head of the American Pharmaceutical Manufacturers
Association had questioned Welch about his financial
relationship to the drug companies supporting his journals and received assurances that he accepted only small
honorariums for his editing work. Editors of similar
journals, usually university professors, were then paid
between $3,000 and $6,000 a year. Welch did not tell
his interrogators that, as half owner of the company
that published the journals, he had made $287,142.40
profit from them between 1953 and 1960.[1] But it came
out at hearings held by Senator Estes Kefauver in May
and June 1960 and seriously damaged the agency's
reputation. FDA Commissioner George Larrick, then
in his sixth year of office, had personally liked and
trusted Henry Welch, apparently accepting the division
chief's reassurances without a second thought. It was
not strange for an FDA official to have a close relationship with drug companies. Commissioner Larrick himself
viewed the drug industry as an ally, as he described to
a former FDA official and friend: "Some strange changes
have taken place. . . . We have good friends among
former enemies and in fact quite a new alignment. When
our appropriation bill got in trouble last week our
supporters ranged all the way from the General Federation of Women's Clubs, American Association of University Women and American Home Economics
Association, to the American Drug Manufacturers
Association, American Pharmaceutical Manufacturers

Association, National Association of Retail Druggists, and the Proprietary Association." [2]

On December 9, 1958, George Larrick received the Pharmaceutical Manufacturers Association's annual award for "devoted service to public welfare" because of his "understanding of mutual problems." [3] In 1963 the Commissioner was made an honorary member of the American Pharmaceutical Association. Commissioner Larrick's own involvement with the drug industry made it impossible for him to understand the conflict of interests inherent in Henry Welch's position as chief regulator of antibiotic drugs for the government and chief publicist of the same drugs for industry. But the Commissioner did understand lying, and Henry Welch had lied. Larrick was interested in building a strong FDA of which he could be proud. He liked having the FDA district office headquarters in Detroit named the George P. Larrick Building. But he never took money, and Henry Welch's $287,000 sickened him. Welch had technically not broken any laws, but his action led to new HEW regulations outlawing this kind of conflict-of-interest activity. Because he had not broken the law, Welch was allowed to retire, much to the chagrin of Senator Paul Douglas and Estes Kefauver, who agreed that HEW Secretary Arthur S. Flemming "was derelict in the performance of his duty" to allow the resignation.[4] Men who have observed the FDA closely for the past fifteen years claim that Commissioner Larrick was a broken man after the Welch incident. He retreated to his office where he vacillated on major decisions while spending hours on the detailed preparation of the new FDA laboratory and office building to be located at the foot of Capitol Hill. As a result, much of what went wrong with the FDA during the decade of the 1960's can be traced to Welch's dishonesty and its effect on the Commissioner.

Larrick had never been a powerful leader. After thirty years as an FDA official, he became Commissioner in August, 1954. The promotion had been arranged through the personal efforts of Mr. Bradshaw Mintener, then general counsel of Pillsbury Mills. Mintener, who respected Larrick, had engineered the Eisenhower write-in primary victory in Minnesota and had the ear of the President. Eisenhower agreed to appoint Larrick if Mintener would become Assistant HEW Secretary with special duties for overseeing the FDA. Mintener assented.[5]

In 1955 the First Citizens Committee on the FDA reported on the agency's weaknesses—including deficiencies in budget, facilities, and personnel—and urged the FDA to do "more educational work and seek more cooperation from industry." [6] As the agency began to gain new responsibilities and more money, Larrick engineered a reorganization to handle the growth. In 1956 he divided the agency into bureaus, primarily to get more money for his staff. Unfortunately, the reorganization broke down clear lines of authority, made it difficult for operating personnel to reach the Commissioner with information, and set into motion "jealousies and maneuverings for positions in the hopes that . . . Mr. Larrick's mantle . . . will fall in the 'right' place." [7] Administrative confusion became serious. The 1960 disclosures of Henry Welch's dishonesty added the Commissioner's personal despair to the administrative confusion he had created and killed any chance of effective regulatory action by the FDA under Larrick. The jockeying of subordinates tugging at the "mantle" gained momentum as strand after strand of authority dropped from the Commissioner's hands.

By virtually destroying Commissioner Larrick's confidence and will, Henry Welch wreaked havoc at the FDA. But his destructive legacy reached even farther. One of the most pressing problems facing the FDA and the American public today is the escalating but unwarranted use of many unsafe or ineffective drugs, particularly combination antibiotics. In 1956, as this market was getting started, a large drug company, Pfizer International Incorporated, devised the slogan "a third era in antibiotic therapy" to sell these suspect combinations. The same year Henry Welch organized an International Antibiotic Symposium which was sponsored jointly by the FDA and one of Welch's economic enterprises—Welch being the representative of both his agency and his company. Welch's welcoming address was submitted to copy writers at Pfizer and their slogan was added to it. "It is quite possible that we are now in a third era of antibiotic therapy," said Henry Welch, throwing the weight and prestige of the United States Government behind a questionable set of drugs. They had been called "shotgun therapy," raising doubts that such combinations "can be justified," according to Dr. Maxwell Finland of Harvard Medical School.[8]

The government has not yet been able to unravel the complex medical and legal situation that Welch labored long and hard to help create, and in the meantime people have died or been injured by the drugs Welch advertised and failed to regulate. In his zeal to push the use of antibiotics, the FDA official supported their use in food-producing animals both to control disease and to enhance growth. Again, potential side effects received only minimal consideration. The drive to use antibiotics went so far that it took the positive intervention of another Senate subcommittee, this one chaired by Senator Hubert Humphrey, to block the use of antibiotics as a preservative added directly to human foods. Commissioner Charles Edwards has said, "I don't want to hear about FDA's past failures. We're starting over from scratch. It's a new ball game." Unfortunately, such wishes have little relation to the shaping of effective agency policy. Unless Edwards and his crew review closely every decision about antibiotics—as human drugs, as additives to feeds, and as animal drugs—that was made under the direction of Henry Welch, people will continue to be injured and to die from the excessive and improper use of antibiotics. If Commissioner Edwards ignores the past the FDA will lose its "new ball game."

In 1962 the Humphrey Committee struck another blow at public confidence in FDA when it revealed the slim margin by which Americans had been saved from the tragic aftermath of widespread thalidomide use. The FDA took credit for protecting Americans from the kind of disaster thalidomide had caused in Europe and Canada, but the facts revealed by Senator Humphrey told another story.

The FDA's involvement with the possible marketing of thalidomide began in September, 1960, just three months after Henry Welch's questionable activities were made public. Dr. Frances O. Kelsey, a newly appointed FDA medical officer, was assigned to evaluate the new drug application of the William S. Merrell Company's brand of thalidomide. Company plans called for marketing the drug before the following spring; estimates are that if they had been successful in their hope, about ten thousand American babies would have been born with gross deformities.[9] That Merrell was not successful is due largely to luck.

Dr. Kelsey's predecessor as a medical officer at FDA, Dr. Barbara Moulton, had resigned seven months earlier in protest over the FDA's careless regulation of drugs and food additives. On June 2, 1960, Dr. Kelsey attended a session of the Kefauver drug hearings at which Dr. Moulton dramatically scored FDA, saying that because of lax drug-control policies "people continue to be injured and even to die." The testimony so impressed Dr. Kelsey that she sought out Dr. Moulton and they became friends, regularly discussing, in general terms, the difficulties of protecting the public from drug hazards. As a result of her conversations, her newness on the job, and her dedication, Dr. Kelsey subjected the Merrell application to a standard of review higher than customary for either the agency or the company. Dr. Kelsey held up approval of the drug for the next year, requiring Merrell to improve the quality of the test data that it had submitted. One section had been made up of "meaningless pseudoscientific jargon" and none of the data had revealed the fact that the drug was associated with peripheral neuritis, which Dr. Kelsey discovered in the *British Medical Journal* in February, 1961. These facts suggested a problem to the new medical officer and she moved ahead cautiously. In spite of her caution, and without filing clear information with the FDA, Merrell arranged to have a number of doctors dispense tablets of the drug to patients as part of an FDA-authorized test of its effectiveness. At the end of November, 1961, the American Ambassador in Germany informed the State Department that the births of from 80 to 150 deformed children had been related to thalidomide. The FDA received this dispatch on January 11, 1962. FDA Commissioner George Larrick did not inform Dr. Kelsey of the dispatch nor did he require Merrell to stop its testing program. On December 5, 1961, Merrell had sent a letter to 137 of the doctors distributing the pills warning them not to give it to women of child-bearing age. On January 6, 1962, and February 3, 1962, Dr. Widukind Lenz, who had originally discovered the problem and warned the American Ambassador, reported overwhelming evidence of the deforming effect of the drug in *Lancet,* another British medical journal.

By February, 1962, the thalidomide problem was clearly documented and circulated in public channels. In fact use of the drug had been officially criticized and curtailed in countries such as Australia, England and Germany. Still neither the American company nor the American agency responsible for controlling its use took action to withdraw the drug from testing on patients. Early in the year Dr. Kelsey attempted to obtain from Merrell a complete list of the doctors experimentally dispensing the drug. The company supplied her with fifty-six names. On March 20, 1962, Merrell informed its investigators that a cause-and-effect relationship between the drug and the deformities had been established. The FDA took no action to discover how many pills were already in circulation or to recall them. On April 11, 1962, Dr. Kelsey sought to obtain from Merrell a more complete list of the doctors dispensing thalidomide; this time she received 1,070 names. The final total after a thorough investigation proved to be 1,276. On May 31, 1962, Dr. Kelsey sounded the alarm directly to her superiors with a memorandum laying out the evidence of thalidomide's danger and the fact of its wide experimental distribution in the U.S.

Still the FDA took no action. It was not until after a July 15, 1962, news story in the Washington *Post* that George Larrick finally sent FDA inspectors around the country to retrieve all thalidomide tablets. On August 1, 1962, Commissioner Larrick appeared before the Kefauver Committee and tried to justify his slow response to the danger. After arguing that the evidence of danger had not been conclusive, the Commissioner said, "Nevertheless, the drug is off the market." Thus the FDA made its first unequivocal announcement that the problem had been serious, simultaneous with the announcement that it had been solved. Even at this critical stage when he admitted the need for vigorous action, the Commissioner could not resist the temptation to put the best face possible on the situation. All the pills had not been found. On August 7, 1962, President Kennedy asked all Americans to remove unlabeled pills from their medicine cabinets. On August 23, the FDA again reported that all thalidomide had been found. This time the agency gave a complete tally: it had recovered 2,528,412 tablets, plus liquids and powders containing the drug (25,176 tablets unlabeled) from physicians.

The drug had never been cleared for sale; it had reached the market through the experimental drug program which FDA claimed kept drugs under strict controls. Once again the agency painted a picture rosier than truth. Seven days later, on August 30, the FDA reported that substantial numbers of pharmacies had stocked thalidomide on their shelves, suggesting how far beyond the FDA's control sale of the drug had gone. Ten babies were reported born with deformities as a result of thalidomide obtained in the United States. Senator Humphrey said, in answer to George Larrick's assertion that the American drug control system had protected Americans, "It surely wasn't a triumph of the system, because the system was not geared to catch this sort of development." Senator Mundt added, "I don't think the system was successful at that time because the system was permitting the use of thalidomide."

On August 27, 1962, in response to questions from Senator Humphrey, the drug company Smith, Kline and French reported that between November, 1956, and December, 1957, the company tested thalidomide and decided not to market it because it "offered no clinical advantages over already available compounds." This evaluation of the drug did not square with the beliefs of either foreign drug companies, which were making thousands of dollars selling the drug, or of Merrell, which hoped to make a great deal of money from its pleasant sedative effect. A September 5, 1962, memorandum from Dr. Kelsey suggests a different reason for stopping testing: "It is now obvious that several cases of phocomelia [the thalidomide effect] occurred during the clinical investigations of the drug in this country, one apparently occurring during the brief period of time that Smith, Kline and French had the drug under observation." Since the case was over by this time, no major effort was ever made to fix responsibility for the drug company's failure to report to the FDA the drug's connection with deformity. In a brief follow-up investigation by FDA, two deformed babies born during the Smith, Kline and French tests could not conclusively be related to thalidomide. They had the appearance of thalidomide-caused deformity, but they had additional problems usually not related to thalidomide. However, Dr. Kelsey still believes that knowing of those tests and the births of two deformed babies while she was considering the drug application might have been a great help in getting strong action sooner. She concludes her memorandum saying, "It is chilling to think that under the present laws, several companies could have suspected the teratogenic effect of the drug and quietly dropped their marketing plans without disclosing the hazard. . . . It should be emphasized that the hazard of [the FDA] passing, through inadequate clinical testing, a drug like thalidomide, might within a short period of time destroy more lives than have been saved by so-called wonder drugs." [10]

Doubts about the FDA's independence from the industries it regulates were intensified by industry statements before the Interstate and Foreign Commerce Committee of the House of Representatives in August, 1962. Industry successfully blocked FDA access to industry records on the grounds that their secrets would be passed on to rival companies employing FDA inspectors in the future.

Unable to view the mounting concern of Congress as a warning to change its policies, the FDA took a defensive position, claiming it was being victimized. In 1962, as criticism mounted, the agency quietly sought to insert into the drug reform amendments language which would block Congress from access to agency files. The attempt had passed in the House, but failed in the Senate when Dr. Barbara Moulton pointed it out to Senator Kefauver. Instead of seeking to protect the public more vigorously from health hazards, the agency

sought to protect itself more vigorously from embarrassment. This attitude was summed up in an October 29,
1965, memorandum to the Commissioner on the FDA
and Congress:

The FDA has been under continuous investigation by the
Congress for almost a decade, and this continuous and contemporaneous surveillance, this congressional "oversight" of
the FDA goes on by and large with little pretense of legislative purpose. The Congress is now prepared to advise and
consent at any and all stages of executive decision-making.
. . . It is the attempts to make headlines for their own sake,
outside of any legislative requirements, to haze and harass
the agency as a sort of public whipping boy, in order to cap-
ture the attention of the news media, that does not arouse
the sympathies of those, at least, who are aware of the neces-
sities of the legislative process.[11]

In October, 1962, the Second Citizens Committee
Report on the FDA, though marred by a strong industry
bias and seeking more freedom from regulation for the
food and drug industries, documented accurately the
serious administrative deterioration of the FDA. But
the report argued that the FDA and industry should be
brought into even closer co-operation. The Kefauver
and Humphrey hearings and the Fountain hearings on
prescription drugs (being held in the House by Congressman Fountain of North Carolina) revealed that the
FDA was in almost complete disorder. It had so lost
sight of its obligations, was so lacking in professional
scientific expertise, and so defensive about its failures
that no effective regulation of major industries was
being conducted. Some FDA "old hands" recall the
Larrick era with a joke popular among agency personnel
at the time. Referring to the deteriorated situation in
agency drug-testing activities, they had said "try it on
the Commissioner. If he doesn't get sick, pass it." On
April 15, 1963, *Drug Trade News* reported an interview
with Senator Humphrey in which the Senator accurately
described FDA disintegration and its cause. "Mr. Humphrey has become convinced from evidence already
adduced before his subcommittee that FDA is in a mess
administratively. He has said it needs dynamic new
leadership. He believes Mr. Larrick has failed to provide
this leadership and must bear the responsibility for

FDA's failures. . . . He [Humphrey] believes that at the appropriate time he [Larrick] should retire." For the next three years the hearings into drug practices continued, revealing case after case of administrative breakdown in agency drug-control activities.

Then in April, May, and June, 1965, Senator Edward Long of Missouri interjected a new issue into the controversy. His subcommittee of the Senate Judiciary Committee revealed that FDA used the most elaborate snooping devices of any government agency. He showed that in some cases convictions of offenders were based on violations of the law by FDA agents and directed at relatively minor crimes and criminals. His report made objective observers doubt the FDA's maturity and responsibility as a law enforcement agency.[12] Finally, in October, 1965, Commissioner Larrick resigned from his job, effective January 1, 1966. He left the agency in November, 1965, and Winton Rankin became Acting Commissioner.

Solomon Friend, a well-known food and drug attorney, reports that Larrick wanted Winton Rankin to succeed him as Commissioner. "Whatever influence I have I'll use for him," Larrick is supposed to have said.[13] Rankin rose to power as Larrick lost confidence and control. His ability to obscure, avoid, or confuse issues before Congressional committees provided the line of defense needed to minimize the FDA's embarrassment at repeated revelations of failure. Rankin worked on the theory that Congress had limited time and resources that could be stretched to the point of ineffectiveness by delays and cleverly worked denials. He would delay the release of documents to committees seeking them, answer specific questions in a ponderous, rambling, and imprecise manner, and if necessary purposely create an impression exactly the opposite of the truth to gain time. Each hour spent with a Congressional committee was viewed as a trial of the moment to be gotten through with the least embarrassment to the agency. If embarrassment could not be avoided, Rankin sought to deflect it from the Commissioner and himself to some other person.

Rankin's closest competitor in the battle for the Commissioner's confidence was Deputy Commissioner

John P. Harvey, who, like Rankin and Larrick, had worked his way to the top of the FDA from the ranks of the inspectors. Harvey was the Commissioner's closest adviser until the Fountain Committee's 1965 drug safety hearings caught him in a conflict of interest charge and his reputation was ruined. Harvey claimed to have dissociated himself from all decisions involving Abbott Laboratories because his brother was an officer of Abbott, but in one important drug recall case involving a sizable investment of Abbott's, the Fountain Committee discovered that at least one very important memorandum had gone directly to him.[14] Harvey had the reputation for impeccable honesty within FDA circles but could not withstand the revelation of his apparent involvement in a conflict of interest and he left the FDA shortly after the hearing. His departure cleared the way for Rankin to become Deputy Commissioner. But when Larrick left the agency in late 1965, Rankin was blocked for the job of Commissioner, chiefly because of pressure from Congress. Dr. James Goddard got the job instead, but Rankin continued to consolidate his control over the agency. Goddard received the job on the theory that a "scientist" in the job would do more for the agency's image than a "cop." He did do a great deal for the image of the agency, keeping it constantly on the newspapers' front pages. But he felt that he had to have help from someone familiar with the agency to keep its internal affairs running smoothly. He appointed Rankin as his deputy.

As a result, the internal workings of the agency fell mainly into Rankin's hands. He gained control of the promotion process. He administered the agency's management-training program, including a one-year management institute course, attendance at which became a virtual prerequisite for promotion; it gave Rankin an opportunity to evaluate the "students," particularly on the basis of their agency loyalty. Rankin saw to it that known critics, particularly those who had co-operated with Congress, were not promoted. Maurice Kinslow was placed in charge of Congressional relations and continued the strategy of foot-dragging and obfuscation with Congress, performing for Rankin essentially the same function as Rankin had performed for Larrick.

The near-unanimous opinion of FDA personnel and observers interviewed during the 1969 Nader Summer Study was that the FDA deteriorated significantly and rapidly under Goddard's leadership, largely because of Rankin's iron grip over internal workings of the agency. Goddard left in July, 1968, and his Director of the Bureau of Medicine, Dr. Herbert Ley, took over the agency. Rankin continued to run the agency internally, it continued to deteriorate, and Ley left in December, 1969. This time Rankin's obstructions and failures were clearly identified and he was removed from the agency with Ley.

The most striking fact about the FDA's obstructionist and unresponsive attitude in Congress was its success. By wasting Congressional time and avoiding important questions, the FDA leadership was able to minimize awareness of the extent of its incompetence and its failure to protect the public interest. The Congressional committees looking at drug failures dealt only super-ficially with the problems they examined. (For example, the problem of antibiotic combinations is still haunting the FDA with reports of deaths and injury from drugs said by the National Academy of Sciences to be inef-fective for their claimed purposes.) And the committees failed to look seriously at anything outside of the drug field. In spite of the fact that a national debate raged over the use of pesticides in the early 1960's, no Con-gressional committee seriously tried to piece together the extent of FDA failure to perform its pesticide con-trol duties. In spite of the fact that the 1958 and 1960 additive amendments had been passed to give power to the FDA to control chemical additives to food, no Con-gressional committee sought an explanation of how effectively the agency was doing. In short, by dragging out the drug investigation, FDA spokesmen like Rankin were able to avoid exposure in the other areas of FDA responsibility. In avoiding embarrassment they also covered up a total breakdown of FDA food protection policies equal to the breakdown in the drug area.

The FDA success in avoiding a close look at its food protection activities must be recognized as one of the great victories of bureaucratic in-fighting. The FDA effectively obscured for the Congress and the public the fact that food protection and drug control are inextricably bound together. Henry Welch's decisions on antibiotics were crucial in getting those drugs into food-producing animals. The fact that he acted as the prime apologist of the antibiotic drug industry, convinced of the drugs' value and doubting their problems, in itself should cause a thorough review of the entire practice of adding antibiotics to animals or their feed. Animal feed amendments were adopted in 1968, but like the food additive and pesticide control laws, they assume that there is a need for the chemicals they are designed to regulate. It is this assumption which the FDA should be evaluating. Dr. Moulton, whose testimony about drug control failure before the Kefauver Committee so damaged and enraged agency officials, left her job not over the question of drugs but rather over the way in which the agency was preparing the Generally Recognized As Safe list of food additives, which was supposedly authorized by the law but which grew to proportions far beyond what the law intended. Dr. Moulton complained to the Kefauver Committee that the list had been prepared without the serious consideration of potential health hazards associated with several of the items on it.[15] John Harvey, whose brother was an officer of Abbott Laboratories, did not exclude himself from a crucial decision on cyclamates, the prime producer of which was Abbott Laboratories. In 1965 he reversed the long-standing FDA policy that sugar and cyclamates could not be used in the same product. This crucial decision, which had been sought by several small and less well-connected companies earlier, made it possible for the industry to produce food products containing cyclamates that were not intended solely for use as special foods for diabetics, causing a major economic breakthrough in the dietetic food business. Harvey probably made his decisions with the best and most honest intentions. But they did raise serious questions. All of these indications of flaws in the FDA's actions in the food field came out simultaneously with the breakdown of the FDA's drug-control activities, but none was actively pursued by the Congressional committees investigating the FDA. They had their hands full trying to pry information on drugs loose from the reluctant and slippery FDA bureaucracy.

Unfortunately, Commissioner Charles Edwards, in charge of the agency since the middle of December, 1969, seems unable or unwilling to change the pattern of the FDA relationship with Congress. Too many of the old Rankin-trained bureaucracy are still in key agency positions. In the agency's first Congressional appearance after Edwards took over, the same old diversions, denials, and distortions studded the testimony. Maurice Kinslow was one major FDA spokesman on that occasion.

Commissioner Edwards seems determined to ignore the past mistakes of the agency, calling them ancient history not important in his "new ball game." But perpetuating the old FDA attitude toward Congress will destroy any hope of effectiveness the agency still has. It must convince Congress that it is responsible if it is going to receive support for the additional authority that it must have to be effective. As part of its campaign to impress Congress with its new vigor and responsibility, the FDA should seek a vigorous and responsible expansion of its authority. In the field of labeling it should propose legislation to require the labeling of all chemical additives to food and prepare a consumer dictionary of food additives so that consumers can be meaningfully informed of what they are eating. All foods should be labeled grade A, B, or C, for example, so that consumers know when they are paying for quality and when they are paying for advertising. They should also be labeled so that the percentage of the most valuable constituent present in the food is clearly identifiable. This would mean labeling 30 per cent meat in frankfurters, 10 per cent orange juice in orange juice drink, or 10 per cent beef in Beef Stroganoff, if that is the case. This kind of labeling would enable the consumer to use his food dollar effectively.

In addition to comprehensive additive labeling laws, the agency should seek more control over additives. The Delaney Clause should be expanded to exclude from the food supply any substance that causes birth defects or genetic damage, as well as cancer in animals, until it is established that such additives will not adversely affect people. Senator Gaylord Nelson of Wisconsin has introduced a bill to accomplish that goal. This Nelson bill also abolishes the Generally Recognized As Safe list in accordance with the observation of the White House Conference on Food, Nutrition and Health Food Safety Panel that long usage is no longer a sure proof of safety. (The panel did not go as far as the Nelson bill but did call for much stronger review procedures of the GRAS list.) A second Nelson bill seeks to set up an FDA testing facility for all drugs. The concept of this bill could well be applied to both pesticides and food additives. The FDA would have a laboratory that conducts evaluation testing of chemicals but whose cost is paid for by the industry seeking the test.

An alternative plan, perhaps more acceptable because it is less bureaucratic, would be legislation developing a chemical testing referral board. Such an organization could be established within the FDA and have the authority to refer requests for testing from the chemical industry to independent laboratories. For example, a company like Abbott seeking to get an evaluation of a chemical like cyclamate would contact the board with a request for testing. The board then would refer the chemical, according to a set of clearly defined guidelines, to an independent laboratory. As the system now stands, the company goes directly to the laboratory; the result is that an unhealthy business relationship tending toward bias builds up between the test lab and the company that retains it. The referral board would avoid this close business contact. The guidelines for operation should include a rotation system that blocks any single laboratory from testing all or even a majority of a given company's chemicals. Also, the guidelines should include accreditation for the laboratories. Presumably, the application presented by FDA-accredited and policed laboratories would be in the proper form and be submitted by the proper procedure. (Currently, approximately one half of all food additive petitions are rejected because they are in improper form or lack proper support.) The referral board would actually benefit the development of the chemical industry and would help, not hinder, the marketing of products that are safe and effective and necessary for their announced purpose.

Information that accurately describes the safety and quality of food products should be available to the consumer. Therefore, in accordance with the recommendation of the White House Conference Food Safety Panel, all TV or radio food advertising that makes claims of safety or nutrition should be filed with a Federal agency (the FDA would be appropriate) prior to broadcasting. This would enable the regulatory agencies to enforce laws against false advertising already in existence and to head off possible violations before advertisers have gone to the tremendous expense of buying and using broadcast time.

There are important methods for informing and protecting the public from potential dangers related to food. The frozen food industry, for instance, could add to its package a device which has now been developed to indicate whether or not the package has been thawed since packing. A small button on the package changes color when the food inside thaws and does not change back if it is refrozen. Some scientists are concerned about the spoilage of baby food if it is opened prior to the time of purchase. A cover which indicates food that has been opened after packaging but prior to purchase has been developed but is not now in widespread use. All drug and vitamin bottles should have the now available cap that cannot be opened by children. These kinds of safety and information devices should be required to give more protection to the consumer and his pocketbook. The FDA should seek additional legislative authority to make such requirements.

In the pesticide area, the FDA should seek legislation to shift the current burden of responsibility for pesticide control. At present, the Pesticide Regulation Division of the Department of Agriculture certifies and registers pesticides on the basis of its judgment as to whether the pesticide will actually work; the division then seeks an advisory opinion from the FDA about the safety of the pesticide, an opinion which it is not bound to follow. Now that the concern about pesticides has shifted from doubts about their effectiveness to doubts about their safety, the authority to certify and register pesticides should be given to the FDA. It should make the determination on the basis of safety, with an advisory opinion from the Department of Agriculture about the effectiveness of the pesticide—an opinion that the FDA should not be bound to follow. In this relatively easy way Congress can legislatively recognize the important concerns about pesticide safety which have until now been minimized.

In the field of enforcement, the FDA needs the authority to conduct much more thorough and vigorous inspection of food-producing facilities—including the authority to inspect plant records showing what ingredients and additives are used. The legal subcommittee of the Food Safety Panel of the White House Conference recommended that the drug plant inspections system be applied to foods. This would require registering the plant with FDA, allowing complete access to all records, including complaint files, batch formulas, and quality control records, and a regular inspection every two years in addition to a number of other important requirements. The recommendation was not adopted by the full panel but should receive further consideration.

These legislative goals are a modest beginning which, if achieved, could open the possibility of serious considerations of the more fundamental problems of food protection and FDA failure. Each of the steps will be vigorously opposed by the food-producing industries which have a vested interest in the current legal arrangements. The FDA could make a grand contribution to its credibility and effectiveness if it forthrightly and vigorously embraced these goals. Unfortunately, the current attitude of the agency is the safe, stand-pat, defensive caution that has led it into repeated mistakes. Unless the new Commissioner seeks new advisers knowledgeable about consumer concerns in the food and drug field (at present he seems unwilling even to make the attempt), the next decade will be a repetition of the last.

12.

The Commissioner

"There are perhaps few men who can for any great length of time enjoy office and power without being more or less under the influence of feelings unfavorable to the faithful discharge of their public duties. Their integrity may be proof against improper considerations immediately addressed to themselves, but they are apt to acquire a habit of looking with indifference upon the public interest and of tolerating conduct from which an unpracticed man would revolt."

—President Andrew Jackson,
First Inaugural Address, 1828

FDA Commissioner Charles C. Edwards is rapidly becoming a practiced man. In three interviews with the author conducted on December 22, 1969 (one week after he took office), January 26, 1970, and February 2, 1970 (the date a major FDA reorganization became official), it was possible to watch the Commissioner's admirable determination to whip the FDA into shape dissolve. The erosion of conviction that results from constant interaction with a professional bureaucracy that values effective self-defense above sacrifice in the public interest has begun to take hold of the "new" FDA. The three interviews were disturbingly like a similar set of interviews, also conducted by the author, with Dr. Herbert Ley while he was Commissioner of the FDA.

The disintegration of resolve that grips each successive FDA Commissioner is best described against this background of bureaucratic insensitivity. The insensitivity has very practical causes. Though charged with the duty of public protection, even the best-intended FDA official must respond to the realities of everyday life at the office. These realities discourage public-spirited action. Two weeks after being ousted as FDA Commissioner, Dr. Herbert Ley told Richard Lyons of *The New York Times* that he had been under "constant, tremendous, sometimes unmerciful pressure" from drug companies regulated by the FDA.[1]

In August, 1969, former Associate Commissioner Kenneth Kirk told *Life* magazine writer Jack Newfield that both the White House and the office of Georgia Senator Richard Russell called the FDA in 1965 to express "interest" in the outcome of the Atlanta-based Coca-Cola Company's campaign to avoid labeling caffeine on its cola product. The campaign succeeded despite nearly unanimous opposition from the FDA staff members. The various FDA food standards and exemptions now in force read like a catalogue of favors to special industrial interests. The red coloring used in maraschino cherries is excluded from all other foods. The presence of MSG must be listed on all products except mayonnaise, French dressing, and salad dressing. Altogether, the fine tailoring of food standards in response to special pleaders has allowed the use of 485 food chemicals and other ingredients without their inclusion on product labels. Pressure from special interests and its results are a constant reality which all FDA officials must routinely consider.

Hundreds of conferences between FDA officials and industry representatives take place every month. The participants decide on pesticide tolerances, determine the use of food additives, exempt certain food chemicals from the usual regulations, and establish food standards. Never is an interest other than that of industry presented to the FDA officials in these conferences. Thousands of decisions are made quietly, confidentially, and without any direct supervised reference to consumer desires. Hearings on the regulation exempting colas and Dr. Pepper from caffeine labeling were never held in spite of over fifty letters (an unusually high expression of interest on a food standard) opposing the exemption. Dozens of items were added to the Generally Recognized As Safe list in spite of specific objections from one or more scientists. In one meeting representatives

of the G. P. Scheerer Corporation, which sold food to
the Sears, Roebuck Company, argued that the GRAS
list should be expanded because of "the attitude of Sears,
Roebuck. That firm does not want anything but GRAS
items on its private-label products." Little was said by
the company about safety. In 1961 Fred Mack and Ed
Harding, attorneys for General Foods and Kellogg, respectively, met with FDA official M. R. Stevens to discuss
a certain labeling requirement. Stevens' memorandum
of that meeting suggests the nature of these closed-door
encounters. "He, Mr. Harding, frankly stated, however,
if we were going to have a negative viewpoint about the
whole affair and felt we could not give them a favorable
answer, he would rather just reach his own decision
without asking for a formal opinion and go ahead and
declare it in that fashion with the feeling and the hope
we would do nothing about it. He asked which approach
I felt was desirable." [2]

Meeting after meeting with industry attorneys and
representatives are recorded in FDA files. Rarely is
there an indication of meetings with consumers. Rarely
is there a statement supporting the consumer interest.
Rarely is there a record of consultation with a critic of
the FDA or the food industry. As a result of this massive and routine interaction with industry, FDA officials
are well informed about industry problems, particularly
aware of industry strength, and organized to cope
with industry dissatisfaction. The FDA cannot effectively
protect a public interest that it does not routinely attempt to discover and therefore is unable to define.

An instinct for protecting the bureaucratic flank
against probable pressure and a familiarity bred by constant awareness of potential industry opponents leads
most FDA bureaucrats away from strong regulatory
action. The stick of possible conflict with industry is
accompanied by the carrot of a possible job in industry.
Their bias is against strong action because it invariably
causes big problems—particularly for the bureaucrat.
An easy to understand but self-defeating rationale is
used to justify this purely practical caution. The FDA
staff constantly tell themselves that theirs is the primary
consumer-protection agency in the country, and that
anything that injures the agency injures the consumer.

Therefore, they argue, their first job is to protect the agency. Using this rationale, they are led to weigh the importance of the public interest against the power of those who oppose it. The public interest then becomes a token to be bargained in negotiation rather than a standard to be protected against all violators.

When Dr. Edwards took over as Commissioner all he knew about were the failures, he knew nothing of their causes. Like Dr. Ley before him, he vowed to clean up the place. In their first encounters with a Nader investigator both were eager, confident, and willing to risk a great deal in a major effort to get an obviously misguided agency back on the right track. Dr. Ley spoke of "finding where the bodies are buried," and getting all the facts that could lead to a cleanup. Dr. Edwards said, "There are a lot of guys behind the drapes waiting to shoot my head off," and insisted he was eager to engage in battle. Both men were well aware that they were in a tough spot where competent and well-intended men had failed before them. By the second interview, each man had been subject to several weeks of eroding interaction with the bureaucracy. Dr. Ley, less secure though still eager for reform, asked Kenneth Kirk, Associate Commissioner for Compliance, to sit in on the interview to gain the advantage of Kirk's more than thirty years experience with the FDA. Each endorsement of reform Ley suggested during the interview was blunted by Kirk. When the Commissioner agreed that a freer public information policy could easily be followed, Kirk reminded him that all FDA files contain "trade secrets" and therefore cannot be made accessible to the public. When Ley showed interest in the fact that certain food additives had been unnecessarily exempted from regulation, Kirk dampened that interest with all the soothing arguments that have issued from the FDA since 1907. Finally, when warned that food and not drugs could possibly be the major problem facing the administration, Ley agreed, saying that he had, at the urging of his staff, planned a trip to each district and would probably look at several food plants. Such a gesture is typical of bureaucratic superficiality. It gives the appearance of looking while assuring that nothing will be discovered. A brief visit to offices manned by bureaucrats practiced in disguising problems is unlikely to reveal basic flaws.

In *his* second interview, Edwards was already as much a captive of the bureaucracy as Ley had been at his second interview. He announced that he intended to appoint Maurice Kinslow, Rankin's protégé and a long-time apologist for FDA failure, as his Assistant Commissioner for Program Co-ordination. Kinslow had served as special assistant to the Commissioner and chairman of the Commissioner's reorganization committee during the six weeks of change-over. Edwards, inexperienced in the treachery of bureaucratic Washington, had been impressed by the ease with which the old hand had led him through the perils. "Three times in the last two weeks I had important decisions I wanted to announce and each time Kinslow pointed out somebody hiding behind the curtain waiting to shoot me down. He's too important, I need him." It would be interesting to know what major decisions Commissioner Edwards had thought so important, what arguments were used to change his mind, and what interests were sacrificed by that change.

In one subsequent interview with Edwards and several with Ley, both men showed the onset of the final stages of bureaucratic paralysis. Each man had lost the ability to distinguish his own personality from that of the agency. Any critic of the agency was a critic of the man leading it. Any failure of the agency was a personal failure which had to be justified and not merely acknowledged as an honest agency mistake requiring immediate attention and correction. So Dr. Ley acknowledged that the evidence he had presented to prove that MSG was safe had, in large part, not really existed, but he still insisted that his conclusion had been correct. He publicly claimed not to have seen the chicken embryos deformed by cyclamates, but privately said he'd seen them but "didn't understand their significance." And he justified the fact that he had not issued a fat labeling regulation, in spite of urging such regulations as head of the FDA's Bureau of Medicine two years earlier, because "things look different from the Commissioner's office." By his seventh week in office, Dr. Edwards had begun to move in the same direction. Presented with a serious indictment of the present caliber of science in FDA district offices, including strong evidence to support the charges, he vigorously repeated his public statement of a few days earlier saying, "I am not interested in dwelling on alleged past failures of this agency." He repeated several times, "These are my decisions and I will have to live with them. If I don't make it then I don't make it." And finally he pointed out that at the urging of his staff he did plan to make a trip to the various district offices to see their condition. If he continues in the direction in which he has started, some time in the next twelve to eighteen months, between the middle and the end of 1971, Dr. Edwards will go the way of Dr. Ley.

Such a tragedy should not be allowed to happen. Dr. Edwards' early resolve must be restored. Some of the intolerance of the unpracticed man that causes outrage at the violation of the public interest must be allowed to triumph over bureaucratic caution. This can only be done if the FDA is opened up to the expression of sentiment from the public so that its future decisions can be arrived at by the joint effort of consumers and producers, citizens and scientists. If the agency is allowed to remain the closed preserve of an isolated Commissioner, privy only to the counsel of Kinslow-type bureaucrats, it, the Commissioner, and the public interest are doomed. Dr. Edwards has made halting steps toward salvation of the organization. He has announced his intention to appoint a consumer advisory group to the Commissioner and has begun looking for people to serve on it. (For some reason even this beginning step may be in danger. A plan to establish two advisory committees, one for drugs and one for foods, is being suggested by some advisers. Such a division would be an unfortunate waste of resources and energy. The same representatives of consumer opinion can easily serve in both areas.) Privately, Dr. Edwards has indicated a willingness to appoint a special assistant for consumer affairs, a person with the confidence of the consuming public, but he has made only limited efforts to find such a person. As slight as these moves toward citizen involvement in the agency are, they do provide at least some hope that under its new Commissioner the FDA might place defense of the public interest ahead of protection of the food industry.

But there are far clearer indications that the change will be superficial. The crucial focal point of the FDA reorganization ordered by Secretary Finch at the end of 1969 was the removal of Deputy Commissioner Winton Rankin and Associate Commissioner Kenneth Kirk. More than any other aspect of the reorganization, their removal from office suggested that HEW, embarrassed by the declining prestige and continuous failure of FDA, seriously intended to reform the agency. Therefore it was with shock and dismay that FDA observers both inside and outside the agency learned that as one of his first acts newly appointed Commissioner Edwards had recalled Rankin to his job. "I've got to have somebody," Edwards said in the December 22, 1969, interview. Only after members of the HEW reorganization team were informed of this attempt, however unwitting, to undermine their major reform, was Rankin permanently moved out of the FDA.

Although Rankin is gone, Dr. Edwards' reliance on Maurice Kinslow continues. Depending on Kinslow's advice will insure short-term bureaucratic survival at the cost of long-term public interest. And Commissioner Edwards' choice of Larry Pilot for special assistant reveals how slender are the hopes that he will institute real change at the FDA. A twenty-nine-year-old lawyer and pharmacist who came from the job of special assistant to Assistant HEW Secretary Egeberg, Pilot previously spent three years on the staff of the American Pharmaceutical Association and three years with the Pharmaceutical Manufacturers Association. While this former association with the major drug industry lobby groups should not disqualify him for service with the FDA, it is not unfair to assume that he does not come to the agency with a consumer bias. He represents a familiar career pattern in which the final goal and reward is a high-paying job in the drug industry. Kinslow's and Pilot's backgrounds, combined with the Commissioner's own record of several years' service in the American Medical Association, cause justifiable apprehension for consumer welfare, particularly when the agency is part of a national Administration which, in two bruising battles, has allowed the drug industry and the AMA to block Secretary Finch's choice of Dr. Warren Knowles for Assistant Secretary for Health and Science, and former Commissioner Ley's choice of Dr. John Adriani for Director of the FDA Bureau of Medicine. Perhaps Dr. Edwards was making a keynote remark in his first public statement, when he said that the FDA should work more closely with industry.

The first regulatory decision signed by Dr. Edwards was ominous, too. During Christmas week of 1969 he delivered a present to the producers of food containing cyclamates by signing into the regulations new labeling requirements that paved the way for foods with cyclamates to reach the marketplace labeled as "drugs" in spite of their unproved safety and in spite of the Delaney Clause, under which cyclamates were withdrawn. So the Commissioner who promised to work more closely with industry as his first regulatory action laid the groundwork to save part of the food industry $100 million in already packaged goods by allowing a substance which has caused cancer in animals to continue in our food supply.

When it is also realized that as part of the HEW reorganization the FDA was removed from the Consumer Protection and Environmental Health Service (CPEHS), which had exposed some of FDA's most gross distortions of fact and law, the future of the consumer interest becomes more bleak. It is true that CPEHS intervened far too much in the day-to-day operations of the FDA. However, it was not necessary to remove the FDA from CPEHS to eliminate their duplication of work. As bad as CPEHS might have appeared, it did force review of the FDA's pesticide monitoring program. It did force a NAS study of cyclamates. It provided an opportunity for routine questioning of FDA decisions at a level below that of the Secretary. The relationship of the two agencies could have been redefined, allowing the FDA to report directly to the Secretary of HEW but requiring CPEHS to oversee and co-ordinate FDA activities with other environmental agencies under its control. This arrangement would have had the significant advantage of subjecting significant problems to varying points of view, providing the Secretary with more than one set of information and one outlook upon which to base his decisions. The removal of the FDA from CPEHS supervision—a move Winton Rankin had campaigned for—has serious negative implications for consumer protection.

The HEW reorganization included the removal of two CPEHS information officers, Thomas Williams and Paul Schutte, for political reasons, who were both knowledgeable about FDA operations and who had steered the FDA away from several policy blunders. The elimination of any meaningful HEW overseeing of the FDA shows with deadly accuracy the direction of the much-touted reorganization.

The next twelve months of the FDA's life will be perhaps the most telling in its confused history. More than once in this century the agency has been the focal point that made and broke powerful political interests; now, with the battle for a clean environment underway, with President Nixon already singling out the agency for specific attention in his consumer message (something rare in Presidential messages), the FDA is clearly going to be at the center of major political battles once again. In this context, the beginning of the "new" FDA is ominous.

Fortunately, Dr. Edwards' current entrapment by old bureaucrats and old bureaucratic ways is not necessarily permanent. During the next twelve months it will be well within the Commissioner's power to make decisions that can reverse the course of FDA history. Of course he will have to have the support of his political superiors, HEW Secretary Finch and President Nixon. But if the active leaders of the movements to clean up the environment and protect the consumer recognize the crucial role the FDA plays in their campaigns, they can bring the kind of public pressure on the President and the Secretary that will cause them to support the proper decisions of the FDA Commissioner.

The FDA is charged with the enforcement of the most potent set of laws designed to control the input of chemical pollutants into the environment. It regulates drugs, cosmetics, pesticides, and food additives. Any effort to clean the dangerous chemicals out of the environment must focus in great part on cleaning up the FDA. Too often the agency has expended its limited resources in untangling the details of a complicated regulatory decision that deals with a single specific problem such as the safety of individual GRAS-list items, the evaluation of food additives petitions, or the setting of a specific pesticide tolerance. What is needed is a basic reorientation of the agency's approach to its major programs, particularly those affecting food.

Specifically, the FDA should face up publicly to what it knows privately about food additives regulation—that the program is a mess. It should establish as its basic guideline the observation of the Food Safety Panel of the White House Conference on Food, Nutrition, and Health: "It is essential that the chemical environment be controlled as completely as possible. The traditional or long-continued use of any additive can no longer be considered to be sufficient evidence of safety." With this statement as its guide, the agency should move to gain control of food additives. It should recommend that Congress abolish the Generally Recognized As Safe concept and the list that goes with it. In the meantime, it should by regulation drastically decrease the number of items on the present list, removing each chemical about which there is even a single doubt. Next, it should explore procedures to decrease the current rate of food additive petitions submitted by industry which do not meet requirements (almost 50 per cent), and break down the close relationship between developers of food additives and the laboratories that test them. This could be accomplished by establishing a referral board within the agency. Similar procedures could easily be developed for color additive and pesticide testing. Of course the FDA must recommend the extension of the Delaney Clause principle to those chemicals that cause birth defects or genetic damage in animals. None should be allowed in human food until proven safe.

The food standards program must be treated in the same over-all way if any meaningful reforms are to be achieved. Again, the White House Conference provided the basic guideline for labeling, the prime function performed by food standards. In addition, the current quibbling about what consumers think a good chemical name on the label means should be eliminated by the simple

expedient of creating a food chemical dictionary or
compendium—also recommended by the White House
Conference. Made easily available to consumers, the
compedium could list in alphabetical order all the chemical names that appear on any can of food and explain
their functions and any possible dangers in consuming
them.

The most important general policy that the FDA must
adopt was also enunciated by the White House Conference: "Inasmuch as the consumer is the primary consideration in deliberations on the safety and adequacy
of the food supply, the consumer must be represented on
panels convened to examine these problems." [3]

In everything the FDA does, whether it be re-evaluation of the food additive program, reorientation of the
food standard procedure, preparation of a food additives
manual, or establishment of a board of referral, the consumer must be part of the decision-making process. To
assure that consumers are not bypassed in the rush of
day-to-day activities, the Commissioner must immediately appoint his Consumer Council and with their aid
and the aid of external consumer advocates find a suitable special assistant for consumer affairs. In addition,
the FDA should make available to the press and the
public the memoranda currently prepared by agency
officials after each of the dozens of meetings every
day with special-interest representatives trying to influence agency actions.

All of this activity must be undertaken immediately if
the direction of deterioration at the FDA is to be reversed. The Food and Drug Administration has not
effectively protected the food supply from pollutants
which are potentially dangerous to the American consumer. In addition, it has not begun to fulfill or even
to recognize its role in combating the alarming effects of
hunger and malnutrition that stem from the economically limited availability of a safe and wholesome food
supply. The first three months of Commissioner Edwards'
administration indicate that the new Commissioner's
philosophy is "business as usual." The same mistakes,
made for the most part by the same people, appear to
be the future of this crippled regulatory agency. If the
agency is effectively to meet the challenge posed by the

need to provide better, safer, and more abundant food to the American public, it will need additional resources —legal, economic, and scientific. However, it is impossible to carry additional sand in a torn sack. Without new imaginative leadership, giving the FDA additional resources will be throwing good money after bad.

Dr. Barbara Moulton pointed out at the Kefauver hearings: "No amount of increased budget will compensate for the gaps in the law, nor will any conceivable appropriations of millions of additional dollars do the job unless it is administered by individuals capable of understanding the real public health significance of the problems with which they must deal, willing to look at scientific fact and able to understand and evaluate them, and interested more in the public welfare than in the financial gains of the industries which they regulate."

The FDA has many dedicated, qualified people at every level, all of whom have enemies within the agency. The dedicated personnel should be singled out and supported; their opponents should be opposed and removed if necessary. But so far Commissioner Edwards has shown an inability to distinguish those advisers who are concerned with the public interest from those who are not. In the classical bureaucratic pattern, he has made the judgment that if they support the Commissioner they are good and if they do not they are bad. As long as protecting the Commissioner and not the public assures success for FDA officials, disintegration will continue.

**Lessons from a
Summer Study**

---

*"I've just told you a great deal of
information which I've never told
anyone else. Can you tell me why?"*

*—FDA official to a group of Nader
student investigators, August, 1969*

The 1969 Ralph Nader Summer Study of the Food and
Drug Administration's food protection activities was
based on the conclusions of a preliminary report prepared during the summer and fall of 1968. Two students,
James Turner, of the Ohio State University College of
Law, and Robert Rideout, of the Princeton University
Woodrow Wilson School of International Affairs, had
been assigned by Ralph Nader to prepare the 1968
report. Based on interviews with present and former
agency personnel, the preliminary report highlighted
major problem areas in the FDA structure, including the
control of cyclamates and other food additives, the failure of decision-makers to use scientific information
effectively, and the misuse of food standards. In 1969
sixteen students or recent graduates (some of the 110
students who worked on the Nader Summer Studies that
year) were divided into teams of two and assigned to
research in depth each of the ten identified problem areas,
with two groups researching two related areas. This
book, *The Chemical Feast,* developed out of research conducted by these students during the summer and by the
author throughout 1968 and 1969.

The procedure of the Nader Summer Study Project
was unique for a research effort. While the students
spent many hours in the traditional library search for
academic explanations of the problems they had discovered, the real heart of the project was the interviews
with responsible agency officials and the collecting of

official documents from them. In their four months of activity the sixteen members of the Nader team conducted over five hundred separate interviews, collected over ten thousand documents, and became regular fixtures in FDA libraries, reading rooms, and offices. Because of their daily presence at the agency, the students had an almost immediate impact upon FDA activities. The agency itself was eager to help. Commissioner Herbert L. Ley, Jr., and C. C. Johnson, his immediate superior in the Department of Health, Education, and Welfare, directed all employees to aid the investigation, and the Commissioner and his staff made themselves available whenever possible to discuss information as it became available. They were glad to co-operate for their own reasons as well as simply to be helpful. In June, 1968, Theodore Cron, then Assistant FDA Commissioner for Information and Education and key adviser to Commissioner James Goddard, said in an interview that he welcomed the Nader investigation because he felt that several divisions of the agency were functioning badly and either intentionally or out of incompetence were providing the agency leadership with inaccurate or incomplete information. Many officials of the FDA who served under Dr. Ley seemed to share this view. The facts uncovered by the students supported it as well.

For the most part, the students who worked on the FDA investigation, both in 1968 and in 1969, began with faith in the quality of the American food supply but also with some skepticism, inspired primarily by (1) Ralph Nader's revelations in 1967 and 1968 that meat and poultry quality was not as high as had been widely assumed and (2) the realization that the FDA was a regulatory agency and therefore probably afflicted with the same bureaucratic density, inefficiency, and self-justification uncovered in other regulatory agencies brought under close scrutiny. It is fair to say that none of the students expected to find in the FDA the shocking disarray and appalling failure of responsibility that their investigations revealed almost daily. As the number of altered documents, misrepresented facts, and suppressed studies began to mount, the students' initial skepticism changed to a deep doubt about all the agency's activities and finally ended in the conviction that most agency efforts were a failure. The fact that most of the distortion and failure related directly to the safety or quality of food served to heighten their concern.

The first specific study the group completed concerned the Coca-Cola–Dr. Pepper fight to obtain a regulation that allowed the addition of caffeine to cola drinks and the Dr. Pepper drink without announcing the addition on the label. Agency documents showed that the overwhelming sentiment of the FDA officials involved in the decision was to require labeling. The record also showed strong reasons for following such a policy. But the first act of Commissioner James Goddard, taken four days after assuming office, was to sign a regulation that allowed the addition of caffeine without requiring that it be listed on the label. After spending ten days going over all the agency documents concerned with the decision, the student investigator involved spent the next days conducting interviews with all the responsible individuals, after which he said, "I will never be able to trust another government official again. Every one of these men lied about their involvement in the decision to one degree or another. If I hadn't had the records, I would have never known there had been any disagreement with the final regulation." The experience of many other students was similar if less dramatic.

Two students discovered that in a January, 1969, memo from Dr. Marvin Legator to Commissioner Ley a recommendation that the marketing of cyclamates be stopped had been deleted from the original memorandum by an intermediary without informing either the sender or the receiver of the memorandum. This discovery was immediately communicated to all parties concerned and was largely responsible for Dr. Ley's acknowledgment on October 18, 1969, that he had a communication problem in his Bureau of Science. Similarly, after Dr. Ley testified to a Congressional committee that his agency had conducted a number of studies, all of which showed that MSG was safe, a student contacted the FDA researchers mentioned and found that two of the four studies cited had not been undertaken and that two others had not been completed. These discoveries were then relayed orally to the individuals responsible. Six weeks later, after no effort had been made by the

FDA to correct the erroneous testimony, a report of the incident was prepared for Ralph Nader to send to the Congressional committee involved, calling attention to the errors.

In December, 1968, the preliminary investigators discovered that FDA studies showed that a very high proportion of deformed chicken embryos came from eggs injected with cyclamates and cyclohexylamine, tending to confirm dangers suggested by studies showing genetic deformities in rats injected with cyclamates. For the next nine months scientists both inside and outside the FDA as well as the study team members tried to get the FDA to conduct some kind of official evaluation of these studies. At the end of September, 1969, Paul Friedman, an NBC news reporter from Washington, specifically asked a member of the study team about the state of cyclamate research at FDA and was informed of the chick embryo study along with other studies. He then arranged to interview the FDA personnel responsible for the studies and broadcast the results on the local Washington news and the Huntley-Brinkley network report. The result was nationwide concern, which eventually led to the banning of cyclamates.*

In various ways the results of the Nader group study were constantly communicated to the responsible officials within HEW. The purpose of the study was and is to contribute the effort of a group of concerned individuals to the solution of a major American problem—how to provide the highest quality, safest food at the most reasonable price to the American people. For this reason the students attempted at every opportunity to point out problems in need of attention and work toward solutions with agency personnel. In the course of this effort they discovered a kind of defeatist attitude which permeates every level of the FDA bureaucracy. There is little belief among the agency personnel that

* It is interesting to note that in an interview with Secretary Finch on October 2, 1969, Ralph Nader, James Turner, and Harrison Wellford of the Nader Summer Project discussed FDA problems, including cyclamates, and did *not* recommend the total banning of cyclamates. What was recommended, based on the research of the students, was suspension of the use of cyclamate until review of the substance could establish its safety. Such an action might have created less confusion than the one taken.

the FDA can really make any difference. Comments of various people associated with the FDA during the past ten years suggest how much frustration and despair grip the agency. Theodore Cron said, while still in office, "We have no idea what is going on in the food standards area. We keep asking them for information and we keep getting nothing in reply." Julius Cohn, chief counsel to Senator Hubert Humphrey's 1960 committee investigating the FDA, said, "I have never seen a bureaucrat take a strong principled stand without being retaliated against for it." One formerly high-placed FDA official who remains within the Federal bureaucracy said, "I am ashamed of the five years I spent at FDA." The successive failures of Commissioners Larrick, Goddard, and Ley, all of whom left the agency (accompanied by a significant number of their high-level advisers) within the past five years, were both the result and cause of rapidly deteriorating agency morale. Their failures suggest that more is wrong with the FDA than its top leadership. Faced with the depressing history of FDA failure and little real prospect for positive change, the students spent much of their time suggesting alternatives to the general situation they found.

It was obvious that the FDA could not be considered in isolation from the politics of HEW and the executive branch, or from Congressional or industrial influence. It would be useless to focus attention solely on a single regulatory agency without also considering the system of which it was a part. In the course of weekly meetings, numerous small discussions, and an almost constant effort to explain the group's activities to curious reporters and other observers, a general plan of how the uses of government could be improved began to emerge.

Any effort at change in this society depends on the faith that there is substance to widespread expression of concern about the way people live. Today more people seem to say more often than they have in the past that something must be done about the quality of American life. There have been other powerful movements directed at curbing the destructive activities of unchecked corporate power, most notably the Progressive movement of the early 1900's. Unfortunately, the current state of disintegration in the food-protection effort—

as well as every other regulatory activity of government —underlines how seriously the earlier movements failed. Simon Lazarus, executive director of New York City's Department of Consumer Affairs, wrote in 1969: "The problem is not simply with the present incumbents of the F.T.C., of the F.C.C., the I.C.C., the C.A.B. and others. The problem is not merely that incumbent officials will not or cannot carry out the grand design of Progressives and New Dealers In large measure, the problem is with the grand design itself. Something is fundamentally askew about the whole regulatory system which the nation adopted to control corporate power in the public interest. Many of the regulatory agencies were doomed to fail from the start." [1] Clearly, more than good intentions are needed if the current efforts to ensure corporate responsibility are to succeed where their forerunners failed. But without good intentions there cannot be even an effort.

The vast majority of students participating in the Nader Summer Project expressed the desire to continue the work for change that the project represented to them. This sentiment is not noticeably different from that of large numbers of students in law school, business schools, medical schools, and most other educational institutions across the country. Their belief is that much more is askew than the regulatory system. The failure of the grand design touches all American institutions—regulatory agencies, Congressional bodies, courts, corporate entities, universities—none has been successful in insuring the highest quality of life possible for the most number of people. All have fallen far short of their professed goals. Now new efforts must be made. The urgency of the problems presented by environmental deterioration, regulatory breakdown, and massive social unrest, combined with the determination of many people (especially students) to solve these problems, provide the reason and the means for the fundamental restructuring necessary.

Once the FDA's regulatory failures are seen as part of a general failure of protection for the public, reform of the FDA becomes only part of a more general problem. The public-interest activities of professionals supported by the activities of large groups of people are examples of actions to be taken as part of an over-all campaign designed to make government more responsive to the real needs of the public. Legislative and regulatory actions will have to be undertaken in conjunction with the private activities of concerned citizens. One of the major failures of previous reforms was the belief that passing laws solved problems: this is rarely the case. However, it is often necessary to pass new laws as part of a more general attempt to solve a given problem. The same is true of the reorganization of all regulatory agencies. There will have to be new legislation passed to define more accurately the role to be played by the government in the food regulations area. The FDA will have to be reorganized so that it represents the public interest. The most important lesson learned during the Nader Summer Study of the FDA was the futility of trying to treat the FDA as an isolated organization. If the nation is going to be provided with the safest, highest quality, least expensive food supply possible, all the public-interest activities necessary in every other area of consumer protection will have to be developed in the food area.

A spirit of concern about the future of America lives among a large segment of American youth. Many are trying in numerous and diverse ways to harness this spirit to the practical tools of change so that life for all Americans can be better. They have great hope, great energy, and with support from others a good chance of success.

Currently, the Food and Drug Administration is trying to get drug manufacturers to organize their management structure so that quality control engineers report their findings, particularly their warnings of danger, directly to high-level management. This attempt to upgrade the awareness of potentially hazardous manufacturing conditions, or low-level decisions which endanger the quality and perhaps the safety of a finished product, is the FDA's effort to rely on the important role that quality control engineers should play in protecting the public. But more is needed. It might be more in the public interest if quality control engineers explored the possibilities of organizing themselves as a quality- and safety-auditing profession independent of big business management. Firms could be organized for the purposes of inspecting and evaluating corporations on the basis of the quality and safety of their products, on how effectively they control the pollution their manufacturing processes produce, and on the cost of their products to the public. Quality control auditors could be organized in a way similar to the accounting profession. This is merely one example of the way in which the raw spirit can be harnessed to the task of making fundamental change. Similar public-interest activities can be undertaken in other professions. Advertisers, mass media communicators, doctors, scientists, and other professional groups have begun to organize themselves into societies and organizations for the defense of the environment, for social responsibility, and for general efforts to protect the public interest. Many law, advertising, and medical firms are making arrangements to allow their associates a fixed percentage of time, perhaps 10 per cent, to work on public-interest projects. Expansion of all of this activity and more is essential to replace the fabric of the failing grand design referred to by Simon Lazarus.

However, none of it will succeed without the support and participation of the consuming public. Each individual consumer and every organization of consumers must make their dissatisfaction known from the local shop level to the national level of corporate managers and government officials. So little is now known about the particular abuses to which American people are subjected daily that it is often impossible to take corrective action. The Consumer Federation of America is organizing consumer chapters for the express purpose of finding abuses and planning action to correct them. Any group of local citizens, effectively organized, can provide a great deal of defense for themselves against the abuses of corporate insensitivity. Cities across the country are beginning to establish consumer-protection agencies which can be a focal point of effort on behalf of the public. Public action must be the primary part of the campaign to restore concern for the public interest in major American power centers, or the campaign will fail.

Notes

Introduction
1. Russett et al., *Handbook of Political and Social Indicators* (Yale University Press, New Haven, 1964), p. 199.
2. The quotations are from "Review of Studies of Vitamin and Mineral Nutrition in the United States" (1950–1968), *Journal of Nutrition Education,* Fall, 1969, Vol. 1, No. 2, Supplement 1, pp. 39–57; and from the November 25, 1969 press release announcing publication of the review and summarizing it. Emphasis added.

Chapter 1
1. New Drug Application, Sucaryl Sodium (Cyclamate Sodium, Abbott) 7258, January 23, 1950.
2. NDA 7258 Memorandum, February 2, 1950. Dr. Lehman's remarks were: "For example, retardation of the growth of rats was observed at 0.05% and 0.1% in the diet. The small number of animals in the experimental groups and the discontinuance of the control group after 36 weeks make the chronic feeding studies some of the poorest I have run across. The chronic experiments on dogs fare a little better but even here only one dog in each group was autopsied.
   "The pathological studies are so poor that there is really nothing presented to express much of an opinion on. Some heart muscle damage was found in rats. The pathological changes in the dogs were nicely taken care of by the statement 'no histologic changes attributable to Sucaryl Sodium' which is not very informative.
   "Diarrhea was observed both in patients and animals."
3. *Ibid.*
4. Morton Mintz, quoting Dr. F. R. Blood of the National Academy of Sciences-National Research Council Committee on Cyclamates, *The Washington Post,* Sunday, October 26, 1969, "Bittersweet Saga: The Rise and Fall of Cyclamates," p. 16, col. 7.
5. Policy Statement on Artificial Sweeteners. Food and Nutrition Board NAS-NRC, 1954, pp. 7–8.
6. NAS Policy, 1954, p. 7.
7. The Safety of Artificial Sweeteners for Use in Foods, NAS Report, August, 1955, p. 8.
8. Policy Statement on Artificial Sweeteners. Food and Nutrition Board NAS-NRC, as revised April, 1962, p. 4.
9. NAS Policy, 1962, p. 7.
10. Non-Nutritive Sweeteners, An Interim Report NAS-NRC, 1968, p. 8.
11. FDA tally of response to published list, December 9, 1958.
12. FDA Memorandum, O. L. Kline to L.P., August 10, 1959.
13. Code of Federal Regulation, Title 21, Chapter 1, Section 125.7. Emphasis added.
14. Food, Drug, and Cosmetic Act, Section 409 (c) (3) (A).
15. NAS Report, 1955, p. 7.

16. S. Kojma and H. Tchibagase, Chemical Pharmaceutical Bulletin 14,971, 1966.
17. Code of Federal Regulations 121,1088.
18. Schubert to Ley, September 23, 1969, and *Family Health Magazine*, October, 1969, p. 43.
19. Summerson Memorandum, February 27, 1968.
20. Verrett, Research Progress Report, July–December, 1968.
21. Verrett, Research Progress Report, January–June, 1969.
22. Abbott release, October 8, 1969.
23. Interview, Ley/Turner, October, 1969.
24. Legator to Banes, January 24, 1969.
25. Schrogie and Kraybill, to Commissioner Ley, December 12, 1968.
26. Finch, cyclamates press conference, October 18, 1969, p. 3.
27. H. Report No. 2284, 85th Congress 2nd Session, 1958. Reprinted in *Cases and Materials on the Food and Drug Law*, Thomas W. Christopher (Commercial Clearing House, Inc., New York, 1966), p. 470.
28. FD & C Act, Section 409 (c) (3) (A).
29. Dr. Jesse Steinfeld, Assistant HEW Secretary, October 18, 1969, cyclamates press conference, p. 5.
30. Finch, press conference, October 18, 1969, p. 3.
31. *Food Chemical News,* November 10, 1969, "Finch Takes Position Against Delaney Clause," p. 3.
32. Press release, HEW News, Thursday, November 20, 1969.
33. *Ibid.*
34. Huntley-Brinkley News, November 21, 1969.
35. FDA Papers, October, 1969, p. 13.
36. *J. Amer. Diet Association,* 23, 327–330 (1954).
37. *Nature,* 221, 91–92 (1969).
38. Dr. Arthur H. Wolff, Assistant Surgeon General, Memo for the Record, October 15, 1969.
39. Steinfeld, cyclamates press conference, October 18, 1969, p. 9.
40. Lieberman to FDA Associate Commissioner for Science, October 28, 1969.
41. Cyclamates press conference, October 18, 1969, p. 5. Text at Note 29.
42. FDA presentation to NAS-NRC Sweetener Committee, October 16, 1969, p. III–30, 32.
43. *Medical World News,* November 15, 1968, p. 27.
44. *Ibid.,* p. 26.
45. *Ibid.,* p. 27.
46. Wolff for the Record, October 15, 1969.
47. *The Washington Post,* December 21, 1969.
48. Interbureau By Lines, November, 1963.
49. Cyclamates press conference, October 18, 1969, pp. 20, 30.
50. NBC in Channel 4, Washington, D.C., interview with Paul Friedman, October 1, 1969.
51. Interview KDKA–TV Pittsburgh, September 4, 1969.

Chapter 2
1. Foreign Service Dispatch 1252, from Oslo to The Department of State, Washington, June 30, 1952.

"The author of the most violent of the attacks on Reich, at one point claimed that Reich did not have a medical degree. A subsequent retraction will be found as numbered item 3 of enclosure No. 2. . . .

"Dr. Reich holds a degree of Doctor of Medicine from the University of Vienna. On completion of his medical studies he became interested in psychiatry and studied with Dr. Sigmund Freud, rising, it is reported, to the position of Senior Analyst in Freud's Berlin Institute. . . .

"It is of interest that all but one of the psychiatrists consulted for information about Dr. Reich spoke of his psychiatric work with the greatest respect, while without exception denying the validity of his biological work."

2. Memorandum from John L. Harvey, Food and Drug Administration to General Counsel Federal Security Administration, October 21, 1953.

"The records show that Wilhelm Reich was instrumental in bringing Ilse Ollendorff into the United States during 1939 and she has since that time lived on the same premises as Reich . . .

"She has also been referred to in various instances, such as in Dunn and Bradstreet Reports, as Mrs. Reich or Mrs. Wilhelm Reich and in at least one instance has signed her name to a letter as 'Ilse Reich.' . . .

"Although he [Dr. Reich] lays claim to having graduated some thirty years ago from the University of Vienna Medical School with an M.D. degree, we have not been able to confirm this and the opinion has been expressed in scientific circles in Norway that the character of his medical education is to be questioned. At our request, the State Department had a considerable investigation made of Reich's former activities in Norway prior to 1939, and we have requested them to follow this up by attempting to investigate his medical education in Vienna."

3. Decree of Injunction, Civil Action 1056, John D. Clifford, Jr., U.S. District Judge for the District of Maine, March 19, 1954.

4. Inspector H. Niss to FDA chief, Boston District, July 13, 1956.

5. Malin, ACLU Executive Director, letter to FDA Commissioner Larrick; released July 11, 1956.

6. Foreign Service Dispatch 1252, from Oslo to the Department of State, Washington, June 30, 1952.

7. Long, Congressional Record, July 9, 1965, p. 14437.

8. Special Subcommittee, Investigation of HEW, April, May and June, 1966, p. 405.

9. Detroit Vital Foods, Inc. vs. United States of America, Supreme Court of the United States, October Term, 1968, Bass and Friend proof brief, April 17, 1969, pp. 1, 11.

10. Long Hearings, Invasion of Privacy (government agencies), Subcommittee on Administrative Practices and Procedures of the Committee of the Judiciary, United States Senate, 89th Congress, 1965, p. 835.

11. Scientology vs. U.S., United States District Court of Appeals for the District of Columbia, No. 21,483, decided February 5, 1969.
12. Barnhard, Food and Drug Law Institute—FDA Joint Educational Conference at Marriott Twin Bridges Motor Hotel, Washington, D.C., December 3, 1968.
13. FDA Program and Financial Plan, 1970, p. 2.
14. *Ibid.*
15. *Food Engineering,* October, 1968, p. 76.
16. "Strategy for a Livable Environment," The Litton Report to HEW Secretary John W. Gardner, June, 1967, p. 21.
17. Memorandum, Goodrich to Harvey, April 12, 1965.
18. Janssen, "FDA since 1962," October 21, 1968, pp. 6, 7, prepared for the Johnson Papers.
19. FDA Reports, December 15, 1969, p. 14.
20. Daniel Tatkon, *The Great Vitamin Hoax* (The Macmillan Company, New York, 1968), p. 98.
21. Consumer Issues, 1966, A Report to the President from the Consumer Advisory Council, 1966, p. 5.
22. James Ridgeway, "The AMA, The FDA and Quacks," *The New Republic,* November 9, 1963.
23. "Strategy for a Livable Environment," The Litton Report to HEW Secretary Gardner, June, 1967, pp. 21, 22.
24. Ann Draper, letter to HEW Secretary Anthony J. Celebreeze, November 2, 1962.

Chapter 3
1. Code of Federal Regulations, Title 21, Chapter 1, Section 31.1, p. 346.
2. Roosevelt to Congress, March 22, 1935, reprinted in Thomas W. Christopher, *Cases and Material on the Food and Drug Law* (Commercial Clearing House, Inc., New York, 1966), p. 183.
3. *The Philadelphia Evening Bulletin,* June 27, 1966, p. 16.
4. FDA Memorandum, Fitzhugh to Ramsey, April 10, 1969.
5. Revised Briefing Memorandum, Roe to Commissioner, October 29, 1964.
6. *Ibid.*
7. FDA Memorandum, McLaughlin to Kirk, June 7, 1965.
8. FDA Memorandum, Kirk to Larrick, March 25, 1965.
9. FDA Memorandum, Rankin to Goddard, January 16, 1966.
10. Austern, "The Formulation of Mandatory Food Standards," *Food, Drug and Cosmetic Law Quarterly,* Volume 2, p. 532 (1947).
11. FDA Memorandum of Interview, Kirk, Larrick, Mintener, Parker and Kittinger of Dr. Pepper.
12. FDA Fact Sheet, "Nutrition, Nonsense, and Sense," May, 1967. Reprinted in the McGovern Hearings, Senate Select Committee on Nutrition and Human Needs, Part 13-A, p. 3956.
13. Federal Register, December 14, 1966.
14. Press release on Survey, November 25, 1969.
15. "Key Science Academy Figure Attacks Proposed FDA Rules

for Diet Food," Morton Mintz, *The Washington Post,* July 20, 1966.

16. *Ibid.*
17. Code of Federal Regulations, Title 21, Chapter 1, Section 3.41, p. 90.
18. *Washington Evening Star,* November 21, 1968.
19. *Time,* January 10, 1969, p. 60.
20. Briefing Memorandum, Food Standards Branch to Commissioner, June 3, 1964.
21. FDA Memorandum, Cassidy to Kirk, July 13, 1967, pp. 1–3. Emphasis in the original.
22. FDA Memorandum, Bellis to Roe, June 23, 1967.
23. FDA Memorandum, McCoy to Gutterman, October 12, 1966.
24. *Ibid.*

Chapter 4
1. FDA Fact Sheet, "Nutrition, Nonsense, and Sense," May, 1967. Reprinted in the McGovern Hearings, Senate Select Committee on Nutrition and Human Needs, Part 13-A, p. 3956.
2. Report of the National Commission on Community Health Services, p. 45.
3. Report of the President's Commission on Heart Disease, Cancer, and Stroke, p. 2.
4. *Ibid.,* p. 5.
5. *Ibid.,* p. 28. Emphasis added.
6. Public Health Service Statistics compiled from the Demographic Yearbook for the year 1966 and updated to 1968.
7. *The Christian Science Monitor,* January 13, 1969, p. 4.
8. Dr. James Goddard, former FDA Commissioner quoted in FDA Fact Sheet, "Nutrition, Nonsense, and Sense," May, 1967. Emphasis in the original.
9. FDA Fact Sheet, "Nutrition, Nonsense, and Sense," May, 1967.
10. FDA Memorandum, Lewis to Ley, October 29, 1969.
11. "An Evaluation of the Salmonella Problem," National Academy of Sciences, 1969, p. 6.
12. Speech delivered at the 54th Annual Meeting of the International Association of Milk, Food and Environmental Sanitarians, Miami Beach, Florida, August 15, 1967.
13. Cliver, D. O., "Implications of Food-Borne Infectious Hepatitis," Public Health Report, 81:159–165, 1966, and "Food-Borne Viruses In Food-Borne Diseases," H. Rieman, editor (Academic Press, 1967).
14. Strong, D. H., speech to the Wisconsin Section, Institute of Food Technologists, Madison, Wisconsin, December 2, 1962.
15. Lennington, 54th Annual Meeting of the International Association of Milk, Food and Environmental Sanitarians, Miami Beach, Florida, August 15, 1967.
16. 54th Annual Meeting of the International Association of Milk, Food and Environmental Sanitarians, Miami Beach, Florida, August 15, 1967.
17. Baylor Law Review, Vol. xvi, 1964, pp. 362–363.

18. Operation Plan for FDA District Offices, Fiscal Year 1970, p. 6.
19. FDA Fact Sheet, May, 1968.
20. Philadelphia for example: Operation Plan for FDA District Offices, Fiscal Year 1970, p. 48.
21. Good Manufacturing Practices included in FDA Fact Sheets on how to avoid various food toxins, May, June, November, 1967.
22. Operation Plan for FDA District Offices, Fiscal Year, 1970, p. 43.
23. Operation Plan for FDA District Offices, Fiscal Year 1970, District Highlights and Comments, p. 47.
24. *Washington Evening Star,* November 21, 1968.
25. Food Nutrition Board, National Academy of Sciences-National Research Council, "Dietary Fat and the Human Health," Washington, D.C., 1966.
26. Dr. Laurence W. Kinsell, Chairman of the American Diabetes Association Committee on Food and Nutrition, to the Food and Drug Administration, November 17, 1967.
27. Press release, November, 1968.
28. Letter to the Food and Drug Administration, May 5, 1967.
29. Circulation 37(3) Supplement 1, 1968.
30. FDA Briefing Memorandum, Dr. Herbert Ley, Director of Bureau of Medicine to Dr. James Goddard, Commissioner of Food and Drug Administration, August 14, 1967.
31. Canadian Food and Drug Directorate Regulations B.09.020 and 021.
32. Joint press release, May 3, 1968.
33. Federal Register, May 27, 1964, Code of Federal Regulations, Title 21, Chapter 1, Section 3.41, p. 90.
34. FDA Memorandum, R. E. Newberry to M. R. Stephens, November 10, 1965.
35. *Ibid.*
36. FDA Memorandum, Kirk to Goddard, December 1, 1967.
37. Goodrich to Deputy FDA Commissioner, April 12, 1965.
38. FDA Memorandum, Weisenberg to Stephens, February 6, 1963.
39. FDA Briefing Memorandum, Bureau of Regulatory Compliance to Commissioner Ley, August 15, 1968.
40. McGovern Hearings on Nutrition and Human Needs, Part 13–B, p. 4286.
41. FDA Briefing Memorandum, Ley to Goddard, August 14, 1967.

Chapter 5
1. Food from Farmer to Consumer, Report of the National Commission on Food Marketing, June, 1966, p. 95.
2. *Ibid.*
3. *Ibid.*
4. Letter, Frandow to Schlossberg, May 20, 1969.
5. Ed Dowling, "To Market We Go . . . Like Lambs to the Slaughter," *The New Republic,* January 28, 1967.
6. Commission Report, p. 9.
7. *Ibid.,* p. 102.

8. Report from the Study Group on Food and Drug Administration Consumer Protection Objectives and Programs, July, 1969, p. ii.
9. *Washington Star,* October 29, 1969.
10. *J.A.M.A.,* Vol. 86; p. 281, 1963, by Dr. Henry A. Schroeder, quoted to the Senate Select Committee on Nutrition and Human Needs by Daniel F. Gerber, Hearing Volume 13-C, p. 4593.
11. *Ibid.*
12. *Washington Star,* October 29, 1969.
13. FDA Staff Paper revised September 22, 1969, McGovern Hearings on Nutrition and Human Needs, Select Committee of the U.S. Senate, Part 13-B, p. 4251.
14. *The Washington Post,* October 24, 1969.
15. *The Washington Post,* December 27, 1968.
16. Anderson to Mayer, September 9, 1969.
17. Charles S. Brown to Wesley W. Posvar, Chancellor, the University of Pittsburgh, July 30, 1969.
18. F. S. Cheever to Charles S. Brown, August 15, 1969.
19. Nelson C. White, President, International Minerals and Chemicals Corporation, November 26, 1969, 9:00 p.m.
20. *Chemical and Engineering News,* December 15, 1969.
21. *The Wall Street Journal,* July 24, 1969, quoted in McGovern Hearings, Part 13-B, p. 4442.
22. Paul Kresh, *The Power of the Unknown Citizen* (Lippincott Company, Philadelphia and New York, 1969), p. 56.
23. *Life Magazine,* November 28, 1969, p. 41.
24. Schramm to Darby, October 30, 1969.
25. Dyestuffs, March, 1967.
26. "Food Additives," *Chemical Engineering News,* October 10, 1966, p. 118.
27. Dairy Council of Savannah, Georgia. Comment against Fat Labeling Proposal included in Summary of Comments, Newberry to Stephens, November 10, 1965.
28. Dairy Council Digest, "Relative Nutritive Value of Filled and Imitation Milks," March, April, 1968.
29. Food, Drug, and Cosmetic Act, Section 409 (c) (3) (A).
30. Hearings on Irradiated Food before a Subcommittee of the Joint Congressional Committee on Atomic Energy, July 18, 1968, p. 43 of draft copy.
31. *Chemical and Engineering News,* October 10, 1966, p. 118.
32. Amendment to 21 C. F. R. 121, Sections 121.7, .9 .50 and .51.
33. Hearings on Irradiated Food before a Subcommittee of the Joint Congressional Committee on Atomic Energy, July 30, 1968, draft pages 118–119.
34. *The Knoxville News-Sentinel,* Tuesday, April 14, 1964.
35. Quoted in Mintz, *The Therapeutic Nightmare* (Houghton-Mifflin Company, Boston, 1965), p. 175.
36. Fred J. Delmore and Kermit V. Sloan, Bureau of Voluntary Compliance, FDA, "FDA's Voluntary Compliance Program, 1963 to 1968," prepared for inclusion in the Johnson Papers. Figures from Sloan, Voluntary Compliance Report, FDA Papers, November, 1969.

37. Fred Delmore, Voluntary Compliance, FDA Papers, February, 1968.

Chapter 6
1. Harvey W. Wiley, *An Autobiography* (The Bobbs Merrill Company, 1930), p. 203.
2. Harvey W. Wiley, Unpublished Speech, 1908, Wiley Collection, Library of Congress.
3. House Report No. 249 of the Committee on Expenditures in the Department of Agriculture, House of Representatives, 62nd Congress, 2nd Session, January 22, 1912 (Moss Committee Report), p. 5.
4. *Ibid.*
5. *Ibid.*, p. 6.
6. William Longgood, *Poisons in Your Food* (Simon and Schuster, New York, 1960), p. 184.
7. *National Observer,* December 11, 1969.
8. Oscar E. Anderson, Jr., *The Health of a Nation, Harvey W. Wiley and the Fight for Pure Food* (University of Chicago Press, Chicago, 1968), p. 210.
9. Wiley, *An Autobiography,* p. 242. Unpublished.
10. Anderson, *op. cit.,* p. 217. Emphasis added.
11. Wiley to Miller, unpublished memorandum. Wiley papers, Library of Congress.
12. Anderson, *op. cit.,* p. 273.
13. Dr. A. L. Winton, Toastmaster of the Harvey W. Wiley Memorial Dinner, September 12, 1944, Hotel Commodore, New York City. Library of Congress, Harvey W. Wiley papers, p. 6.
14. GRAS List comments 1958, FDA Files.
15. Wilson to Robinson, July 25, 1911, Hearing 523.
16. Moss Committee Report, p. 7.
17. Anderson, *op. cit.,* p. 224.
18. Wiley, *An Autobiography,* p. 259.
19. "Wiley Faces Crisis," *Washington Times,* Friday, July 14, 1911.
20. "Was Doctor Wiley a Piker?" *Washington Times,* July 14, 1911.
21. Moss Committee Report, p. 4.
22. *Ibid.*
23. Quotations from *Oil, Paint, and Drug Reporter:* Dunbar's from November 1, 1926 and Wiley's from November 22, 1926.
24. Dunbar, Creed of the FDA, Drug and Allied Industries, 1947.
25. Fred J. Delmore and Kermit V. Sloane, Bureau of Voluntary Compliance, FDA, "FDA's Voluntary Compliance Program, 1963 to 1968," prepared for inclusion in the Johnson papers.
26. Wiley, *An Autobiography,* p. 273.
27. Bernard Sternsher, *Rexford Tugwell and the New Deal* (Rutgers University Press, New Brunswick, New Jersey, 1964), p. 225.
28. Tugwell to Pottle, March 16, 1933, FDA Files.
29. Campbell, Memorandum for the file, March 17, 1933, FDA Files.

30. Tugwell, "Recollections of 1933 and Later," FDA Papers, June, 1968.
31. USDA Press Release, July 3, 1968, USDA, 2149–68.
32. Wallace to Jones, and Wallace to Smith, both on June 1, 1933, FDA Files.
33. Ruth De Forest Lamb, *American Chamber of Horrors* (Farrar and Rinehart, 1936), p. 195.
34. *Food Chemical News*, January 26, 1970, p. 31.
35. Arthur M. Schlesinger, *The Coming of the New Deal* (Houghton-Mifflin Company, Boston, 1959), p. 129.
36. *Ibid.*, p. 130.
37. *Ibid.*, p. 173.
38. Robert S. Lynd, Introduction to *Consumer Representation in the New Deal*, by Persia Campbell (Columbia University Press, New York, 1940), p. 11.
39. Rexford Tugwell, "Consumers and the New Deal," delivered before the Consumers League of Ohio, Cleveland, May 11, 1934, reprinted in *The Battle for Democracy*, by Rexford Tugwell (Columbia University Press, New York, 1935), Chapter 27, pp. 285–86.
40. Tugwell to Richberg, January 24, 1935, Department of Agriculture Files.
41. FDA to Senator J. W. Bailey, April 26, 1935, F.D.R. Library, Hyde Park, New York, Personal Correspondence Files 375.
42. Young, p. 202.
43. Schlesinger, *op. cit.*, p. 359.
44. Sternsher, *op. cit.*, pp. 231–32, quotations from *The Wallaces of Iowa*, by Russell Lord (Houghton-Mifflin, Boston, 1947), p. 346; and *America's Economic Growth*, by Fred A. Shannon, 3rd edition (The Macmillan Company, New York, 1951), p. 799.
45. Tugwell, "Recollections of 1933 and Later," FDA Papers, June, 1968.
46. Ruth De Forest Lamb, *op. cit.*, p. 290.
47. Sumner Welles, "Review of *The Stricken Land*, by Rexford Tugwell," *The Saturday Review*, December 28, 1946, p. 9.

Chapter 7
1. Hillman and Fraser, *Pediatrics*, August, 1969, p. 299.
2. "Nitrosamines as Environmental Carcinogens," Lijinsky and Epstein, *Nature*, Vol. 225, January 3, 1970.
3. *Medical World News*, April 26, 1968, p. 27.
4. *Ibid.*, pp. 21, 22.
5. "Simple Chemicals May Harm Genes," *The Washington Post*, April 28, 1968, p. 1.
6. Rachel Carson, *Silent Spring* (Crest Books, Fawcett World Library, New York, 1964), p. 164.
7. *Ibid.*, p. 166.
8. "Alternate Methods of Controlling Insect Pests," Edward F. Knipling, FDA Papers, February, 1969, p. 16.
9. *Ibid.*
10. *The Christian Science Monitor*, December 11, 1969.
11. G. Q. Lipscomb, *Proceedings of the Pesticide Analytical Workshop*, March 10–14, 1969, Atlanta District.

12. William C. Purdy, Letter to Consumer Protection and Environmental Health Service officials, April 8, 1969.
13. *Ibid.*
14. Draft Memorandum, September 24, 1969, meeting between Dr. Purdy and FDA officials, prepared by FDA, FDA Files.
15. Personal letter to William C. Purdy, July 24, 1969.
16. FDA's answer to William C. Purdy inquiry following the September, 1969 meeting.
17. Summary of the Delaney Committee, Report from Thomas W. Christopher, *Cases and Material on the Food and Drug Law,* Food and Drug Law Institute, p. 473.
18. Food, Drug, and Cosmetic Act, Section 2015.
19. *Ibid.*
20. Division of Pharmacology and Food, FDA, September 2, 1959.
21. FDA GRAS List Files.
22. FDA press release, August 17, 1965.
23. Food, Drug, and Cosmetic Act, Section 201(s). Emphasis added.
24. Bureau of Medicine to Checchi, March 2, 1959, FDA Files.
25. Statement by George P. Larrick before House Committee on Interstate and Foreign Commerce, February 26, 1961.
26. McGovern Hearings, July 17, 1969, Part 13-A, p. 4029.
27. *The Philadelphia Evening Bulletin,* October 21, 1969.
28. Rankin to Depew, August 25, 1960, FDA Files.
29. Bureau of Field Administration to Directors of Districts on Ethyl Alcohol, May 5, 1960, FDA Files.
30. Winton B. Rankin, quoted in *The Philadelphia Evening Bulletin,* October 21, 1969.
31. Food, Drug, and Cosmetic Act. Section 409 (b) (2).
32. Hearings on Irradiated Foods, held by a Subcommittee of the Joint Congressional Committee on Atomic Energy, July 18, 1968, p. 103.
33. FDA Report on Enforcement and Compliance, February, 1963, pp. 3–5.
34. Hearings on Irradiated Foods, Subcommittee of the Joint Congressional Committee on Atomic Energy, July 30, 1968, p. 98.
35. Dr. Daniel Banes, Hearings on Irradiated Foods, Subcommittee of the Joint Congressional Committee on Atomic Energy, p. 104.
36. *Food Irradiation: An FDA Report,* by Alan T. Spiher, FDA Papers, October, 1968, p. 16.
37. FDA Memorandum, Goodrich to Kirk, February 19, 1961, FDA Files.
38. Food, Drug, and Cosmetic Act, Section 409 (c) (3) (A) provisio.
39. *The Washington Post,* November 6, 1969.
40. Report of the 8th session of the Joint FAO/WHO Expert Committee on Color Additives, Geneva, Switzerland, 1964.
41. Archives of Dermatology, Vol. 88, December, 1963.
42. *Chemical and Engineering News,* October 10, 1966, p. 106.
43. *Ibid.,* p. 104.
44. FDA Program and Financial Plan, 1970–1974, p. 3.

Chapter 8
1. Introduction to the Kinslow Report, by Maurice D. Kinslow, Chairman, Study Group on FDA, Consumer Protection Objectives Director, FDA Baltimore District, July 14, 1969.
2. Walter Cronkite, CBS Evening News, August 7, 1969.

Chapter 9
1. Citizens Advisory Committee Report on the FDA, 1955.
2. Bayne-Jones et al., The Advancement of Medical Research and Education Through the Department of Health, Education, and Welfare. Report of the Secretary's consultants, 1958.
3. Quotation from Day report reprinted in Hearings, Agency Coordination Study, Subcommittee on Reorganization and International Organizations of the Committee on Government Operations, U.S. Senate, Senator Hubert H. Humphrey, Chairman, Part 2, p. 343.
4. Humphrey Hearings, Part 2, p. 323.
5. Second Citizens Advisory Committee (CAC), 1962, I-3.
6. Second CAC report, 1962, II, pp. 10–11.
7. Second CAC report, 1962, I-3.
8. Day speech reprinted, Humphrey Hearings, Part 2, p. 350.
9. Letter to Purdy, July 24, 1969.
10. Hearing held before Subcommittee on Public Health and Welfare, Chairman Paul Rogers, FDA Draft Report on Consumer Protection, August 12, 1969, p. 111 of stenographic copy.
11. Rogers Hearings, p. 161 of stenographic copy.
12. Humphrey Hearings, Part 2, p. 341.
13. HEW press conference, October 18, 1969, pp. 25, 27.
14. FDA Memorandum, May 7, 1969.
15. MSG Staff papers #2 pp. 2, 3.
16. Ley to McGovern, September 22, 1969, p. 2.
17. Adkins and Hove, February 13, 1969.
18. Fitzhugh, Nelson and Frawley, "A Comparison of the Chronic Toxicities of Synthetic Sweetening Agents," *Journal of the American Pharmaceutical Association,* Scientific Edition, Vol. XL, P. 583, pp. 46–47.
19. Nonnutritive Sweeteners: An interim report to the USFDA, Prepared by the Ad Hoc Committee on Nonnutritive Sweeteners, Food Protection Committee NAS-NRC, November, 1968.
20. Dr. S. S. Epstein, Response to Questions Raised by Senator Muskie in his Letter of August 2, 1968, McGovern Hearings, Vol. 13-A, p. 3933.
21. "Improving the Environment for Science in HEW," a report to the Secretary, December 23, 1968, p. 12.

Chapter 10
1. Memorandum of telephone call, February 5, 1953, Taber to Crawford—4-669L Dried Black Raspberries File FDA.
2. Janssen, "FDA since 1938, The Major Trends and Developments," *Journal of Public Law,* Vol. 13, No. 1, p. 216.
3. C. W. Crawford to Canning Machinery, Inc., March 5, 1948, FDA Files.
4. Harvey to Buffalo District, March 31, 1953.

Division of Food reports that "Beet Balls" are much smaller and more regular, although tougher than the "Tiny Whole Beets." . . . The "Beet Balls" are so spherical and uniform in size that there is a question that many individuals would be likely to mistake them for whole beets. . . . We believe that we have to conduct a consumer survey before undertaking to proceed against the product. . . . Under the circumstances we have decided to class 44-487-L [the beet seizure case] as disapproved and put in permanent abeyance.

5. Code of Federal Regulations, Part 130, p. 22.1, printed October 4, 1967, 32 Federal Register 13807.
6. Cron, "The Talmud and the FDA," National Convention of the American Medical Writers' Association, Chicago, Illinois, September 23, 1967.
7. Finkel to Byck, January 31, 1969, printed in McGovern Hearings 13-A, p. 4032, January 31, 1969.
8. Daniel Tatkon, *The Great Vitamin Hoax* (The Macmillan Company, New York, 1968), p. 180.
9. September 2, 1959, Bureau of Pharmacology and Food to Checchi.
10. FDA Fact Sheet, May, 1967, reprinted in McGovern Hearings, Senate Select Committee on Nutrition and Human Needs, Part 13-A, p. 3956.
11. *The Washington Post,* December 27, 1968.
12. *The Great Vitamin Hoax,* p. 175.
13. *Life,* November 28, 1969, p. 44.
14. Federal Register, Vol. 31, No. 241, December 14, 1966, p. 15732, entered by FDA.
15. Goddard, personal communication to Soret and Scholengarth, September 6, 1969.
16. *Ibid.*
17. *The Washington Post,* February 8, 1970.
18. *The New Yorker,* February 7, 1970, p. 50.

Chapter 11

1. Kefauver Hearings, Administered Prices, Kefauver Subcommittee on Antitrust and Monopoly of the Committee on the Judiciary, United States Senate, May and June, 1960, Parts 22 and 23.
2. Larrick to Atkinson, April 8, 1957.
3. Mintz, *The Therapeutic Nightmare* (Houghton-Mifflin, Boston, 1965), pp. 95–96, 181.
4. *Ibid.*, p. 134.
5. *Ibid.*, p. 128.
6. *Stephens Rippey Drug Trade News,* July 13, 1959.
7. *Ibid.*, September 17, 1962.
8. Mintz, *op. cit.*, p. 566.
9. *Ibid.*, p. 25.
10. FDA Memorandum, Kelsey to Commissioner, September 5, 1962.
11. FDA Memorandum, R. Berles to the Commissioner, October 29, 1965, The Food and Drug Administration and the Congress, 1958–1965.
12. Invasion of Privacy, Government Agencies, Hearings, Sub-

committees on Administrative Practice and Procedure of the Committee on the Judiciary, United States Senate, Part 2, April to June, 1965.

13. Interview, Friend/Turner, 1969.
14. Fountain Hearings, Drug Safety, Subcommittee of the Committee on Government Operations, U.S. House of Representatives 89th Congress, Part 4, July, August, September, 1965.
15. Kefauver Hearings, Administered Prices, Part 22, p. 1248.

Chapter 12
1. *The New York Times,* December 31, 1969.
2. Stevens, Memorandum of Interview, November 29, 1961.
3. White House Conference on Food, Nutrition, and Health, Introduction, Panel III-3.

Conclusion
1. Review, *The Nader Report on the Federal Trade Commission, The New York Times Book Review,* October 19, 1969, p. 3.

INDEX